SOUNDINGS IN TIME

THE FICTIVE ART OF
KAWABATA YASUNARI

Kowabata Yasunari contemplating a Nō mask – photographed at his home in 1954, following publication of *The Sound of the Mountain*.

SOUNDINGS IN TIME

THE FICTIVE ART OF
KAWABATA YASUNARI

Roy Starrs

JAPAN
LIBRARY

SOUNDINGS IN TIME
THE FICTIVE ART OF KAWABATA YASUNARI

First published 1998 by
JAPAN LIBRARY

*Japan Library is an imprint of Curzon Press Ltd
15 The Quadrant, Richmond, Surrey TW9 1BP*

© Roy Starrs 1998

British Library Cataloguing in Publication Data
A CIP catalogue entry for this book is
available from the British Library

ISBN 1–873410–74–3

Typeset in Plantin 11 on 11½pt by LaserScript, Mitcham, Surrey
Printed and bound in England by Bookcraft, Avon

CONTENTS

ACKNOWLEDGEMENTS

I would like to express my deep gratitude to the Social Sciences and Humanities Research Council of Canada, whose award of a postdoctoral research fellowship enabled me to devote time to this work.

I would also like to extend thanks to the editors of works in which parts of this book have previously appeared: Søren Clausen and Anne Wedell-Wedellsborg, co-editors along with myself of *Cultural Encounters: China, Japan, and the West* (Aarhus, Denmark: Aarhus University Press, 1995); Mika Merviö, editor of *Modulations in Tradition: Japan and Korea in a Changing World* (Tampere, Finland: University of Tampere, 1993); Kinya Tsuruta, editor of *An International and Comparative Perspective on Kawabata Yasunari* (Vancouver: Institute of Asian Research, 1986); Bernard Saint-Jacques and Matsuo Soga, editors of *Japanese Studies in Canada* (Ottawa: Canadian Asian Studies Association, 1985); Hirakawa Sukehiro and Tsuruta Kinya, editors of *Kawabata Yasunari Yama no oto kenkyū*, (Tokyo: Meiji shoin, 1985).

Finally, a deep *gasshō* to my wife, Kazuko, and to my children, Sean and Serena, for their patience and support.

INTRODUCTION

It is now precisely a quarter of a century since I published my first tribute to Kawabata, a rather naïvely gushing review in the Toronto *Globe and Mail* of *The Sound of the Mountain* (in Edward Seidensticker's award-winning translation, of course), to which an equally gushing editor had given the headline: 'Secret Riches in Paraphrased Haiku'.[1] A brash young reviewer who had not yet been to Japan or made any formal study of the country, its culture or its language, and who was reading a modern Japanese novel for the first time in his life, I was nonetheless captivated by the '*haiku*' quality of Kawabata's prose and by the obvious depth and subtlety of his art of fiction. Indeed, even if I were asked today for a quick, on-the-spot account of the reasons for my appreciation of his work, I doubt that I could improve much on that first 'innocent', 'intuitive' response to his greatest novel. (Did not an ancient wit say that most of us are geniuses at twenty and mediocrities at fifty?) But the study which follows represents a more extended response, at least, and hopefully a more informed and considered one. Although undoubtedly inadequate to its subject, it is, after all, a product of the intervening quarter century's reading of and rumination on Kawabata's work. My enthusiasm for that work has only deepened, even if now I am somewhat less gushing in my expression of it.

Although I analyse works here from the whole span of Kawabata's career in more or less chronological order, I do not attempt to give anything like an exhaustive history of that career. At almost all stages of his long creative life Kawabata was a very prolific writer. Rather than offer summary accounts of a great many of these works – something which a number of other writers have already done well enough, even in English – I have chosen to concentrate in more depth on a few representative works from each stage of the five decades of his active career, from the 1920s to the 1960s. With only one or two exceptions, the works I have singled out are rather obvious choices, those generally regarded as his most significant 'serious' works of literature. To some extent Kawabata himself

1

makes these choices easy: though prolific, much of the fiction he wrote was 'sub-literary', intended as 'throw-away' popular entertainment for women's magazines – a kind of writing for which, to the benefit of his pocket-book if not his reputation, he seems to have possessed a great facility. This is not to say, however, that I have managed to give due consideration here to all of those works I consider 'worthwhile'. Besides innumerable short stories of very high quality, one omission I particularly regret is of his short short stories or 'palm-of-hand stories' (*te no hira* or *tanagokoro shōsetsu*). These really constitute a separate genre to his fictional works *per se*, belonging as much to the realm of poetry or prose poetry as to fiction, and there are so many and such a variety of them that it would require another full-length study to do them justice.

Another significant way in which this study differs from a straightforward 'critical history of a writer's career' is that my methodology and critical approach tend to vary somewhat from chapter to chapter. To a large extent these variations are determined by what I perceive to be the nature of the works analysed and the critical approach each seems to call for – or, in a wider perspective, the different character of each stage of Kawabata's career. Roughly speaking, I divide his career into five major stages. From about 1914 to 1925 was a period of 'self-discovery' during which Kawabata, like many writers before him, grew to self-awareness as both a man and an artist through the writing of autobiographical sketches and stories. The period culminated in his first masterpiece, *The Dancing Girl of Izu*, which firmly established his position as an important up-and-coming writer, and was in this sense his real 'debut work'. From about the mid-1920s to the mid-1930s was a period of 'experiment and expansion', during which, under the influence of the European modernism which, by a fortunate coincidence, was flourishing exactly at that time, the young writer ventured far beyond the traditional style and themes of his early 'lyrical' writings. Although the creative products of this period were of varying success – inevitably, given the risks attendant upon experimentation – Kawabata grew enormously as an artist through these experiences and learned much that would prove of lasting value to him. Thus, during his next phase, from the mid-1930s to the mid-1940s, which I would describe as that of his 'early maturity', he was able to return to a style that was to some extent traditional but considerably enriched by what he had learned from his 'modernist experiments'. The representative work of this period is, of course, his first great '*haiku* novel', *Snow Country*.

2

The fourth phase of Kawabata's career, resumed after the brief hiatus in his writing caused by the Pacific War, consists of the great flowering of his art which occurred in the immediate postwar period. This may be described as his period of 'late maturity', in which his *haiku* novel achieved a new level of significance and perfection with *The Sound of the Mountain*. The works of this period are pervaded by a mood of gentle, elegiac melancholy, something like the *mono no aware* pathos of traditional Japanese literature, and this may be read as a response to both a historical and a personal situation: on the one hand, Japan's defeat and the threat this seemed to pose to the native cultural tradition and, on the other, Kawabata's own sense of the incipient encroachment of old age.

The fifth and final stage, which could perhaps be described as that of his 'post-maturity', was in several senses a period of decline: from the late 1950s onwards Kawabata wrote relatively little and the deterioration in his physical and psychological health led ultimately to his tragic suicide in 1972. But this period of his 'decadence' was nonetheless marked by an appropriately dark florescence, in the form of two remarkable 'flowers of evil', *Sleeping Beauties* and 'One Arm'. These two studies in the dehumanization of sex at the service of male narcissism are as masterful in their style and fictional technique as anything Kawabata ever wrote.

Dealing with the first of these stages, that of 'self-discovery', Chapters One and Two adopt a rather 'biographical' approach – an approach which seems justifiable in this instance both because the early stories are more directly autobiographical in the mainstream *shishōsetsu* (literally, 'I-novel') tradition and because, of course, the formative years of Kawabata's childhood and youth, which he describes in these stories, had an incalculable impact on the rest of his life and work. For this reason, too, I pay far more attention here than in later chapters to Japanese Kawabata scholarship, which tends overwhelmingly to be preoccupied with biographical issues and speculations about parallels between the writer's life and work. At the same time, though, I offer a critique of some of the excesses and even absurdities of what has been, until quite recently at least, the most common form of Japanese literary scholarship.

Chapter Three, dealing with the period of 'experiment and expansion', naturally takes a more comparative and analytical approach in trying to evaluate what Kawabata learned from his encounter with European modernism. In the work perhaps most representative of this period, the novella *Crystal Fantasies*, for instance, Kawabata makes use of Freudian psychology and a Joycean stream-of-consciousness technique to provide a striking psychological portrait of a 'new breed' of modern, educated and alienated Japanese housewife.

Chapter Four analyses the masterpiece of Kawabata's period of 'early maturity', *Snow Country*, as a product of his 'return to tradition' but also as an excellent example of how he integrated modernist and traditional styles and techniques to create a powerful new mode of expressing his own distinctive world view. In particular, I examine his extensive use of techniques of juxtaposition on all levels of the novel, techniques familiar from traditional Japanese genres such as *haiku* but also from Western modernist poetry and fiction. On the level of theme and character, I also analyse the protagonist, Shimamura, as Kawabata's most convincing portrait of a male narcissist, but one that is made so convincing mainly because of the powerful presence of his suffering female partner, Komako.

Chapters Five and Six deal with three works representative of Kawabata's postwar period of 'late maturity'. In Chapter Five *Thousand Cranes* and *The Master of Go* are analysed not just as symbolic expressions of Kawabata's elegiac mood in the wake of Japan's defeat but also as complex psychological studies of particular human beings. I examine, for instance, how *Thousand Cranes* uses a style of ambiguity to reflect the state of mind of its protagonist, a man who enters into a relationship with his dead father's mistress and is thus troubled, as Kawabata males often are, by the guilt of incest. *The Master of Go* is analysed as an exemplary study of the psychology of an artist, a man so devoted to his art that he loses 'the better part of reality'.

Chapter Six deals with the work I, among others, regard as the culminating masterpiece of Kawabata's career, and one of the great novels not only of Japanese but of twentieth-century world literature, *The Sound of the Mountain*. In line with the international stature of this work, my approach here again becomes partly comparative, exploring how Kawabata's integration of the theme of resistance to time into the very form of his novel compares with that of Proust in one of the defining novels of European modernism, *In Search of Lost Time*.

Chapter Seven tries to come to terms with the two difficult but fascinating stories which seem best to represent the darker mood of Kawabata's 'post-maturity', the novella *Sleeping Beauties* and the short story 'One Arm'. In an attempt to throw some light on this latter, perhaps Kawabata's most baffling story, I explore some remarkable affinities which seem to me to exist between this work and Dostoyevsky's novel, *Crime and Punishment.*

At the same time that I adopt these various approaches in response to the changing character of the works analysed, however, I also seek to identify the main areas of continuity and development throughout Kawabata's long career. There are, of course, many of these. Principal among them are probably the continuities and developments in his major themes. Perhaps like most writers, Kawabata was preoccupied with basically the same questions from the beginning to the end of his career – although, of course, there were some significant changes in the way he formulated those questions and in the answers he found for them. Contrary to those Japanese critics who fault Kawabata for lack of seriousness or depth, for contenting himself with the play of surfaces – and for an amoral, dehumanizing world view which makes no distinction between, say, the beauty of women and of objects of art – an analysis of his major themes shows him to have been preoccupied with important psychological, philosophical and even moral issues.

It is perhaps true that one would have to dig rather deep to find much social or political relevance in his work. Nevertheless, even that is not entirely absent: *The Sound of the Mountain*, for instance, could be read as a bitter commentary on the nihilism of young war veterans and the consequent breakdown of the family in postwar Japan. More generally, despite his 'apolitical' stance, Kawabata's cultural nationalism and nostalgia for traditional values would seem to place him somewhere to the right of centre in the current Japanese political spectrum. Certainly present-day left-leaning Japanese writers tend to regard him as a spokesman of right-wing 'nativist' attitudes towards Japan – a kind of gentler version of Mishima – and as already a voice of the past. This emerged clearly in a very public way, and in an international forum, in late 1994 when Ōe Kenzaburō, who followed Kawabata as the second Japanese to win the Nobel Prize in literature, called his acceptance speech 'Japan the Ambiguous and Myself' (*Aimai na Nippon no watakushi*) precisely to dissociate himself from Kawabata's brand of cultural nationalism. (Kawabata, of course, had entitled his speech, 'Japan the Beautiful and Myself', *Utsukushii Nippon no watakushi*.) Said Ōe: 'As someone living in present-day Japan and sharing bitter memories of the past, I cannot join Kawabata in saying "Japan, the Beautiful, and Myself"'.[2]

But even if the social/political relevance of Kawabata's work is not immediately apparent, certainly he does address, as all major writers do, more general questions about the human condition, questions of eternal relevance regarding such matters as the experience of time, the nature of the ego and its attendant problem of narcissism, the loss of innocence and purity and the attempt to recapture these, the experience of old age, the relation between men and women, human beings and nature, art and life, life and death, and the possibility of spiritual enlightenment and liberation from suffering. Surely such questions are important enough to confer sufficient depth and significance on any literary work which addresses them in a serious and original way – as Kawabata's does.

Indeed, when we look to the early phase of Kawabata's career, we find that he held an almost too-lofty and too-serious view of the function of literature. He began very optimistically with the Arnoldian belief that literature would replace religion in the new age of scientific materialism that was dawning the world over. In order to make his own work adequate to this spiritual or salvational role, he tried to imbue it with a mystical/ monistic vision which drew upon such diverse sources as Western occultism and surrealism as well as his own religious and artistic tradition. Although his expression of this vision became less explicit and less optimistic in his later work, it always remained with him as a longed-for if unattainable ideal – and thus as an important element of continuity throughout his total *oeuvre*.

On the moral and psychological level, the main questions Kawabata explores in his work derive from his view of the problems endemic to relations between men and women: for example, male narcissism, eroticism and aestheticism, which all lead to the dehumanization and exploitation of women, even to the extreme we might describe as 'the male as vampire' – a theme which became increasingly important in late Kawabata.

A more particular set of questions arises from Kawabata's interest in and exploration of the nature and fate of the artist, the aesthete, the passive man of sensitivity, more an observer of life than an active participant in it. These questions clearly have an autobiographical relevance: it is obviously no coincidence that the central protagonist of most of Kawabata's major works is a man of this type and of about the same age as Kawabata when he wrote the work. If we follow the progress of this 'Kawabata hero' from an early work like *The Dancing Girl of Izu* to a late work like *Sleeping Beauties*, we may construct a kind of 'metanarrative' out of the entire *oeuvre*, the life-story of the Kawabata hero from his lyrical and innocent if troubled youth to a bitter and despairing old age tinged by more than a hint of evil. Along the way we may follow the course of his relations with women and the self-discoveries and spiritual struggles which result from these. As with the writers of *shishōsetsu* – often regarded as the mainstream genre of modern Japanese fiction – there is thus a continuing correspondence and interaction between Kawabata's life and his work – if not always with literal equivalences then at least symbolically.

Finally, although one must take account of the negative and, for any reader, potentially depressing aspects of Kawabata's work, one should also acknowledge that his work ultimately triumphs over all of these – not by any facile 'happy ending' nor by any explicit statement of an optimistic philosophy but, as great writing should, by the power and beauty of its language. There is a quiet, meditative, poetic quality to Kawabata's language which speaks more eloquently of a victory of the spirit over suffering and of a serene joy in life than any explicit statement could do. In this respect, certainly, it shares something with the language of *haiku* and of Zen. In trying to describe this mysterious power of Kawabata's style, even a critic may be tempted to wax poetic.

> Each word casts
> a sound into silence
> and the shimmer of silence
> casts a shadow on time.
>
> Each word ventures
> a sounding in time
> unto depths that are soundless
> and timeless.

CHAPTER ONE

AN ORPHAN PSYCHOLOGY

1. The Diary of a Sixteen-Year-Old

Readers of Kawabata often come away with a general impression of coldness – as if 'snow country', the title of one of his most famous novels, were also an appropriate description of the whole world of his fiction. His novels possess a certain beauty, such readers usually agree, but it is a cold, inhuman beauty, a beauty of surfaces, of an exclusively aesthetic world in which the fine sheen of a woman's skin is savored in exactly the same way as the fine sheen of a piece of pottery.[1] These readers seem tempted to say of Kawabata what Cézanne once said of Monet: 'He is only an eye ...' – though they too may allow, as Cézanne did: 'but what an eye!'

Other readers, more sympathetic and perhaps more perceptive, speak not so much of coldness as of a longing for warmth, a longing in itself 'warm' enough to melt the ice of aesthetic detachment which forms the surface glaze of Kawabata's work. The aesthetic detachment itself, in fact, is seen as only the obverse side of a profoundly human sensitivity: either in a negative sense, as a defence mechanism against further emotional wounds, or, in a more positive sense, as a compensation in the currency of beauty for the major losses Kawabata sustained in the currency of love. Such 'sympathetic' readers often notice too that Kawabata's 'longing for warmth' also assumes, quite early in his writings, a spiritual and even a religious dimension: as if universal love, or the mystical experience of union with all creation, might replace the lost love of his mother. In this spiritual search which seems to animate Kawabata's work at its deepest level, there is also, such readers feel, a profoundly human pathos which belies the pose of aesthetic detachment.

Whichever of these very general views of Kawabata's work one takes, in trying to account for either the 'coldness' or the 'longing for warmth' one is inevitably led back to his childhood. Frequent readers of literary biography no doubt have heard enough of the unhappy childhoods of great writers, of Dickens' blacking factory and Proust's hay fever, and of the lasting effect of these childhood traumas on both the writer's character and work. But Kawabata's childhood sufferings certainly were not merely the product of the kind of abnormal sensitivity common among future artists. Even by the extreme standards of literary biography, his childhood was an unusually painful one. Though it is always impossible to measure such things with anything like scientific accuracy, the conclusion seems as inescapable as it is obvious that this 'wounded childhood'[2] had a profound and lasting impact on both the man and his writings. And one may see this impact in its most explicit form, of course, in Kawabata's more directly autobiographical writings, such as his very first publication of significance, *The Diary of a Sixteen-Year-Old (Jūrokusai no nikki*, 1925).

The title of this early Kawabata work may seem self-explanatory in a rather bland way, but actually it is deceiving on several counts. In the first place, the work should not be regarded as a mere piece of juvenalia. To say that it is not an ordinary 'teenager's diary' is an almost humourous under-statement. Kawabata, of course, was no ordinary teenager: if the *Diary* itself is to be credited, already at fourteen he possessed, to an almost frightening degree, the necessary detachment of the artist from the object he would depict – even if that object happened to be his own grandfather. On the other hand, the actual age of the author when he wrote the work is a matter of dispute, in spite of the open declaration of the title. Some critics are convinced that the *Diary* is a kind of literary fraud, that it was written, by and large, the same year it was published, eleven years after the events it describes, by an ambitious twenty-six-year-old up-and-coming writer, eager to prove himself, retro-actively, to have been a child prodigy.[3] There is a further complication, in fact, in that the author was 'sixteen' at the time of his grandfather's death only by *kazoedoshi*, the old Japanese way of computing age, according to which a person is one at birth and two at the start of the following new year. By Western and modern Japanese count, Kawabata was fourteen. Thus one critic, who accepts the author's assurances that the diary proper was written contemporaneously with the events it describes, suggests that the title should now be changed to *The Diary of a Fourteen-Year-Old*.[4]

More significant, though, than these questions regarding the author's age are the ambiguities which arise from the other term of the title, 'diary'. The work hardly conforms to our usual (Western) notions of what constitutes a diary, although many precedents for it could be found in the long Japanese tradition of 'diary literature' (*nikki bungaku*). It is more like a short story in the way it focuses on a single dramatic action – the death of the diarist's grandfather – and presents vivid portraits of two 'characters' distinct from the diarist himself: his grandfather and the maid, Omiyo. Regardless of the age at which it was written, this is a work which deals with weighty themes and is the product of a mature, disciplined artistry. Published in a leading literary journal, the *Bungei Shunjū* (*Literary Times*) just four months before the publication of *The Dancing Girl of Izu* (*Izu no Odoriko*, 1926) catapulted the young author to overnight fame, the *Diary* is Kawabata's first really significant creative work. Though in some ways unique, it may justifiably be regarded, when viewed in the context of his total *oeuvre*, as the fountainhead of much that was to follow.

2. The Boy Diarist

Of the *Diary*'s three portraits, the liveliest and fullest is not, as we might expect, of the boy diarist himself but of his grandfather. This has led some critics to assign the boy an entirely subordinate role, comparing him to the *waki* or deuteragonist in a Nō drama, vis-à-vis his grandfather as *shite* or 'doer'.[5] Though both the boy and the maid, Omiyo, do perform the *waki*-like role of drawing the old man's 'story' out of him (perhaps Omiyo more so than the boy), in the work as a whole the grandson's role is surely more central and active than this. Much of the drama, in fact, arises from the clash of two male egos, the boy's and his grandfather's. This is a rare thing in Kawabata, since generally he is more interested in male-female than in male-male relations, and it is exactly this which gives the *Diary* more open dramatic tension than the usual Kawabata story or novel. Another conspicuous exception, of course, is a much later work, *The Master of Go* (*Meijin*, 1954), in which also two males clash – only, in this case, over a game of *go*.

If the *Diary* is concerned, as is the typical Nō play, with spiritual salvation, then it is the spiritual salvation of the boy at least as much as of his grandfather. This is not true of the *waki*, who is usually a Buddhist priest who brings salvation to the *shite*, often a discontented ghost. Indeed, if the boy's role were confined to that of a mere 'witness', as Arthur Waley calls the *waki*,[6] then Kawabata's claim that the *Diary* was his 'one and only frank autobiography'[7] would be a strange one indeed. In an autobiography, needless to say, one expects a little more self-revelation. I do not wish to argue that an author is always the final authority on his own work, but it seems to me that, in this case at least, the author's claim is not so greatly exaggerated. The *Diary* does tell us much about the diarist, albeit often in an indirect way. To be sure, we are told far more about his grandfather but, after all, this is partly a function of their respective ages: there is inevitably more to tell about a seventy-five-year-old man than about a fourteen-year-old boy. Thus, whereas we are given an impression of the whole life and character of the old man, the boy's life and character are defined mainly in relation to his grandfather. While it is true, as some critics have pointed out,[8] that the boy does not often give free vent to his thoughts and feelings, there is enough in what he says and does to give us an adequate idea of these, and there is much that we can read 'between the lines'. Furthermore, in the two postscripts – which, as several critics have argued,[9] form an integral part of the total work – the thoughts and feelings of the now mature diarist are presented explicitly as one of the major themes.

From the very beginning of the *Diary*'s first entry, for 4 May [1914], we are quickly and vividly introduced to the boy and his unfortunate situation: he returns home from school to a closed, silent house in which his blind, ailing grandfather is asleep all alone. No-one answers his friendly call of *tadaima* ('I'm home!'), making him feel, as he tells us, 'sad and lonely'.[10] The boy must repeat this greeting several times before the grandfather finally responds. But, rather than answering with the usual warm greeting of *okaeri nasai* ('welcome back!'), the old man immediately begins to complain: no-one has helped him to relieve himself since morning, he has been waiting in agony, and he needs to be turned to face another direction. He then demands impatiently that the boy make some tea and bring him the glass urinal. Confronted by this irascible, demanding old invalid, the boy understandably begins to lose his temper. He makes it clear that the duty of fitting the old man's penis into the glass urinal and holding it while he urinates is particularly distasteful to him. But, since 'it can't be helped', he performs this onerous task with admirable equanimity. Then, as he is doing so, there seems to occur a sudden and remarkable transformation in his psychological state:

> 'Ahh, ahh, it hurts! ouch! ouch! ahh! ahh!'
> It hurts when he urinates. Along with his voice, which sounds like that of a man whose painful breathing is about to stop, the sound of the clear water of a valley stream on the bottom of the glass urinal.

11

'Ahh, it hurt!'
Hearing his voice, which sounds as if he can't bear
the pain, I am moved to tears.[11]

In the small drama of this opening scene, which reaches a
'mini-climax' in the above passage, we may see that, while the
grandfather plays the role of passive sufferer and insensitive
provoker of the boy's suffering, it is with the boy's feelings and
psychology that we are mainly concerned. And these are by no
means simple, even in so short a scene. Already, in fact, the
basic pattern which they will assume throughout the entire
work is clearly evident: the pendulum swings between anger,
resentment and despair on the one side and shame, pity and
compassion on the other.

Actually, there are two forms of tension here, each of which
contributes to the overall dramatic tension which structures the
Diary into a literary work. Firstly, there is the overt tension
between the boy, a mere fourteen years old, who has his own
legitimate boyish needs and desires, and the old man, as
helpless and demanding as any infant. It should be noted that
this is in addition to the in-built, natural opposition which
already exists between the boy and the old man merely by their
being juxtaposed against each other: innocent, healthy youth
opposed to corrupt and decrepit old age. This kind of passive,
contrastive opposition would become an important part of
Kawabata's method in his later works. And, even in the *Diary*,
it is used to good effect. As the work progresses, the contrast is
strengthened and clarified, and it functions not only on a
physiological level, as in the above scene of the boy taking the
old man's urine, but also morally and intellectually: the boy
seems strong-willed, unsentimental and clear-sighted in contrast to his weak-willed, n'er-do-well, self-pitying and self-
deluded grandfather. Thus we can see that, in this sense also,
the boy's role is indispensable: he is one side of a polar
opposition at the core of the work's structure. As already noted,
though, to an extent rare in Kawabata this 'passive' opposition
erupts into an active and dramatic one. And, secondly, there
are the tensions in the boy himself: between, on the one hand,
his sense of duty and the love and compassion he feels for his
grandfather, and, on the other, his natural desire to escape
from a terrible burden. But what is also of great significance is
the psychological process by which both these overt and inner
tensions are momentarily resolved in the above passage.

The sentence which contains the implied metaphor equating
the sound of urine with the sound of stream water has probably

been more commented on than any other part of the *Diary*, and, indeed, is one of the most celebrated sentences in the whole of Kawabata. How each critic interprets this metaphor depends ultimately, of course, on his or her view of the work as a whole. But most seem to agree, at least, that it contains an important key to the overall significance of the *Diary*. Indeed, one could even argue, without too much exaggeration, that Kawabata, throughout his entire career, never strayed far from the poetic and philosophic vision embodied in this metaphor contained in a single sentence written, supposedly, when he was fourteen years old.

Donald Keene may betray a characteristically Western viewpoint when he calls the metaphor 'ironic'.[12] Japanese interpreters seem to consider it anything but that. In general, they tend to take it more seriously, and more literally. Hasegawa Izumi, for instance, who was the first critic to analyse the *Diary* at length, views the metaphor first as a manifestation of the extraordinary poetic sensibility of the young Kawabata. But, more than that, he sees it as an example of how the writer's indomitable spirit, through poetic inspiration, may rise above the sorrows of life.[13] A number of early critics, in fact, assign to the metaphor this double-edged moral/aesthetic function: it is an 'aestheticization' of an ugly reality which, at the same time, serves to strengthen and purify the boy's spirit.[14] Yamamoto Kenkichi makes the poetic quality of the metaphor seem even more convincing by showing how it anticipated a modernist *haiku* of Ishida Hakyō (1913-69): 'Autumn dusk: the chamber pot sounds with the voice of spring water'. (*'Aki no kure shubin izumi no koe o nasu'*.[15])

Perhaps the most thorough treatment of the psychological and philosophical basis of the metaphor is given by Sasabuchi Tomoichi. According to this critic, the metaphor is not merely an example of 'beautification' but reveals a Buddhist/surrealist 'metamorphosis', realized in the deepest part of the imagination, and necessitated by the boy's unconscious desire to resolve the dualism between pure water (representing life) and urine (representing death).[16] Tsuruta Kinya also sees the image as resolving a life/death dualism but in a more concrete way: the water image psychologically washes clean the physiological stain that comes from the approach of death.[17] This whole process, according to Tsuruta, is made possible by the child-like simplicity of the boy, for whom 'water is water', as well as by his deep-down love of his grandfather, which moves him thus to try to oppose the old man's coming death with the power of beauty. 'The reason why we cannot receive a feeling of impurity [*yogore*] from this work, even though it deals with death, is because the author's incomparable naïveté and his devotion to his grandfather support the work at its deepest level'.[18]

However we evaluate the metaphor aesthetically (and certainly Kawabata later created more sophisticated and more beautiful ones), its importance to any understanding of the boy's psychology is quite evident. I would agree with those critics to whom it signifies the overcoming of a duality, but it seems to me that this duality exists primarily within the boy himself: it arises more from his struggle against his own ego than from his struggle against his grandfather's imminent death. We have already seen that, immediately prior to the appearance of the startling metaphor, the boy was in a state of inner tension: his repugnance at the task before him was at war with his sense of duty towards his grandfather. The way in which he resolves this inner tension, as signified by the metaphor, is by cutting off all discriminative thinking, all thoughts of 'pleasant' and 'unpleasant', 'dirty' and 'clean' and, by a leap of poetic imagination, identifying the urine of a sick old man with the pure water of a valley stream. If he can convince himself, in this way, that one is as good as the other, that such diverse-seeming phenomena are fundamentally the same in essence, then he will be able to undermine the resistance of his ego to performing such a 'disagreeable' task.

This psychological strategy of nondiscrimination or non-dualism is not unique to the boy, of course; most famously in East Asian culture, it is given profound philosophic expression in the Mahayana Buddhist teaching of the identity of *samsâra* – the realm of physical existence – with *nirvâna* – the realm of enlightenment. This is a teaching which, as Nakamura Hajime has shown,[19] the Japanese in particular, with their 'this-worldly' temperament, have taken closely to heart. The development of a non-discriminative consciousness is the avowed purpose of many forms of spiritual discipline in Japan – from Zen meditation to the Tenrikyō practice of cleaning out, without charge, other people's non-flush toilets. Thus it is hardly surprising that the boy diarist, feeling himself trapped in a hellish situation, and suffering also from severe inner tensions, should seek relief in the way sanctioned by his cultural tradition: by changing, not the situation, but his own consciousness. This is made all the more convincing by the fact that Buddhism in particular looms large in his home environment and in the thematic structure of the *Diary* itself. Indeed, the very metaphor he uses calls to mind the twenty-first 'case' (*kōan*) of the *Mumonkan* (*The Gateless Gate of Mumon*), a famous Zen scripture of the Sung dynasty (thirteenth century) still used in the training of Zen monks:

> A monk asked Ummon: 'What is the Buddha?'
> Ummon replied: 'A dried shit-stick'.[20]

Needless to say, this *kōan* provides one of the most extreme – and humourous – expressions of Mahayana non-dualism, identifying the highest spiritual reality with a dried (therefore useless) 'shit-stick' (the Chinese of the day used bamboo sticks in lieu of toilet paper). Kawabata's metaphor, we might say, moves in the opposite direction, but ultimately with the same purport: 'the shit-stick is Buddha' – that is, 'the old man's urine is pure valley water'.

From the same Buddhist perspective, it is important to note also what follows the boy's *satori*-like realization that urine and pure water are one. Not only does his rancour at the unpleasant task subside but he also opens himself, for the first time, to feelings of compassion for the old man's suffering: 'Hearing his voice, which sounds as if he can't bear the pain, I am moved to tears'.[21] His momentary state of non-duality thus proves to have wider implications: it reconciles not only urine and pure water but also boy and old man. As if to demonstrate this point, the boy's first act, after he sheds tears of compassion, is to serve the old man tea – which, of course, will soon necessitate that he again perform the 'disagreeable' task.

Though the diarist's metaphor – and Ummon's – is a particularly startling case of the 'union of opposites', one could argue quite cogently that a monistic world view actually forms the basis of all metaphors, and even of poetry itself. Thus, when one critic describes the urine/water metaphor as 'surrealistic' on the basis of its non-duality,[22] his logic must be faulted: surrealism may be monist, but it does not follow that all literary expressions of monism are surrealistic. Many of Bashō's haiku express a nondualistic world view, but obviously it would be anachronistic to call Bashō a surrealist.

Even in the Western context, surrealism itself may be properly viewed as an extreme development of romanticism and, as R.H. Blyth has exhaustively demonstrated, elements of monism may be found in all of the great romantic poets.[23] And one could go further afield than that: all poets with 'mystical' inclinations, from Dante to Blake to Yeats, have written some of their greatest poems from the perspective of a non-dualistic consciousness. Dante's final great vision in the last canto of the *Paradiso*, his 'beatific vision', is a monist vision on the grandest scale imaginable:

> I saw gathered there in the depths of it,
> Bound up by love into a single volume,
> All the leaves scattered through the universe;
>
> Substance and accidents and their relations,
> But yet fused together in such a manner
> That what I am talking of is a simple light.[24]

Commenting on the unitive vision of the *Divine Comedy*'s last canto, T.S. Eliot remarked: 'It is the real right thing, the power of establishing relations between beauty of the most diverse sorts: it is the utmost power of the poet'.[25] If this power of 'establishing relations', of finding unity in diversity, is, as Eliot suggests, the poetic power *par excellence*, then Kawabata is one of the most poetic of novelists. He is poetic not merely because, as many have remarked, he writes *haiku*-like sentences, but because his total world view is a quintessentially poetic one. The celebrated metaphor of the *Diary* is only a small augury of all that was to follow.

In his seminal essay on the subject, Hadori Tetsuya has amply demonstrated the young Kawabata's attraction to various forms of monist philosophy, both Western and Eastern, and his liberal use of these as thematic material in many of his early works.[26] The young writer was drawn to these philosophies, according to Hadori, by his search for some way to transcend death, a search made urgent not only by his personal experience, the early loss of all members of his immediate family, but also by the general history of the age: the death of so many in the First World War, and then in the Great Kantō Earthquake of 1923. It was an apocalyptic age; many were convinced that worse disasters were imminent, perhaps even the end of the world.[27]

Kawabata's early preoccupation with death may thus be seen as a natural expression of the spirit of the times, as well as of the series of tragic losses he suffered in his own life. In an article he wrote in the early 'twenties, 'Eternal Life and Immortality', he clearly expressed the hope which he felt a monist philosophy held out for the transcendence of death: 'To save the human being from personal death, it seems that the best way is to blur into vagueness the boundaries between one individual and another, and between the human being and all other objects of the physical world'.[28] In other words, the more one identifies oneself with the species as a whole, or with nature as a whole, the more one partakes of their 'immortality' and the less one feels the heavy burden of one's own fate as an individual doomed to die.

16

We can see, then, that in the more concrete terms of the *Diary*, by identifying human urine with natural water, the boy not only 'purifies' the urine and thus overcomes his revulsion towards it, but also he identifies the old man with the larger world of nature and thus, if only for a moment, frees him from the grip of death. There is thus a philosophic as well as an aesthetic significance to the metaphor: it opposes death not only with its beauty, but also with its monist world view. In this sense, it operates as what Cleanth Brooks has called a 'functional metaphor', as opposed to a merely illustrative one.[29] And Kawabata would continue to use the monist world view in this way, though in ever more sophisticated and ambiguous forms, right up to such a late work as 'One Arm' (*Kata ude*, 1963-64). It seems that he never completely lost his faith that 'man's salvation', as he put it in an early story, lies along the 'retrogressive road' which leads back to the primeval 'world of unity in diversity'.[30] And, in his first significant work, the *Diary*, it is the boy diarist, supposedly Kawabata himself, who is assigned the important role of expressing this non-dualistic point of view.

It may be noted, though, that by identifying his grandfather with nature, the boy to some extent depersonalizes him. There are even more obvious examples of this depersonalizing tendency in some of his later descriptions of the old man's physical appearance. When, for instance, immediately after the above scene in which he has helped the old man to relieve himself, he serves him some tea:

> I helped him to drink drop by drop. Face bony, white-haired head mostly bald. Trembling hands all skin and bone. The Adam's apple in the long, crane-like neck bobs up and down as he drinks each gulp. Three cups of tea. [31]

This is the kind of coolly detached, clear-sighted objectivity that Kobayashi Hideo, the most distinguished of modern Japanese critics, referred to as the 'terrible quality of the child' (*kodomo no osoroshisa*),[32] and many subsequent critics have also remarked upon it: for example, Hadori even claims that the fact that the boy describes his grandfather's death so coolly may indicate that he did not love the old man as much as he loved his grandmother.[33] His dispassion may indeed seem at first sight incompatible with the compassion towards the old man which he expresses on other occasions. But without this objectivity the *Diary* would be far less of a work of art; it might easily degenerate into the sort of sentimental, commonplace 'teenager's diary' that is of interest only to the diarist himself.

Thus it seems important that we distinguish between the boy's two main roles: as creative writer and as loving grandson. The former role obliges him to stand back, to observe dispassionately, with unflinching honesty. Anything less would compromise his mimetic function as artist. The 'terrible quality' is not so much of the child as of the artist – it is the same quality which so disturbed the friends of Leonardo da Vinci when they observed him coolly sketching the final spasms of a hanged man. The latter role, that of loving grandson, obliges the boy to participate fully in the unfolding events, to experience to the utmost all the emotional ups and downs attendant upon his relationship with his dying grandfather. Needless to say, the balance struck between these two roles is a delicate one, and it is difficult for the reader not to confuse them at times. This can lead to some misinterpretations of the boy's character, but not necessarily so; in fact, his two roles are not entirely contradictory. By calling upon his objectifying powers as a writer, the boy is better able to cope with his grandfather's suffering. As Isogai Hideo writes:

> One imagines the figure of the boy who, for the very reason that he suffers within a hell from which there is no escape, tries to regain his spiritual composure by capturing the surface level of that reality as seen from a cool third-person point of view. Since escape from reality was impossible, he had no choice but to find his way out of the situation by changing his own consciousness.[34]

In this sense, his writing of the *Diary*, like his embrace of a monistic world view, may be regarded as a psychological strategy for coping with the agony of his grandfather's debilitation and death. Thus, paradoxically, his moments of detachment may be seen as a sort of inverse measure of the love he holds for his grandfather, as the necessary other side to his moments of compassion – in the same way as his 'coolness' or longing for warmth may be seen to bespeak a great underlying capacity for warmth. And his two roles, apparently in opposition, may ultimately be reconciled. This is, indeed, one of Kawabata's major achievements in the *Diary*. It was a necessary achievement, because neither of the boy's roles could be relinquished. Without the grandson's feelings, the work would lack emotional depth; without the writer's detachment, it would lack aesthetic integrity.

If, then, there is no fundamental contradiction between the boy's compassion and his detachment, neither is there between his detachment and his monism. Monism, after all, implies egolessness: to experience oneness with all things, the individual consciousness itself must be 'depersonalized'. The boy-as-artist achieves something of this state when he becomes an objective 'camera eye', able to record with sharp-focused precision whatever comes into view. Isogai even goes so far as to say: 'The form of human life which is naturally revealed through selfless eyes – there, in a word, lies the power of this work'.[35] Perhaps he exaggerates a little here: the work does possess other forms of power, such as the dramatic power engendered when the boy, in full possession of his ego, comes into conflict with his grandfather. (For the boy, after all, is not a full-fledged mystic; his brief moments of monistic 'enlightenment', though no doubt refreshing to his troubled spirit, do not resolve his tensions forever.) But certainly the great power of the boy's portrait of his grandfather, for instance, derives from its unsparing objectivity.

If we distinguish, then, between the boy's two roles, as writer and as grandson, we may trace clearly how each of these is developed and concluded throughout the course of the *Diary*. His dualistic tensions are not conclusively resolved by his metaphoric *satori* – they are an important part of the work's ongoing drama. One may find throughout other such 'poetic moments' created by him which also resolve various other forms of duality. When the boy brings a lamp close to the old man's face and the light shining on his eyelids creates the illusion that he has opened his eyes and can see again, there is a momentary resolution of the duality of light/darkness: 'It was a happy thing, as if a ray of light had shined into a world of darkness'.[36] Again, in the boy's description of the impression he receives from his grandfather's voice as it calls out in the quiet of the night, there is an attempted resolution between the dark hell of his grandfather's present condition and heaven itself: 'From a room plunged in the midst of pitch darkness, a voice was spat out in spasms, a voice that seemed to appeal to heaven'.[37] On the other hand, this duality is turned in the opposite direction by Omiyo when she accuses the old man of trying to pull 'the stars down from heaven'.[38] When the grandfather cries on being told by Omiyo of the overwhelming generosity of the villagers in sending congratulatory gifts on the birth of her first grandchild, the boy remarks that 'in his tearful voice, somehow, real tears were mixed with tears of joy',[39] thus resolving the duality between the joy of the new baby's birth and the sorrow of the old man's imminent death.

A more subtle kind of dualistic leap, like that of electricity between a positive and a negative pole, occurs after the old man has recited the *nembutsu* ('Hail to Amitabha Buddha!'), signifying that he is near death, and the boy writes: 'By the light of the lamp grandfather's long beard shone golden. I felt lonely'.[40] This form of resolution of a subject/object duality – the boy's loneliness being somehow intensified by the eerie glow of his grandfather's beard – was a conscious part of the young Kawabata's 'neo-perceptionist' method,[41] and would become quite common in his later work. We may see it again, though in a less directly metaphorical form, in another passage of the *Diary*: 'There is a long, high groan. It is an evening of early summer rain'.[42] In such *haiku*-like or *renga*-like 'leaps', the correspondence between the two terms verges on the non-rational, the inexpressible – one might call it suprametaphorical – but it exists nonetheless, and the reader is convinced of the underlying coalescence, in Kawabata's mysteriously animistic world, of human and natural phenomena.

One might also note that as the distance between the two terms is stretched almost to breaking point, there is created the kind of resonant, kinetic space or interval which Japanese aestheticians have long referred to as *ma*.[43] These 'pregnant pauses' serve much the same function in literature as do the 'blank spaces' in Zen-inspired ink painting: they afford the mind an intuition of the emptiness from which all form arises, and they invite the imagination to fill in what is missing. I shall discuss in more detail Kawabata's particular use of this device – not only in his 'suprametaphors' but also in his transitions from scene to scene – when I analyse some of his later works, but for now I shall simply point out that, since *ma* is a manifestation of *mu* (the Buddhist nothingness), it also points to the ultimate resolution of all dualities.

It is important to note also that all these moments of duality-resolution are accompanied by at least an implied sense of compassion for the old man. And there are more direct expressions of this: most conspicuously, when the boy discovers a book his grandfather has written on *kasō*, the art of fortune-telling based on the aspect and position of a house. Since the book was rejected for publication, it reminds the boy of his grandfather's whole pitiful life, a life full of losses and disappointments:

> Ah, what must be the feelings in grandfather's heart,
> he not having attained his one goal in life, and having
> failed somehow at whatever he set his hand to. But,

fortunately, he lived on for us to his seventy-fifth year through all these adversities. His heart was robust. (I thought that grandfather was able to live a long life, though enduring many sorrows, because his heart was robust.) He has outlived everyone's child and grandchild, he has no-one to talk to, nothing to look at or listen to (he was blind and almost deaf) – this is complete solitude. The sorrow of solitude – that is grandfather's condition. In his case, the common expression 'living in tears' is quite literally true.[44]

But even this outburst of deeply felt compassion does not signal the end of moments of equally deep resentment. In his diary entry for the very next day, 8 May, the boy tells of the conflict which occurred the night before:

Morning: grandfather eagerly awaits Omiyo's coming. Although he has repeatedly complained about my unkindness last night, he still feels he hasn't said enough. I also think that I acted rather badly. But when one is awakened any number of times during the night one tends to get angry. On top of that, I hate to have to assist him in relieving himself. [45]

These pendulum-like swings in the boy's mood only increase in intensity as the work progresses; simply because, as the old man's condition deteriorates, he naturally becomes more demanding, thus arousing more resentment as well as more pity. The dramatic role of the boy is thus to struggle not only against his grandfather's death but also against his own rebellious ego. The pendulum swings to its most extreme reach in the direction of resentment or egotism on several occasions after the compassionate outburst of 7 May: on 8 May, when the boy calls his grandfather a 'silly old dotard' after the old man doubts that he will achieve success in life;[46] and then, on 16 May, the final day of the diary proper, when the boy calls out to his grandfather that he is going to visit someone and, without waiting for an answer, dashes out of the house as if he can no longer bear his heavy responsibility.[47] When he returns later that night, he is met by only more demands for food from the old man. The final words of the diary proper leave us with a negative image of both grandfather and grandson, the growing senility of the one opposed to the growing impatience of the other:

He kept repeating time and again the same trivial, foolish things. Whatever I said just went straight in one ear and out the other, and he would ask me the same thing over again. What has become of his mind? [48]

Observing his grandfather with such clinical detachment, the diarist now seems remote from the caring, compassionate grandson of 7 May. It is a chill note on which to end.

Evidently Kawabata himself felt so on reading the diary over before its publication eleven years later, because he thought it necessary to add a substantial postscript, the obvious purpose of which is to swing the pendulum in the opposite direction. In this first postscript, the boy diarist's initial 'reincarnation', as the up-and-coming writer of twenty-five, he assures us that: 'I had a belief, however indistinct, in the dead man's wisdom and loving-kindness'.[49] And, as if to counteract the final impression left by the diary proper and to prove his underlying devotion to his grandfather, he recalls three incidents which occurred at about the time of his grandfather's death. Firstly, when his dying grandfather gratefully welcomed the ministrations of a Western-style doctor, even though, as a practitioner of traditional Chinese-style medicine, he had always held such doctors in contempt, the boy at first felt betrayed, but then felt 'a painful sense of pity for him'.[50] Secondly, on the day his grandfather died the boy attended a memorial service for the dowager empress at his school. After the ceremony was over, the boy was filled with an uneasy premonition. Taking off his wooden clogs, he ran barefoot all of the five miles home. Sure enough, his grandfather had died shortly after he arrived. Thirdly, after the old man's death, when the house which had belonged to their family for generations had to be sold, the author tells us 'it was painful to think of the love grandfather had towards it'.[51] Needless to say, each of these three memories reflects well on the boy as a filial grandson, thus redressing the image we might have formed of him from the conclusion of the diary proper, and finally resolving the dramatic conflict between his resentment and his compassion in favour of the latter.

This *ex post facto* resolution is further strengthened when the boy's second 'reincarnation', the forty-nine-year-old author of the second postscript, addressing the problem of 'why did I write this kind of diary?', concludes that: 'Undoubtedly when I saw that grandfather was soon to die I wanted to preserve an image of him ...'.[52] Surely, again, this is a commendable sentiment in a grandson.

This emotional drama in the boy's relation with his grand-father has a lesser parallel on an intellectual level: namely, the struggle within him between the forces of an ancient tradition of folk beliefs, represented by his grandfather and Omiyo, and the forces of a modern, sceptical, 'scientific' education, represented by his school. Here the particular historical moment – 1914 – plays a considerable role, as does also the particular place – the countryside of the Kansai area, the main centre of traditional Japanese culture. As the *Diary* clearly shows, the old folk traditions were still very much alive in Toyokawa, the village of Kawabata's boyhood. Furthermore, his own grandfather was a prime representative of those traditions: with his seemingly accurate fortune-tellings and his almost miraculous cure of a mass outbreak of dysentery, he had gained respect as something of a local *shaman*. He was, in fact, an educated and cultured man, but only in the old-fashioned sense: an expert in folk medicine, fortune-telling, house-divination and so on. Since the boy had already been given the foundations of a modern education, his attitude to his grandfather's special 'expertise' was already ambiguous. As the twenty-six-year-old author tells us in one of his bracketed notes:

> (I remember that, at this time, my feelings towards grandfather's fortune-telling and house-divination were uncertain – I neither believed nor disbelieved. Even so, no matter how countrified we were, the fact that I, a fourteen-year-old third-year student in middle school, didn't have a doctor look at grandfather, although he'd been constipated for thirty days, but rather consulted with the diviners at the Inari shrine, thinking that he might be possessed by an evil spirit – when I consider this fact now, I find it hard to laugh about.)[53]

We see, then, that the boy's attitude towards the old ways, his grandfather's ways, is by no means one of outright rejection, despite all his new-found sophistication as a 'third-year student in middle school'. This is particularly evident in his struggle with the idea mentioned in the above quotation, that his grandfather's illness is caused by an evil spirit. Encouraged in this 'superstition' by Omiyo, his mind becomes obsessed by it and, despite his skepticism, he agrees to perform a sword-waving ritual in an attempt to exorcise the evil spirit. Thus we may conclude that, if anything, the 'old ways' gain an ascendancy in the boy's mind, and this also may be considered a result of his own monistic tendencies: the practice of such rituals, after all, leads to a sense of oneness with one's fellow men – including one's ancestors – with the natural world and with a higher spiritual reality, whereas the 'new ways' of modern science and intellectual skepticism often lead to a sense of alienation. This is why even later, in his 'twenties, Kawabata was strongly attracted to various forms of occultism and theosophical spiritualism, as well as to the more orthodox religions, and allowed these to influence his work.[54] In this respect too the *Diary* is an important augury of what was to follow.

If, in this way, the author finally proves himself a loving grandson in the two postscripts, he also more consciously addresses and clarifies there his role as creative writer. His main concern in this regard seems to be to reconcile the two roles: how is it possible that a loving grandson, faced by the dreadful prospect of his grandfather's imminent death, still is able to achieve the detachment necessary for turning any subject into an aesthetic object? Or, more to the point: why would he want to do so, if not for his self-centred ambition as a writer? Are his ambitions as a writer, then, more important to him than his feelings for his grandfather?

In both the *Diary* proper and in the two postscripts, the apparent contradiction is resolved by viewing the act of writing itself as an act of love. According to a note in the diary proper, the boy was able even to assign a kind of occult, shamanistic power to the act of writing, so that he felt that, if the diary reached a hundred pages, his grandfather's life would be spared.[55] And he also believed in writing as a preserver of life in a more conventional sense: though his grandfather might die, the *Diary* would capture his image forever. Repeating this latter sentiment in the second postscript, the forty-nine-year-old author adds that, even so, 'when I think of the fourteen-year-old me sitting beside a dying man and writing a sketch-like diary about him, from my present perspective it seems strange'.[56] In other words, he himself is surprised that, though a loving grandson, he was able to describe his grandfather with such sketch-like objectivity. But, as I have already indicated, what this really shows is not that he was lacking in filial affection but that his aesthetic instincts were already quite sound: he knew that, without this objectivity, the image he created of his grandfather would lack staying power as literature. As he says towards the end of the second postscript: 'the fact that it can be read as a literary work is on account of this sketch-like quality'.[57]

As one would expect, the sudden changes from the writer as fourteen-year-old in the diary proper to the writer as twenty-five-year-old in *Postscript One* and forty-eight-year-old in *Postscript Two* bring with them appropriate changes in the quality and level of sophistication of the authorial point of view. The fourteen-year-old lives almost entirely in the present; he records his grandfather's words almost directly as they are spoken. Needless to say, this does not allow him much time to reflect on his role as writer (and it will be noted that even the above statements regarding his motives were written either in a note by the twenty-five-year-old or in *Postscript Two*). The two postscripts, by way of contrast, contain some sophisticated, Proustian meditations on the writer's relation to passing time. In *Postscript One*, he remarks that when he first discovered the diary ten years after it was written, what struck him as most strange was that he could not remember a thing about the daily life described therein;[58] fortunately, this forgotten life still survived within the pages of the diary. But his purpose here is not simply to sing the praises of the art of writing as a way of redeeming lost time. For his next point is that, confronted by the 'now-forgotten sincere feelings of the past', he found that 'the figure of my grandfather presented in the diary was more ugly than the one I held in my memory. My memory had continued to wash clean its image of my grandfather for ten years'.[59] And, in *Postscript Two*, he goes further, claiming that: 'I, whose memory is bad, do not believe firmly in memory. There are times when I feel that forgetfulness is a grace'.[60]

Thus, just when it seems that the whole question of the apparent contradiction between his roles as grandson and as writer has been resolved, the author reopens it in a new and more general way, a way that seems to have important implications for his later work. *Postscript One* seems to say: forgetfulness, the enemy of the writer, is the ally of the grandson, who does not really want to be reminded of the uglier aspects of his grandfather's character. *Postscript Two* seems to raise this to a more general principle: forgetfulness being a 'grace', perhaps it is the ally of the writer as well as of the grandson. Perhaps the writer's work will express a purer, more poetic truth if he allows his memory to 'wash clean' every image that is to be admitted into its confines. Undoubtedly, such was, to some extent, the method of the later Kawabata: as he himself insisted, the Izu dancer of his story is not the same girl he met on his travels, nor is Komako the same hotspring *geisha* he encountered in the snow country – both were 'washed clean' by the writer's memory.[61]

The modest statement of *Postscript Two*, then, may be regarded as concealing a bold manifesto of the writer's creative freedom: he would not confine himself in the future to such 'naturalistic' or 'sketch-like' realism. Those critics such as Isogai who regret this fact may regard the above statement as a confession of Kawabata's unabashed romanticism: he seems to declare boldly that he prefers the idealizations of memory to the bitter truth. But it is not really as simple as that: an artist's choices in such matters may be based more on aesthetic than on philosophic grounds and, from this point of view, more may be gained than is lost. But this thorny question of Kawabata's 'romanticism' may be better dealt with in relation to some of his later works. Perhaps, for now, we should remind ourselves of what Samuel Beckett once said of Proust: that if it were not for his bad memory, he would never have felt the need to write *In Search of Lost Time*![62]

Given the prominence of the two themes of the diarist as grandson and as writer, it should be apparent that the *Diary* is as much his story as it is his grandfather's. Perhaps the work is best regarded as a 'story within a story', the grandfather's story coming within the framework of the grandson's. Since the boy diarist is the narrator, his story naturally forms the outer frame. And, though we are given a much stronger sense of the grandfather's character, and a more panoramic view of his life, this is, as already noted, a natural function of his far greater age; the boy, after all, does not have much of a past history to recount, nor has he had much time to develop personal idiosyncracies. Even in longer works of fiction, children generally are not given much 'character': typically, they are portrayed either as naughty pranksters or as passive victims. But Kawabata's boy diarist is given far more character than this; in his struggles with his grandfather and with his own recalcitrant self, he enacts his own individual drama. Indeed, as a portrait of a sensitive, intelligent boy suffering through an extreme crisis, the *Diary* contains scenes powerful enough to invite comparison with such classic Western portraits of the writer's troubled childhood as *David Copperfield*, *Tonio Kröger* and *A Portrait of the Artist as a Young Man*.

3. The Grandfather and His Influence

Though any literary work may be used as a tool for probing its author's psychology, for indulging in what Leon Edel, perhaps the most eminent contemporary practitioner of this form, calls 'literary psychology',[63] the temptation to use it in this way is particularly strong if the work is, like the *Diary*, largely autobiographical. Thus the fact that much of the 'serious' Japanese fiction of this century has presented itself and been accepted by its readers as more or less autobiographical may well account for the strong predilection for 'biographical criticism' among Japanese literary scholars and critics during most of this same period. Or perhaps it would be more accurate to say that both the 'autobiographical fiction' and the 'biographical criticism' issue from the same cultural source: the ancient 'lyrical heart' of Japanese literature. In the case of the *Diary*, Kawabata himself may be said to have encouraged these tendencies by describing it as 'my one and only frank autobiography'[64] and by insisting that the entire diary proper was a *bona fide* diary written by him as a fourteen-year-old. At any rate, given the fact that the *Diary* is, beyond doubt, more directly autobiographical than most of Kawabata's other works, it seems inevitable – and even justifiable – that critics should treat it as a rich source of biographical data.

Probably the most frequent use made of the *Diary* by such critical biographers is as evidence of the origins of Kawabata's so-called 'orphan psychology' (*koji no kanjō*). The phrase was coined by Kawabata himself,[65] but has become something of a catchphrase, the use of which seems *de rigueur* for anyone analyzing the relation between this author's life and work. If one looks for it, one may detect this 'orphan psychology' in many of Kawabata's early autobiographical stories but, as Hayashi points out,[66] because the *Diary* in particular was presented as written by the teenaged Kawabata, it has always been considered as closest to the source of this condition.

Several writers, though, have argued against a too-easy acceptance of Kawabata's self-image as an 'orphan'. Perhaps, they suggest, this is more of a useful literary pose than a deeply felt reality. Since he lost his parents at such an early age that he had no memories of them, he can hardly be thought to have missed them. And, on the other hand, his grandparents made excellent and, it seems, even overly indulgent substitute parents. As Hayashi remarks: 'Kawabata was a parentless child but, until the time of the *Diary* at least, he was not, to use his own words, a "stranger in a strange land" in terms of real relatives (and even after the time of the *Diary* there were still relatives he could rely on)'.[67]

Indeed, Kawashima Itaru goes so far as to claim that Kawabata, being raised by his grandparents, enjoyed an over-protected childhood, sheltered from the other village children and the outside world in general, and treated with much indulgence (*amae*, which some social psychologists regard as the key lubricant of Japanese social relations).[68] Attendance records show that the young Kawabata was often absent from school and, as he himself tells us in one of his early works, his grandfather even conspired to help him when he wanted to play truant.[69]

This brings us to the second major theme of biographical treatments of the *Diary*: the predominant role of the grandfather in the early, formative years of Kawabata's life. And a related question: what was the old man's true character? If we are to gauge the exact nature of his influence on his grandson, this is obviously something we must try to determine.

As has often been pointed out, Kawabata's real orphanage, at least in emotional terms, came not with the loss of his parents but with the loss of his grandfather, his last remaining relative and the relative who undoubtedly had the most profound impact on the boy's mental and emotional development. Indeed, Isogai Hideo goes so far as to say: 'I view as more important than Kawabata's orphan experience the fact that his boyhood was spent living with his grandfather'[70] – and certainly one could make a good argument for such a view. This fact alone, of course, gives to the *Diary*, Kawabata's main testimonial to his grandfather, a central importance from a biographical if not from a literary point of view. But how accurate a testimonial is it?

One may answer this question, first, by saying that the image of the grandfather which emerges from the pages of the diary proper, at least, is probably somewhat unfair to the man as he was throughout most of his life. As we have seen, Kawabata himself seemed to feel so later on and thus, we may surmise, felt compelled to add the mitigating postscripts. After all, few men are at their best on their deathbeds. In the grandfather's case, the combination of physical suffering and helplessness with encroaching senility was not calculated to bring out his best qualities. (On the other hand, 'man's extremity is God's opportunity', and, with his deathbed turn towards Buddhism, this proves to be so in his case too.) Thus some critics have tried to balance the picture by filling in some of the more positive aspects of the grandfather's character as he was in his healthier years. Furthermore, when certain of his failings are admitted to, some extenuating factors are found which would not have been evident to the young diarist. The general picture which emerges is of a good-hearted, well-intentioned if somewhat ineffectual man who, to some extent, was a victim of circumstance.

On the positive side, Hadori Tetsuya, for instance, emphasizes an aspect of the old man we are given little sense of in the

Diary: in a very traditional way, he was a man of culture; he tried his hand at painting as well as writing and he was something of a scholar of such *kangaku* ('Chinese learning') subjects as astrology and divination. 'Kawabata has said that an artist is not born in one generation, and probably we cannot ignore the role of this cultural refinement of the grandfather in producing the writer Kawabata'.[71] On the other hand, while admitting that Sanpachirō (the grandfather's personal name) managed to squander during his lifetime the quite large assets which the Kawabata family had amassed over many generations, Hadori advances some persuasive arguments to at least partly excuse the old man's prodigality and improvidence: basically, he sees him as a sort of sacrificial victim to the new Meiji god of capitalism.

The changeover from the feudal Tokugawa system to the new Meiji capitalism had a drastic effect on many small landowners: their taxes now had to be paid in cash rather than in rice and, since they could not raise sufficient funds for their taxes and other expenses by selling their rice, they had to begin to sell off their land. As the headman of his village and as a landlord directly in charge of collecting taxes, Sanpachirō was continually pressured from above to raise more money; thus he was obliged not only to sell his land but also to embark on various business schemes such as the cultivation of tea and the production of isinglass and folk medicines. He became totally caught up in the capitalist fever of the early and middle Meiji period (the last quarter of the nineteenth century). But Sanpachirō lacked the hard-headed business acumen and ruthless competitive spirit of the successful capitalist. Like Yasunari, he had been raised by indulgent grandparents and tended to see the world through rose-coloured glasses. This excessive optimism extended also to his estimate of his own abilities: he did not agree that 'the fault, dear Brutus, is not in our stars,/But in ourselves, that we are underlings'.[72] For Sanpachirō the astrologist, the fault was precisely 'in our stars'. Spurred on not only by tax collectors but also by his own ambition to restore the Kawabata family to its former glory, he engaged in one grandiose money-losing scheme after another until there was nothing left for the young Yasunari to inherit.

In this way, historical circumstances conspired with personal foibles to produce the financial collapse of a venerable family of *shōya* (village headmen).[73] Nevertheless, and regardless of Hadori's Marxist-tinged rhetoric about the 'cruelty of the modern capitalist system' which demands 'sacrificial victims',[74] we might say that, if Yasunari's first misfortune was the early death of his parents, his second misfortune was his grand-father's character, the end result of which was that the boy was left not only an orphan but a 'charity boy', dependent on the favours of more distant relatives. In other words, his childhood was pervaded not only by the sorrow of bereavement but by the humiliation of hurt pride. If one were to look in Kawabata for the source of that determined ambition which any writer must have to drive him on to great achievements, one might look first at this sorry tale of his grandfather's failures. It was left to the grandson to restore the Kawabata name to an even greater glory than it had previously known – and this at a moment when it seemed that the family was on the verge of extinction! When Yasunari became the first Japanese to receive the Nobel Prize in literature, one might imagine that it consoled him somewhat to accept it also on behalf of the unfortunate Sanpachirō.

But there were no doubt other, more subtle ways in which the old man left his mark on his grandson. By giving the boy an exaggerated sense of his family's importance as *mura no kizoku* (village aristocrats),[75] as well as by shielding him from unpleasant contacts with the outside world, Sanpachirō not only left Yasunari singularly unprepared to face the world alone after his grandfather's death but probably also helped to lay the foundations of the author's lifelong 'alienation' from society at large. One need not be a doctrinaire Marxist to recognize Kawabata's general lack of interest in society and social problems. The leading Japanese critic of the age, Kobayashi Hideo, for instance, once claimed that this author was so unconcerned with social, moral and ideological questions that he was, by nature, 'disqualified as a novelist'.[76] Of course, in the more than half century which has passed since Kobayashi made this claim, our idea of what constitutes a *bona fide* novel has expanded sufficiently so that it is doubtful whether anyone would make such a statement today. We might recognize, for instance, that Kawabata's fiction has much in common with the modern Western tradition of the 'lyrical novel' as it has been so well delineated by Ralph Freedman.[77] In a purely Japanese context, some critics would now argue that Kobayashi's idea of fiction was too Eurocentric and that Kawabata's *'shōsetsu'* should not be confused with the Western 'novel' anyway. At any rate, if one were looking for a biographical source for Kawabata's 'subjectivism' or even 'solipsism' as a writer of fiction, one certainly might consider as a major factor the closed, inward-turning, claustrophobic atmosphere of his grandfather's house – as evoked so well in the *Diary*.

The fact that Yasunari was not very thoroughly inculcated with the austere social virtues demanded of a citizen of prewar Japan was evident also in other areas of his life. His cavalier attitude towards money and property, for instance, was legendary. Isogai relates this to his grandfather's financial irresponsibility as described in the *Diary*.[78] And, in a society which tended to emphasize the value of group solidarity, he remained a loner, difficult to approach and taciturn about his private life.[79] Like the hero of his story, *Kinjū* ('Of Birds and Beasts', 1933) Kawabata, at least at some periods of his life, seemed to prefer the society of animals to that of his fellow men. Still, one might hesitate, in these speculations on the grandfather's influence, to go so far as the critic who suggests that Kawabata's lack of parental discipline accounts for his attraction to the anarchic avant-garde movements of the Twenties![80] Here, perhaps, we come dangerously close to that tendency towards *reductio ad absurdum* which often threatens to undermine any critical argument based on biographical data.

But it does seem reasonable to assume that Kawabata's own 'anti-social' tendencies were only exacerbated by his grandfather's death. Indeed, it might well be argued that the old man's influence on his grandson derived more from his death than from his life. Although Kawabata's childhood was darkened by a whole series of deaths – his father's, his mother's, his older sister's, his grandmother's – it was his grandfather's death, as the *Diary* clearly shows, which affected him most profoundly. This was such a devastating event to the fourteen-year-old Kawabata that, as we have seen, he was still trying to come to terms with it thirty-five years later, writing the second postscript to the *Diary*. And, actually, it is an open question as to whether he ever really did succeed in coming to terms with it. Kawabata remained almost morbidly obsessed with death, and with ways of escaping or transcending death, for the rest of his life. Indeed, considering the way he ended his own life, one might surmise that he was determined to the last not to submit to the agonizing, humiliating form of death, the slow process of mental and physical deterioration, that had victimized his grandfather.

One must also recognize, however, that there was a positive as well as a negative side to Yasunari's response to his grandfather's death. His early search for ways to transcend death led him to the earnest study of various kinds of religious and occult literature, Western as well as Eastern.[81] The monistic/mystical doctrine of the oneness of all things seemed to offer his best hope, as he himself asserted. To quote again from an essay he wrote the same year that the *Diary* was published: 'To save the human being from personal death, it seems that the best way is to blur into vagueness the boundaries between one individual and another, and between the human being and all other objects in the physical world'.[82]

As a literary programme this implied a new form of 'subjectivism' in which subject/object dichotomies would be dissolved; the writer would write of a lily, for instance, not as if it existed separately from him but as if he and the lily were one.[83] A traditional Western 'realistic' novelist, of course, trying to present an 'objective' view of human society, did everything in his power to individualize his various characters, so that the 'boundaries' between them were as well-defined as possible. But, as Kawabata himself already vaguely recognized,[84] his 'new programme' actually put him in touch with the contemporary European avant-garde, the dadaists, surrealists, expressionists and other experimental artists of the Twenties, who were also, by the kind of strange coincidence that almost persuades one of the reality of the *Zeitgeist*, proclaiming a new 'subjectivism' based on a monist philosophy. More pertinently perhaps, it also put him in close touch with the whole movement towards the 'subjectification' of the novel which had been in progress in the West since about the turn of the century.[85] And finally, of course, it put him in touch with his native literary and religious traditions, for much of what the young Kawabata was expounding in his 'Essay on Expressionist Cognition' and other 'avant-garde' manifestoes could be regarded as nothing more than a retailored Zen. And, though none of Kawabata's later works discuss the monist world view as openly as does, say, his short story of 1932, 'Lyric Poem' (*Jojōka*), still one may sense its presence everywhere, as a distant ideal if not as an attainable reality.

Furthermore, we must acknowledge that even the negative side of Kawabata's response to his grandfather's death – the increase of his anti-social tendencies – was turned by him to positive literary use. Many twentieth-century writers, Western as well as Japanese, have found it profitable to cultivate the persona of the alienated man, the 'outsider'.[86] For Kawabata, however, the condition was natural, a 'given' – though this is not to say that he did not consciously cultivate, for literary purposes, his image as an outcast, an 'eternal traveller',[87] an orphan, a 'stranger in a strange land'.[88] He also transposed this image to his fictional *alter egos*, from the wandering student of *The Dancing Girl of Izu* (*Izu no odoriko*, 1926), who strongly identifies with those 'social outcasts', the *tabi geinin* (vagabond entertainers), to that strangely detached traveller of *Snow Country* (*Yukiguni*, 1935–47), Shimamura, to that pathologically alienated, solipsistic inhabitant of a bachelor apartment, the vampirish protagonist of 'One Arm' (*Kataude*, 1964).

While it may be true in large part, as some critics have claimed,[89] that there is no direct treatment of the theme of 'family life' in Kawabata's works, a theme which has been so central to modern Japanese literature since the turn-of-the-century 'Naturalists' (although Kawabata's greatest work, *The Sound of the Mountain* [*Yama no oto*, 1954], is a conspicuous exception to this), the general lack of social breadth, it may be argued, allows for a more profound philosophical/psychological depth. Kawabata's social isolation compelled him to confront the basic problems of human existence without the usual social comforts that people take refuge in.[90] Thus it is a mistake to claim, as some critics have, that Kawabata's work lacks philosophic depth (*shisō*) and is distinguished only by its lyrical beauty. On the contrary, as a more sympathetic critic has argued, he is an existential thinker *par excellence*, since his thought concerns 'the existence of a self after its social nature has been torn away'.[91] In other words, while he may present us with little sense of the social/moral problems of man in society – the staple of the traditional novelist – he does present us with an acute sense of the ontological/existential problems of 'man in the universe', of the man who, as Rousseau said, is born naked and must die naked.[92]

Kawabata seems to perceive the basic problems of human existence in terms of a number of great antithetical dualities, and his works often take their structure from the contrastive interplay of these: being and nothingness, beauty and ugliness, youth and age, purity and corruption and so on.[93] Yet there is always, as in the *Diary*, a countervailing aspiration towards transcendence of these dualities and the spiritual liberation which this might bring. And since this liberating and blissful state of union is attained by Kawabata's heroes, if at all, only for the briefest of moments, a sense of melancholy and frustration pervades his works, and a vision of the tragic nature of man's fate. As Sasabuchi Tomoichi has written:

> In Kawabata's Nobel Prize acceptance speech, he expressed his respect for Eastern traditions, especially Zen. But, if Westerners think that his writing has attained the state of Zen, this is, needless to say, a great misunderstanding. One may say that his work comes from almost the opposite of the spiritual clarity and serenity of a Zen monk; rather it is the

product of illusion (*meimō*). It comes not from the world of the higher self but from the world of the small self, the individual. It is not from the world of the unconscious but always from the conscious, the perceived. Thus, even if the world of the unconscious, the transcendent self, comes into consciousness, this appears, until the end, as an object to be longed for, aspired for. In this sense, the view that Kawabata's writing is more Western than Eastern is perhaps quite defensible.[94]

Perhaps so. But, on the other hand, the view of a critic such as Katō Shūichi, who insinuates that Kawabata's interest in such things as Zen was only feigned to impress Westerners after he won the Nobel Prize,[95] is just as misinformed as would be any naïve Western perception of Kawabata as an enlightened Zen master. Kawabata's preoccupation with the themes of illusion and enlightenment began, as we have seen, with his first significant work, the *Diary*, and lasted throughout his entire career. And I would not be quite so categorical in this matter as Sasabuchi. It seems to me that much of the power of Kawabata's work, as I intend to show, derives from the author's being deeply in touch with the unconscious, the transcendent self. To mention here but one example: witness the important function of dreams in a work such as *The Sound of the Mountain*.[96] As Donald Keene has remarked in another connection, one of Kawabata's definite fortes lies precisely in 'the successful evocation of the world of dreams, where the impossible can occur with irrefutable authority'.[97]

While 'illusion' is often a central theme of Kawabata's works, it is usually counterbalanced, as in the *Diary*, by the theme of enlightenment, so that it seems a mistake to characterize the whole work as a 'product of illusion'. Nevertheless, looking over the author's total life-work, one must agree with Sasabuchi that it seems to be illusion which usually, in the end, gains the upper hand. And one cannot help but think that, for Kawabata, the prototype of man suffering under the power of illusion was his unfortunate grandfather, Sanpachirō.

4. The Diary and the Critics

A Western reader reviewing much of the Japanese critical debate which surrounds the *Diary* – or, indeed, many other works of Japanese literature – often has the feeling that he has stepped through Alice's looking-glass into an intellectual version of her absurdist wonderland, or perhaps that he is witnessing a furious Lilliputian debate between two parties who disagree as to which end of a boiled egg is the proper one to cut. Some of this impression is no doubt a natural result of one's different cultural values and prejudices and, as cultural anthropologists are constantly warning us, one must thus beware a too-easy dismissal of the foreign cultural product. On the other hand, one obviously cannot accept a complete surrender of one's critical faculties whenever one studies a foreign culture. There must be some fair limits to one's tolerance of arguments which seem absurd or illogical or a violation of common sense – even in the name of crosscultural openness. And it seems to me that Western writers on Japanese literature will contribute very little if they merely accept Japanese critical debates on their own terms. Furthermore, one parenthetical but important point: in my experience it is not only Western readers but a number of Japanese too who, in the name of a basic and to some extent universal common sense, question the appropriateness of some of this Japanese scholarly or literary-critical debate.

At any rate, that debate is often an interesting cultural/ anthropological study in itself, and some of that which surrounds the *Diary* is a prime example of its excesses. We may begin, for instance, with Kawashima Itaru's suggestion that, since Kawabata's unfortunate experiences with his grandfather soon became a rich mine for literary materials, Kawabata may have regarded his 'orphan psychology' as a 'heaven-sent blessing unavailable to other writers no matter how they wished for it'.[98] Perhaps, suggests Kawashima, his discovery that his orphan experience could be used as material for creative work was even the primary factor in his deciding to become a novelist![99]

Such speculations lead to the main Japanese critical debate surrounding the *Diary*, which addresses the question of the extent to which the work may be accepted as a *bona fide* diary – a question more urgent in a Japanese than in a Western literary context, because of the status of 'sincere' autobiographical writing as one of the sacred shibboleths of Japanese criticism. One of the most curious of the arguments in this debate concerns the author's motives in writing his diary: was he being a mere literary opportunist, shamelessly exploiting his grandfather's sufferings in order to establish himself as a writer? Or was he completely innocent of any literary motives in writing his diary, and simply wished to preserve and commemorate his grandfather's memory?[100] Some readers may be tempted to respond with two questions of their own: who knows? and, who cares?

But certain critics, it seems, do care. For them the *Diary*'s status as a work of literature is much less important than its status as a kind of 'sincere' personal confession by the author. And an accusation of 'insincerity' against Kawabata carries far more weight in a Japanese literary critical context than it would in a Western one. In particular, given the immense prestige of the autobiographical *shishōsetsu*, at the time Kawabata was writing regarded as the 'purest' form of literature (*jun bungaku*),[101] especially as exemplified by the 'god of the *shōsetsu*', Shiga Naoya,[102] and given the always suspect status of mere fiction in Japanese literature since the age of Murasaki Shikibu, any author who mixed the two indiscriminantly was playing a dangerous game, calculated to raise critical passions to a feverish pitch.

Kawabata, in fact, seems almost to be consciously teasing the critics (and mocking their *shishōsetsu* pieties) when, on the one hand, he describes the *Diary* as 'my one and only frank autobiography' and, on the other, confesses that the postscript at least was first 'intended as fiction'. Even his most devoted apologist, Hasegawa, admits that he was given a 'great shock' by this confession – as if the adulteration of autobiography with fiction were a major and culpable crime![103] But Hasegawa soon resolves his own doubts on this score. Quoting Kawabata's rejoinder to the skeptics, in which he insists that the *Diary* is 'just one person's straightforward sketch, and very difficult to change', Hasegawa concludes: 'From the sincere tone of these statements, we cannot smell the odour of novelistic fiction ...'. [As if fiction were a kind of noxious gas!] 'Thus, the ripple of doubt stirred up by his confession of fictional intent in writing the postscript ... is made to disappear in a very natural way'.[104]

But, unfortunately, not all critics were satisfied with Hasegawa's (and the author's) assurances. An intense debate raged around the question of the *Diary*'s 'authenticity' – a debate which Kawabata himself felt so strongly about that he abandoned his customary reclusion and 'came out fighting'. His main opponent was Kawashima, who claimed that the *Diary* was overvalued simply because everyone naïvely accepted the author's assurances that he wrote it at fourteen.[105] Isogai Hideo then restored peace by working out a compromise solution, though one that ultimately seemed to favour the Kawashima over the Kawabata camp: although much of the diary proper was no doubt written by the fourteen-year-old, the *Diary* as a whole, since it is so dependent for its effectiveness on its notes and postscripts, must be regarded as a <u>literary</u> <u>work</u> of the twenty-five-year-old.[106] Isogai, however, differed from Kawashima in one crucial way, a way which must have done much to recommend his arguments to the author: he placed a high value on the *Diary* as a well-structured, autonomous and realistic work of art.

I exhume these arguments here not to poke fun at the Japanese critics, who of course have every right to set their own critical priorities and who will naturally do so in accordance with their own cultural values. Rather my aim is to suggest something of the critical milieu in which Kawabata was writing and, more to the point, the effects of this on what he was writing. The very fact that Kawabata himself felt impelled to act against his grain and join in this particular debate shows that he was by no means free of this milieu: he was imbued with its standards, even though, at times, he may have satirized them, as he seems to do in the postscripts to the *Diary*.

A good many Japanese critics of the *Diary*, then, seem to be disturbed by its generic ambiguity, the intrusion of fictional elements into a work which first seems to present itself as straightforward autobiography. Either they suppress their doubts, as does Hasegawa, and accept the author's 'sincerity', or, at the other extreme, they conclude, as does Kawashima, that, in exposing the work as a literary fraud, they have undermined the basis of its value. It does not seem to occur to them that, detached from the largely moral issue of the author's sincerity, this very ambiguity may come to seem an aesthetic virtue, which only adds to the final value and significance of the work. This claim may appear rather far-fetched, but actually there are many historical precedents, both Western and Japanese, to support such a view.

Since the beginnings of the novel in Europe, generic ambiguity has been its hallmark: countless novels have presented themselves as actual journals, letters, biographies, histories and so on. And this ambiguity serves a definite aesthetic function: being presented as 'fact' heightens, of course, the work's power to convince but, more than that, the very play of fact with fantasy becomes a source of pleasure and instruction and has often been the explicit theme of novels from *Don Quixote* onwards. Precedents for this may also be found in Japanese literature. Indeed, in fictionalizing his diary Kawabata may be said to have returned to the ancient Japanese tradition of the literary diary, the *nikki*. Long before the so-called 'naturalists' of early twentieth-century Japanese literature made such a fetish out of 'sincerity' in their autobiographical writings, great literary diarists from Ki no Tsurayuki (869–945) to Bashō (1644–1694) did not hesitate to take liberties with the facts in the interest of aesthetic effect. And the same held true in other genres. Chikamatsu's theory of the *jōruri*, the puppet theatre, seems particularly apropos here: 'In writing *jōruri* one attempts first to describe facts as they really are, but in so doing one writes things which are not true, in the interest of art'.[107] Furthermore, the art of *jōruri* is to be found in 'the slender margin between the real and the unreal'.[108]

Besides being supported by such historical precedents, the generic ambiguity of the *Diary* may also be seen to serve an important function in the specific context of modern Japanese literature. By violating the inner sanctum of the *shishōsetsu*, Kawabata calls into question some of the most inhibiting dogmas of the Japanese literary establishment of his day, and thus already declares his independence from them with this, his first important work. This independence is to function on both the critical and the creative levels: as an artist, he objects to biographical fact-finding taking precedence over the appreciation of the aesthetic qualities of his work; and, conversely, he declares his right to select, arrange and even change the 'facts' of his life in the interest of a higher aesthetic truth.

After the *Diary*, Kawabata would give more and more free reign to his imagination in the creation of his literary works. Few of them would be as directly autobiographical, as literal or even as 'realistic' as the *Diary*. A critic such as Isogai, who deplores the 'romanticism' of Kawabata's later works, may regret this fact. And even an admirer of the later works must concede that something indeed is lost: one misses, for instance, the presence of a wise, earthy older woman such as Omiyo – Kawabata's later heroines, his female *bodhisattvas*, are all young and beautiful in a way which, with any lesser writer, might seem shamelessly romantic. But beneath the romantic, lyrical beauty of his later works the troubled world view of the *Diary* still lingers. One senses it especially in the male characters: like the boy diarist and his grandfather, they tend to be alienated figures longing for an experience of union – with other people, with nature, with art or simply with themselves. As Kawabata himself grew older, naturally enough the figure of the frustrated, illusion-ridden old man moved to centre stage in his fiction. There was no longer any need for a boy diarist to serve as *waki* or intermediary. The greatest works of his late maturity, *The Sound of the Mountain* and *Sleeping Beauties* (*Nemureru bijo*, 1961), present this old man's consciousness directly; and Shingo and Eguchi, their protagonists, are old men who, at least in their feelings of frustration with their entire lives, are reminiscent of Sanpachirō. There is thus a remarkable continuity throughout the whole long span of Kawabata's career, and the importance of the *Diary*, not only in its own right but as a precursor of all that is to follow, cannot be overstated.

After his grandfather's death, the now completely orphaned Yasunari became a boarder in the Ibaraki Middle School residence until his graduation from that school in 1917. The most significant event of these middle school years was the 'love affair' of sorts he carried on with his room-mate, one Ogasawara. Kawabata provides some details of this homoerotic but essentially Platonic and idealistic relationship in a work written more than thirty years later, *The Boy* (*Shonen*, 1948–49). From this and from some diary entries he made shortly after the event, we may discern in his 'first love' the beginnings of what we might call his transcendental romanticism vis-à-vis the love-object. As is also often the case with the Kawabata protagonist's heterosexual relationships, the love-object here is idealized as a model of purity and admired dreamily from a safe distance. A 'safe distance', that is, psychologically if not always physically: he does enjoy lying down beside the boy and touching him while he is sleeping, but only then to drift off into a state of self-absorbed reverie. The essentially spiritual or psychological function the love-object always has for Kawabata is expressed in a revealing diary entry he made on 23 January 1918: 'That pristinely pure Ogasawara has bequeathed to me an eternal sense of salvation'.[109] This sentiment is echoed in a letter he writes to the same youth in *The Boy*, addressing him ecstatically as the 'god of my salvation'.[110] In fact, Ogasawara's pseudonym in *The Boy* is 'Kiyono', which means literally 'field of purity', a name which emphasizes the quality in all of Kawabata's love-objects that he prizes most: the 'purity' which will wash his own soul clean.

After graduating from the Ibaraki Middle School in 1917 Kawabata went up to Tokyo to attend the most prestigious university preparatory school in all of Japan, the First Higher School, attendance at which would almost guarantee his admission, in turn, to the most prestigious Japanese university, the Imperial University of Tokyo.[111] The educational establishment had clearly begun to recognize the remarkable gifts of this precocious if rather shy and gloomy young man. It was while he was a student at this prestigious school, in the autumn of 1918, that he defied convention by joining up with a troupe of vagabond entertainers while on a solitary walking tour of the

Izu Peninsula – an experience later recounted in his most famous early work, *The Dancing Girl of Izu*.

But Kawabata continued his struggle towards 'self-discovery' and towards the development of his own particular world view in a number of other significant short works written prior to the publication of *Izu*. Among the shortest of these were the so-called 'palm-of-hand' or 'palm-sized' stories (*tenohira* or *tanagokoro shōsetsu*), the short short stories which often read like surrealistic prose poems and which Kawabata began to write as early as 1916 and continued writing throughout his whole career. The earliest of these, according to Kawabata himself, was 'Gathering Ashes' (*Kotsu hiroi*, 1916–49), which describes how he had to perform the depressing duty of going to the crematorium and, as is the Japanese custom, use chopsticks to pick up his grandfather's incinerated bones and place them in an urn.

While at the First Higher School Kawabata also published a short story, 'Chiyo' (*Chiyo*, 1919), in the school's literary magazine. This is a strange, rather melodramatic story which abounds in untoward coincidences and even features a haunting by a ghost – in fact, rather like one of the ghost stories or tales of the supernatural in traditional Japanese literature and theatre. But it also contains the first use Kawabata made of his Izu experience: one of the three girls named Chiyo the hero mysteriously meets is the Izu dancer. Obviously, though, Kawabata himself was not completely satisfied with this first fictional use of the experience, since he went on to handle it in a very different way in his later novella. His interest in the supernatural, in reincarnation and even in Western spiritualism persisted, however, and, as we shall see, appeared in more sophisticated forms in later stories. When the narrator remarks casually: 'The three Chiyos are, of course, ghosts', one is reminded that Kawabata said the same thing about some of his later characters – even, surprisingly, about the most 'fleshed out' and 'full-bodied' of all his characters, Komako of *Snow Country*.[112]

In 1920 Kawabata graduated from the First Higher School and entered the English Literature Department of the Imperial University of Tokyo.

CHAPTER TWO

AN AMBIGUOUS REDEMPTION

1. The Dancing Girl and the Model-Hunters

The second major work which Kawabata published in his mid-twenties, *The Dancing Girl of Izu* (*Izu no odoriko*, 1926) seems, initially, to form a striking contrast with the first. One might be tempted to surmise that, having relieved himself of the burden of his unfortunate childhood by writing his 'song of experience', the young author now felt free to give vent to his natural youthful exuberance by writing a joyful 'song of innocence'. His new-found 'liberation' seems to be made clear by the very setting of this second work: in contrast to the dark, closed, static environment of his grandfather's house, which naturally evokes feelings of claustrophobia and paralysis, we now have the bright, open, ever-changing landscape of the beautiful southern Izu peninsula, which naturally suggests an uninhibited freedom and movement. Also there is, of course, the even starker contrast between the two central characters with whom the protagonist comes into contact: in the *Diary*, a physically repulsive old man whose constant demands drive the boy to rebellion; in *Izu*, a beautiful girl who seems eager to serve the young man in any way she can. It is as if the protagonist of the *Diary*, in one of his darkest moments, had fallen asleep and dreamt the compensatory dream of *Izu*.

At any rate, it was this 'bright', 'youthful' side of *Izu* which was emphasized by its first critics, who characterized it as 'lyrical' and even 'sentimental' and used words such as 'pure', 'clean', 'fresh' and 'healthy' to describe its general effect.[1] And no doubt it is this aspect of the work which accounts for its tremendous popularity among several generations of Japanese readers, far exceeding that of the author's 'darker' works, and for its continuing status as an icon of the popular culture. (An *Odoriko Express*, for instance, still takes honeymoon couples down to the hotspring resorts of southern Izu, where they pose to have their pictures taken in front of the very inn where Kawabata stayed in 1918.) In short, the popular image of the work as a romantic story of innocent first love between a high-class Tokyo youth and a kind of vagabond 'gypsy' girl, no doubt abetted more by the numerous film versions than by any close reading of the text itself, offers an irresistible potpourri of old-fashioned exoticism, sentimental romance and the nostalgia of lost innocence. And who among us does not respond to such a charming concoction – at least in our weaker moments?

Perhaps no one would deny that much of the surface appeal of *Izu* lies exactly in this direction. But what distinguishes it immediately from other such popular, 'romantic' works is that its appeal does not stop there. The fact that it has a 'deeper' and 'darker' side is, indeed, indicated even on the surface level of its narration. To explain his exhilaration on simply being called a 'good person' by two of the vagabond performers, the narrator points to his conception of his own character at this time, his view of himself as 'warped' by an 'orphan's psychology'; indeed, it was to relieve the melancholy caused by this 'severe self-introspection' that he had undertaken his trip to Izu.[2] Taking a hint from this brief 'confession', latter-day critics have emphasized the underlying 'orphan psychology' of the protagonist as the 'shadow side' of *Izu*, concealed just below its bright, 'lyrical' surface. Seen from this perspective, *Izu*'s surface-level lyricism may seem 'deceptive' in the same way, for instance, as is the lyricism of Hemingway's story, 'Big Two-Hearted River'.[3] In both stories the hero has set out on a journey away from urban civilization into the freer, more natural countryside where he hopes to be cured of his deep psychic malaise. The exact nature of this malaise is never specified in the Hemingway story, and only briefly referred to in Kawabata's, but still it may be felt lurking as a continual, ominous presence in the background – inevitably so, since both stories are filtered through the states of mind of their respective protagonists. The 'lyricism' in both cases has an almost desperate quality about it: the war-scarred Nick Adams being desperate to lose himself in the mindless rituals of fishing; the orphaned protagonist of *Izu* being equally desperate to lose himself in the group of vagabond performers. By hardly being mentioned, the underlying malaise assumes an even greater presence and poignancy. This is the phenomenon which Hemingway referred to as the power of the 'thing left out', and it is a power which Kawabata also often made good use of in his elliptical style.[4]

At any rate, we may already begin to see that the psychological atmosphere of *Izu* is not really as remote from that of the *Diary* as we might first surmise. And critics of the past several decades, taking their lead from the narrator's own description of his psychological state, have devoted much effort to the illumination of the work's 'shadow side'. Though it is now generally accepted that the basic theme of *Izu* is the narrator/protagonist's 'liberation' from his 'orphan psychology', there is, of course, no general consensus about what exactly this 'orphan psychology' consists of, nor even about whether his 'liberation' is actually achieved.[5] As is often their wont, the Japanese critics marshal to their respective sides heavy barrages of biographical data, supplemented by copious cross-references to other of the author's 'autobiographical' works, but most seem to feel little compunction to support their arguments by evidence culled from the text itself. Indeed, one might say, with little exaggeration, that those two troublesome words, *koji konjō* (orphan psychology), have opened a veritable Pandora's box of literary/biographical speculation, not only in regard to *Izu* but concerning the interrelations between the whole of Kawabata's life and work.

Furthermore, because these critics rarely make any distinction between the author and his literary *alter ego*, the concept of 'orphan psychology' itself is almost infinitely expandable, far beyond the borders of *Izu* – indeed, it is made to include even some of the author's experiences which occurred long after his encounter with the dancing girl in 1918! This startling feat of critical legerdemain is made possible by the fact that Kawabata did not write the prototype form of *Izu* until 1922, and in the meantime he had undergone the painful experience of being jilted by a girl whom, apparently, he had loved far more deeply than the *Izu* dancer. Thus, argue some critics, his memories of the former were bound to colour his memories of the latter. And there is one other 'love experience' which these critics feel must be taken into account: the homosexual 'affair' which, as Kawabata confessed in *The Boy* (*Shōnen*, 1948), he had carried on with his room-mate at the Ibaraki Middle School dormitory where, as an orphan, he had lived from 1916 to 1917. The general view of the way these three 'love experiences' came to be related in the author's mind is that, after having suffered the great shock of being jilted, he consoled himself by an imaginative reliving of his two more 'satisfactory' love experiences.[6] The work in which he accomplished this was *Memories at Yugashima* (*Yugashima de no omoide*, 1922), which contained the prototype form of both *Izu* and *The Boy* (though this work itself was never published and, according to Kawabata, was destroyed by him after he had extracted *The Boy* from it). Though all this sounds quite plausible, the question still remains: does an understanding of the author's 'motivation' in writing a certain work, presuming that such be possible, improve at all our understanding or appreciation of the work itself? Or, on the other hand, is there a danger that such speculations may even distort our perception of the work's true nature? In dealing with much of the Japanese critical literature devoted to Kawabata, one feels obliged, willynilly, to raise such questions again and again.

The most thoroughgoing and convincing defence of what might be called the 'retroactive' view of *Izu* is made by Hasegawa Izumi, who points out that in the short story 'Chiyo' (1919), which contains Kawabata's first treatment of his Izu experience of 1918, there is no mention at all of his psychological malaise or 'orphan psychology'.[7] It seems then that this theme was developed only in retrospect, under the influence of later experiences. Above all, it was the experience of being jilted which drove home to Kawabata the fact of his 'warped' nature, since he was convinced that the girl had rejected him for this very reason.[8] 'I had wanted to be a child in her arms', Kawabata had confessed.[9] But the girl was only fifteen and, cast out into the world like an orphan herself, she was hardly prepared to play substitute mother to this strange twenty-two-year-old intellectual. At any rate, concludes Hasegawa, by evoking his happy memories of the Izu dancer and of his former room-mate, Kawabata was performing a requiem (*chinkon*) for the repose of his own soul, so grievously wounded by his loss of a later love. Writing thus became a 'device for salvation'.[10] (It is interesting to note, in this connection, that Hasegawa considers the homosexual love experience as having been the deeper and more satisfying of the two, as evidenced by the fact that it occupies much more of the author's attention in *Yugashima*.[11])

Hasegawa's speculations are of definite biographical interest and, though it is debatable how much they are directly applicable to *Izu*, they at least do not seem to greatly distort our view of the work. The same cannot be said, however, for the speculations of another critic, Kawashima Itaru, which clearly manifest some of the dangers inherent in this whole approach. Here again, as with the *Diary*, Kawashima plays the role of *enfant terrible*, sparking off a hot debate over 'image influence' which, again, involved even the author. For Kawashima goes much further than Hasegawa: in writing *Izu*, he claims, Kawabata was not simply evoking the dancer's memory in order to pacify his mind after being jilted; he was actually writing about the girl who had jilted him, using the Izu dancer as a sort of pretext. By making the girl, disguised as the dancer, far more devoted to himself than she was in reality, he was able to achieve a sort of fantasy union with her which assuaged his wounded spirit.[12] Thus Kawashima turns *Izu* into a disguised *Chiyomono* or *Michikomono*, one of a whole series of autobiographical stories Kawabata wrote dealing with his experiences with 'Chiyo' or 'Michiko' (both pseudonyms which he assigned, in his stories, to the girl who had jilted him).

The evidence Kawashima offers to support this startling proposition is flimsy, to say the least. His main arguments are that since, when Kawabata wrote *Yugashima*, he was much closer in time to his experience with 'Michiko' than to his experience with the Izu dancer, it is inevitable that the dancer's image was coloured by Michiko's; and, further, that certain key scenes of *Izu* – the 'nude scene' and the final scene in which the protagonist is confronted by another student – are similar to scenes in other stories dealing with 'Michiko'.[13] To the author's objections that the images of the two girls had been quite distinct in his memory, and that similar encounters actually did happen on separate occasions, Kawashima answers by expressing doubts as to the reliability of the author's memory – an argument *ad hominem* if ever there was one![14]

Instead of recapitulating this debate over issues which can never really be proved one way or another, however, perhaps we had best judge Kawashima's theory by its fruit: that is, by its applicability to the text itself. When put to this test, it seems to me that its inherent contradictions and its potential for distortion soon become apparent.

For instance, Kawashima claims that by applying his 'interpretation' we can understand why the *Izu* protagonist so lustily pursues the dancer at first, misconstruing her age: it is because he perceives her not as the fourteen-year-old dancer but as the sixteen-year-old Michiko.[15] If this is so, we might wonder why then the lusty young man feels relief after seeing her nude and discovering that she is merely a child. The reason, claims Kawashima, is that Kawabata himself is happy to perceive the child in Michiko![16] This seems rather like the critical equivalent of 'having your cake and eating it too'. Also it seems to me that it distorts and even trivializes some of the key scenes in *Izu*, those related to the central theme of 'liberation from orphan psychology'. But more on this later.

The 'after-image' of 'Michiko', however, is by no means the only 'ghostly image' which critics have claimed to find lurking in the background of *Izu*; nor is it the only one the 'discovery' of which is supposed to throw light on the protagonist's 'orphan psychology'. Fujimori Shigenori, for instance, is an even more

45

obsessive 'model-hunter' – or perhaps we should say 'ghost-hunter' – than Kawashima. Intent on showing the orphan youth as literally haunted by the ghosts of his dead relatives, Fujimori goes to great – perhaps one should say absurd – lengths to prove that every character in *Izu* corresponds to a real person from the author's past. Some prize specimens of his 'line of reasoning' run as follows: the image of the dancer throughout *Izu* is a sexually neutral one because superimposed upon it is the image not only of 'Michiko' but also of Kawabata's homosexual lover;[17] furthermore, since the dancer is the same age as was Kawabata's older sister when she died, she is also the 'ghost' of that older sister.[18] As for Eikichi, the dancer's older brother, he is twenty-two, the same age that Kawabata was in 1921, when he was supposed to marry 'Chiyo', and Chiyoko, Eikichi's wife, as we can calculate from information given about her two pregnancies, was sixteen at the time of her marriage, the same age 'Chiyo' would have been had she married Kawabata in 1921: thus it is obvious that the marriage of Eikichi and Chiyoko is a fantasy version of the marriage that was not realized in actuality, between Kawabata and 'Chiyo'; but, at the same time, since 'Eikichi' was also Kawabata's father's name, we must not forget that the dancer's older brother is also the ghost of Kawabata's father! etc. etc.[19] All of which reminds one of nothing so much as Stephen Dedalus's long mock-argument proving that Shakespeare was the ghost of Hamlet's father![20] Though doubtless not intended as such, Fujimori's exegesis makes a fine *reductio ad absurdum* of the whole 'biographical' approach to criticism.

No form of literary criticism, of course, is an exact science; close textural analysis, for instance, also produces its share of absurdities. Nor would I reject biographical criticism outright; when handled with delicacy and common sense, as by such Kawabata critics as Hasegawa and Hadori, it can provide us with a good general sense of the relationships between an author's life and work. The fact that Japanese critics have a particular penchant for this form of criticism is no doubt attributable, as I have already pointed out, to perfectly legitimate cultural imperatives. Though they often seem blissfully unaware of the pitfalls inherent in this approach, the Western reader should not make the complacent assumption that this is an exclusively Japanese phenomenon. As W.H. Auden once remarked, probably 'more nonsense has been talked and written, more intellectual and emotional energy expended in vain, on the sonnets of Shakespeare than on any other literary work in the world' – and for a purpose much the same as Fujimori's: to uncover the true identity of the male Friend, the Dark Lady, the Rival Poet, Mr. W.H., and so on.[21] Of course, had Auden been able to read Japanese, he might not have stated so boldly 'any other literary work in the world', but what he has to say on this subject might well have been directed at certain Japanese critics as well:

> The relation between [an artist's] life and works is at one and the same time too self-evident to require comment – every work of art is, in one sense, a self-disclosure – and too complicated ever to unravel. Thus, it is self-evident that Catallus's love for Lesbia was the experience which inspired his love poems, and that, if either of them had had a different character, the poems would have been different, but no amount of research into their lives can tell us why Catallus wrote the actual poems he did, instead of an infinite number of other poems he might have written instead, why, indeed, he wrote any, or why those he did are good. Even if one could question a poet himself about the relation between some poem of his and the events which provoked him to write it, he could not give a satisfactory answer, because even the most 'occasional' poem in the Goethean sense involves not only the occasion but the whole life experience of the poet, and he himself cannot identify all the contributing elements.[22]

One need not be as pessimistic as Auden on this subject, but certainly anyone venturing into the treacherous area of 'biographical' criticism would do well to keep his words in mind.

The fact is, though, that even in attempting to come to terms with some Japanese critics' general interpretations of *Izu*, one cannot always ignore their preoccupation with 'models', since this preoccupation, as we have seen in both Hasegawa's and Kawashima's case, has such a pronounced impact on their hermeneutical method. In the case of Fujimori too, his final view of what he calls *Izu*'s 'structure' is contingent upon his model-finding. We see this very clearly in his view of the role of the old lady with her grandchildren whom the protagonist encounters in *Izu*'s final scene. At first Fujimori seems to argue that she is an extraneous element, with no role integral to the work's structure,[23] but then, when it occurs to him that she is perhaps the 'ghost' either of Kawabata's mother or grandfather – just as, in an earlier scene, the old man at the teahouse is supposed to be the 'ghost' of Kawabata's grandfather – then he accepts her as performing the role of *waki* ('witness') in the final scene.[24] Thus we find that, for a critic of Fujimori's ilk, a work such as *Izu* ultimately takes shape and 'works' for non-aesthetic, extraliterary reasons: it 'justifies' itself as a kind of grand exorcism of the ghosts of the author's past. The protagonist's euphoria in the final scene is explained as showing his relief at no longer being haunted by these ghosts. And, in a final, almost bizarre, confusion of the boundaries of literature and reality, Fujimori implies that, having exorcised himself by writing *Izu*, Kawabata was then prepared to marry his real, lifelong wife, Hideko. This is a remarkable piece of mind-reading on the critic's part, one must admit![25]

The preceding three critics, then, and others of their kind, are concerned mainly with answering the question of what drives the *Izu* protagonist to embark on a walking trip into the country, away from Tokyo, and what impels the author to write about it – in other words, both questions of motivation. Treating the work as straight autobiography, they are able to answer these questions by expanding the narrator's confession of his own 'orphan psychology' to include everything that seems relevant in the author's own personal history: not only the obvious parallel of his own 'orphanage' but even such seemingly unrelated incidents as his later experience of being jilted. Their claim would seem to be that, without the benefit of such biographical expansion, the full significance of the work would not be apparent. Indeed, Fujimori goes so far as to claim that we cannot even conceive a true idea of the work's structure unless we know its parallels with the author's own life.[26] But, one might ask, does this not belittle the author's achievement and diminish our sense of the aesthetic integrity of the work itself? If *Izu* is shown in this way to be incapable of 'standing on its own', then inevitably it comes to seem less a work of literary art and more a mere fragment of autobiography. And even a cursory reading of this finely crafted novella is enough to convince one that this is a serious misrepresentation.

The pertinent question here, it seems to me, is whether or not the term 'orphan psychology', used by the narrator in a rare moment of self-analysis, is explicable only by an 'outside' reference to the author's own life, or is its full meaning amply manifested 'inside' the work itself – so that, from a purely aesthetic viewpoint, its mention is by no means extraneous or superfluous, as if it were a casual, offhand remark, but functions as an integral part of the fabric of the work, perhaps even as the keystone of its thematic structure. Since I am confident that the latter is, in fact, the case, I will attempt to examine the work from this point of view.

2. An Orphan's Odyssey

> But thou, contracted to thy own bright eyes,
> Feed'st thy light's flame with self-substantial fuel,
> Making a famine where abundance lies,
> Thyself thy foe, to thy sweet self too cruel.
>
> Shakespeare, Sonnet I.
>
> Love is too young to know what conscience is:
> Yet who knows not, conscience is born of love?
>
> Shakespeare, Sonnet CLI.

During the first two chapters of the story, the young man's alienated state of mind is suggested only in a subtle, indirect way and the reader is generally led to expect a typical 'romantic' story of young love. The hints, nonetheless, are already present. Firstly, the very fact that the youth is travelling alone is unusual in the Japanese context, where group travel is the norm for pleasure trips, especially considering the fact that he is a student at the First Higher School in Tokyo, an elite institution. One would expect him to travel with at least a small group of friends. The first suspicion that might occur to us, then, is that he is friendless. Secondly, his behaviour in regard to the dancer and her group is somewhat contradictory. Though he is obviously eager to make contact with them, he is tongue-tied when they meet at the Amagi Pass teahouse. And later, after he has made a great effort to catch up with them on the road, he pretends indifference until addressed by the man of the party. This is partly, of course, the natural pride and shyness of youth but, in this extreme form, it seems to go beyond that. Thirdly, we are given a sense of the young man's extreme self-absorption from almost the beginning, when we are told that, although he was 'charmed', to some extent, by the mountain ranges, virgin forests and deep gorges which surrounded him, he really had no time to pause and admire them, since his heart was 'aflutter' with a 'certain expectation' which made him hurry along the road. Although, in this case, the 'certain expectation' has to do with his meeting and perhaps bedding down with the dancer, the point is that the young man is here so preoccupied with his subjective state that he is 'closed' to his surroundings. And the same might be said of him throughout the entire work.

An odd fact about *Izu* is that, although it is often described as a 'lyrical' work, there is very little lyrical feeling in it towards nature, the kind of feeling we associate with Kawabata's later '*haiku*' style. Such lyricism as does exist lies mainly in the young man's feelings towards the dancer, and hers towards him. Even though southern Izu, with its almost tropical lushness, is one of the beauty-spots of Japan, the descriptions of it in this work are all quite perfunctory. This in itself obviously tells us something important about the protagonist's state of mind – but I shall return to this point later.

Apart from these few gentle hints as to the youth's true mental state, however, the instincts he displays during the first two chapters seem to be those of any 'normal', red-blooded young male. In the emotional high-point of the first chapter, he is aroused to lustful thoughts when the old woman at the teahouse implies that the vagabond performers are available for the night to whomever will pay for them. The second chapter ends with another such 'climax' in which the young man is raised to a fever pitch of jealousy when he hears the dancer's drum in the distance and imagines that she is spending the night with someone else. Needless to say, these are the expected reactions of any healthy young male in 'hot pursuit' of a female.

The same certainly cannot be said of his reactions on the following day, however, when, on seeing the dancer nude, he discovers that she is not the ripe young woman he had taken her for but a mere child. Coming after the 'climaxes' of the first two chapters, this scene in the third chapter is something of an anticlimax to the reader, whose own expectations of witnessing a 'romantic' sexual adventure have been fully aroused. What is even more disconcerting, however, is the young man's reaction to this discovery. Rather than disappointment – the reaction one would expect from any 'normal' youth whose desires had been frustrated – the *Izu* protagonist displays the most intense sense of relief, as if a great burden has been lifted from his shoulders. Indeed, his euphoria has almost the character of a purifying religious experience: 'I felt fresh water wash over my heart. My head seemed to be wiped clear'.[27] And his irrepressible smile seems like that of a suddenly enlightened *bodhisattva*.

This, then, is the first noticeably peculiar reaction of the protagonist, the first which impels us to recognize that there is something out of the ordinary about his state of mind – something which may well be related to what he later calls his 'orphan psychology'. If so, then not only does the incident tell us something about the nature of this psychology, it also indicates one way in which he hopes to transcend it. In the first place, his intense sense of relief implies that, although he was physically attracted to the girl and even conceived 'lustful' thoughts towards her, some deeper part of his nature resists the idea of a physical consummation of his desire. Why this should be so is suggested by the other side of his reaction: accompanying his relief, as we have seen, is a joyful sense of self-purification, as if he had directly imbibed the girl's purity – which has the power, it seems, of returning him, at least for the moment, to a childhood state of innocence prior to the development of his 'orphan psychology'. As Mishima Yukio pointed out, this is an important early expression of the 'virgin theme' which would become a keynote of Kawabata's works, and the manner of its expression certainly makes it one of the lyrical highpoints of *Izu*.[28] But, despite the fact that it is expressed in such a pleasant and positive way, we should not ignore its other, more negative side, a side which would emerge with more clarity in later Kawabata works, but whose unfortunate results we can already ominously perceive, it seems to me, in *Izu*. I am referring, of course, to what might be termed the 'spiritual egotism' of the Kawabata male. The desire to use the female not as a sexual object but as a sort of 'purifying agent' might be regarded as a highly refined form of egotism, but it is egotism nonetheless, since it is concerned solely with the male's own psychological liberation and is totally oblivious to the needs of the other. Because there is none of the sort of mutual giving and sharing which is the basis of mature relationships between the sexes, the self still remains essentially alienated from the other, encased in an impenetrable solipsism. We may note in the above scene, for instance, that the physical distance between the young man and the woman seems a fitting objective correlative of the psychological distance he wishes always to maintain between them: she is safely across the river, so that he is able to observe her as one would an aesthetic object, without fear of personal entanglement: 'She was completely nude, without even a towel to cover her. I gazed at her white nudity with her legs stretched wide like young paulownia trees ...'.[29] Furthermore, while she literally 'exposes' herself to him in this absolute way (even her posture as she stands before him is 'wide-open'), he himself remains safely concealed within his bath, closed up within his thoughts. Thus, while he may receive some momentary aesthetic pleasure or spiritual refreshment from his contemplation of the girl, one wonders whether, as some critics claim, he is really on the right path here towards 'liberation from his orphan psychology'.[30] Since his solipsism remains essentially intact, such a 'liberation' would at best be momentary and thus illusory.

This inescapable fact, and the consequences of it, becomes abundantly clear throughout the remainder of the work. His lack of interest in any real, person-to-person relation with the dancer becomes increasingly obvious, and there is now a reversal of roles: the dancer becomes the pursuer, the protagonist the pursued. What also becomes increasingly obvious is the dancer's suffering as a result of this – but, ironically, it is a suffering which only feeds into the orphan protagonist's need to feel wanted and loved. We must examine these developments more closely.

There is a striking contrast between the protagonist's mood at the end of Chapter Two and his mood at the end of Chapter Three. Whereas Chapter Two ends with him in a state of extreme confusion and insecurity, unable to decide whether or not he should run out barefoot into the night in a frantic search for the dancer, Chapter Three ends with him full of energy and self-confidence, in spite of the fact that the dancer has just left him alone for the night. Now, it seems, he has no more need for her presence and, as if he has won some sort of victory by this, he feels 'extremely bellicose' as he prepares to play checkers all night with a travelling salesman.[31]

This newfound 'independence' of his is confirmed by the events of Chapters Four and Five, in which the protagonist is shown drawing closer to the group of travelling performers as a whole, at the same time that he detaches himself more and more from the dancer. Since he is no longer exclusively interested in the dancer, there is a certain 'opening out' of the story to include other characters as well: in particular, Eikichi, the dancer's older brother, and the older woman referred to as '*Ofukuro*' ('Mother'), Eikichi's mother-in-law. Having been 'released' from the imperative of a sexual relation with the dancer, the protagonist now seeks a relation of 'friendship' with the entire group. But what form of friendship is it?

As Chapter Four opens, the young man is shown exchanging his school cap, symbol of his elite status, for a hunting cap or deerstalker, thus preparing himself to draw closer to the low-class performers. Then, no longer feeling the shyness and restraint he had felt while actively pursuing the dancer, he marches confidently up to the performers' room, only to find them all still in bed. It is the dancer who now shows deep embarrassment, while the protagonist is able to contemplate her with detachment, noticing even the most minute details of her appearance: with traces of heavy makeup still on her face, and smudges of rouge around her lips and eyes, she is almost comically 'cute', like a small girl who has dressed up as a mature woman. And since this quaint little figure can no longer be the object of his sexual desire, he is able to casually invite her over to his room for a game of checkers. But the dancer herself, despite her 'childishness', does not seem to be similarly free of all romantic intentions towards him, nor does she appear to agree that any liaison between them would be out of the question. Thus, in Chapter Four, she thinks it improper that they play checkers alone in his room; after her hair almost brushes against his chest, she flushes scarlet and runs out of the room; she stops playing the *samisen* when he appears later at her inn; she asks him shyly to read her a story, 'as if it were Ofukuro's request'; she aligns his *geta* (wooden clogs) for him when he leaves the inn (already acting like a good Japanese wife), and she asks him to take her to a movie when they arrive in Shimoda.[32] While the girl thus seems to grow more active in her pursuit of him, the young man increasingly assumes the role of detached if appreciative observer: while reading her the story too, he derives aesthetic relish from her 'best feature', her large, double-lidded eyes, whose lines he finds 'inexpressibly clean' (as if admiring a work of calligraphy); and he is charmed by her 'flower-like laugh' (again objectifying her in nonhuman terms).[33]

The reversal of the pursuer/pursued roles, however, becomes even more evident in Chapter Five, which describes the last leg of the group's journey, from Yūganō to Shimoda. Indeed, the girl here becomes the pursuer quite literally, manifesting in the physical realm what is true also in the psychological, as she chases after the young man up the steep mountain road. Early in the chapter, she invites him to come visit her at her home on the island of Ōshima, but his reply is not given. Later, when they reach the summit of a mountain, she dusts off the skirt of his *kimono* and invites him to sit down. A strange scene transpires:

> 'Why do you walk so fast?' the dancer asked. She seemed very hot. I tapped on her drum several times with my finger and the small birds flew up and away. 'Ah, I'd like some water', I said. 'I'll go look for some', she answered. But a while later she came back empty-handed through the yellowing trees.[34]

The scene has obvious sexual overtones, suggesting in this, the first time the girl and young man are really alone together, a symbolic attempt at their union – an attempt initiated by the pursuing girl. Dusting off his *kimono*, she kneels before him in a posture of self-surrender. It is she who is 'hot' and who seems to rebuke him for escaping from her: 'Why do you walk so fast?' He cooperates for a moment, absentmindedly tapping his finger on her drum. One need not belabour the physical resemblance of the girl's drum – a taut membrane – to her maidenhead, to conceive of it as the synecdochic image of her virgin self: it is the image most often associated with her throughout the entire work. As for the young man's finger – anyone who has read *Snow Country* need not be told of the suggestiveness of the male finger in Kawabata.[35] At any rate, since real sexual union is impossible between this couple, not only because of her age but because of his resistance, this symbolic enactment represents the closest they are able to approach it. But even this is soon 'aborted': after briefly fondling her 'drum', the protagonist calls for water. We remember that, after he had seen the dancer naked, he had felt as if his heart were washed by 'pure water'. Water is for him the symbol of the 'purity' he craves. But the significant point here is that, now that she has pursued him so actively, and has even – howevermuch on a purely symbolic level – tried to initiate sexual relations with him, she can no longer provide him with the 'water' he needs, and returns empty-handed through the yellowing trees (symbols of barrenness and death). The older woman Ofukuro, however, does not so naïvely misconstrue the true needs of the young man: shortly after the above scene, she offers him water that is still 'undirtied' by women.[36]

After this scene of 'aborted union', the protagonist betrays an increasing sense of distance between himself and the dancer. As she prattles on about her life and friends on Ōshima, he confesses that it all means nothing to him.[37] When the rest of the group catches up with them, he stays behind purposely to talk with Eikichi – obviously now more interested in a personal relation with him than with the dancer. Indeed, he even betrays, for the first time, a sense of irritation with her when she combs her puppy's hair with a comb he had once planned to ask for as a memento. The reality of the girl thus threatens to impose upon his dream-like image of her: he had wanted to take away not the girl herself but an aesthetically pleasing memory of her, a 'memento' to be relished at leisure. An aesthetic object such as the comb, from an aesthete's point of view, has several advantages over a flesh-and-blood girl: above all, its formal perfection is changeless, timeless, and will never disillusion by such a lapse of taste as the girl displays in using it to comb the dog's hair. Since the 'vulgarity' of the actual girl, then, threatens to sully even the memory he had hoped to take away of her, the protagonist's increasing detachment from her becomes not merely fated but necessitated. And we begin to suspect that there is another side to this whole 'orphan psychology' business. Perhaps his isolation from others is not merely a condition imposed by fate but is reinforced also by his own deeper will. The protagonist, we must remember, is an artist, the fictive writer of this 'autobiographical' novella, and alienation is as much a necessary condition of the artist's work as is the capacity for union: he must be able to unite with the object of his attention in order to know it intimately, in its essence, but he must also be able to detach himself from it in order to use it as the raw material of his art. And the *Izu* protagonist does want to use the dancer as 'raw material', as we know from the work before us. As a human being, of course, he may desire momentary relief from his isolation, but as an artist he cannot afford any ultimate 'liberation' from it.

As all possibility of his romantic involvement with the dancer fades away, however, the possibility of his friendly union with the group as a whole seems to grow – and to promise 'salvation' in a milder form. In Chapter Four, after he has agreed to stay on an extra day at Yūganō in order to travel with them, the older woman, Ofukuro, who appears to be the *de facto* leader of the group, expresses her approval by saying that their meeting seems 'strangely fated' (*fushigi na goen*) and asking him to offer a prayer at Shimoda for Chiyoko's dead baby – as if he were now accepted as a family member.[38] This impression is further heightened shortly after when Eikichi opens himself completely to the protagonist, disclosing his own unfortunate personal history as well as that of other members of the group. Similarly, the three young women invite him to take a bath with them, and they press him to come visit them on Ōshima. In Chapter Five comes what might be regarded as the climax of this trend towards his 'incorporation' into the group when he overhears the dancer and Chiyoko remarking on what a 'good' person he is. Again, as in the earlier 'nude scene', the young man's reaction to this casual remark seems vastly out-of-proportion, so that one feels obliged again to refer to his 'orphan psychology' in order to explain it. Only a young man whose mind had been full of self-doubt and even self-loathing could be thrown into such raptures simply by being convinced, for a moment, that he is regarded as 'a good person in the ordinary sense of the word'.[39] And, indeed, this is the passage in which the narrator himself, in retrospect, refers to his 'severe judgement' of himself as having been 'warped by an orphan psychology', and thereby implies that, with this experience of approbation by the dancer and Chiyoko, he was given at least momentary relief from this oppressive state of mind; it was, as he says, 'inexpressibly welcome'. Released now from his inner tensions, he comes alive to the beauty of the surrounding nature, noting the brightness of the mountains as the ocean draws near.[40] Full of a new self-assurance, he marches forward, lopping off the heads of the autumn grasses with his bamboo staff. Does this mean, then, that the orphan has at last found the family he never had, in the form of a group of vagabond performers who, as he himself notes, are held together by warm familial feelings?[41] Having relinquished all hope (or desire) of overcoming his alienation by a close relation with the dancer, does he now opt for achieving the same purpose in a 'safer' way, by a comradely union with the group as a whole?

If so, there are two factors already apparent at the end of Chapter Five which imply that, as with the dancer, any hopes of a 'healing union' are ultimately bound to be dashed. Firstly, his own essential isolation and self-absorption are no more broken through in this scene than when he observed the dancer in the nude. Just as then he observed the dancer from a 'safe distance', so now he overhears the conversation of the two girls – there is still no direct, person-to-person relation between himself and the others. Likewise, the euphoria he feels is not a shared thing, a mutual experience; he enjoys it in complete isolation. Nor does he become more sociable in its aftermath: he turns his attention not to the girls but to the beauties of the natural world – and one might even detect a hint of unfeeling arrogance in the way he lops off the heads of the autumn grasses. (The gesture may perhaps be excused as an expression of youthful high spirits, but certainly it would be out of character with the later Kawabata, the *haiku* poet always in deep communion and sympathy with even the humblest life-forms of the natural world.)

The second impediment to any real union between the young man and the performers is an objective one: the discrepancy in their social status. Significantly, we are given a rude reminder of this immediately after his 'euphoria' by the signs which, we are told, he saw outside some of the villages he passed: "'Mendicant vagabond performers keep out!'"[42]

This ominous omen, of course, is quite justified by the events of the final two chapters, Six and Seven. Upon arrival in Shimoda, a gathering place for vagabond performers, both the protagonist and the performers are each drawn back inexorably into their own social spheres. While they were 'on the road' a certain liberty could obtain; but now, back in 'civilization', social discriminations must again prevail. There is an almost immediate cooling in their relations after the performers settle into a cheap flophouse filled with others of their kind, in an attic-like room in which the protagonist cannot even sit down comfortably: Ofukuro denies permission for the dancer to go to the movies with him; the dancer herself becomes uncommunicative; most of the women do not come to see him off when he boards the boat back to Tokyo; and even Eikichi, though still friendly, is duly respectful, wearing ceremonial dress in his honour. As a final gesture symbolizing his return to his own proper sphere, the protagonist gives Eikichi the hunting cap and puts his own school cap back on.

Has he, then, merely been indulging in a form of 'slumming', enjoying a temporary holiday from the pressures of his elite status by playing at being a 'vagrant' and flirting with an exotic 'gypsy girl'? This view seems to have some currency, especially among critics of a Marxist/feminist persuasion.[43] And no doubt there is some truth in it – I would be the last to deny the essential selfishness of the Kawabata male, especially in his relations with women. But it is unlikely that this view will be accepted as the last word by anyone who reads *Izu* with sensitivity, since it scarcely does justice to the work's full psychological complexity. There is much more to the *Izu* protagonist than male egotism or an elitist mentality. As I have already suggested, he is a veritable cauldron of contending forces, including a deep human need for union with others in constant conflict with a psychological and artistic need for detachment. And, though his 'orphan psychology' may serve his needs as an artist, this does not make it any less painful to him as a human being. His human need for union with the dancer and her group is still a sincere and even a desperate one.

How then does his 'orphan psychology' reveal itself in the final two chapters? And are we convinced, in the end, that the protagonist has achieved a final liberation from it?

The last complete exchange of words between the young man and the dancer is a seemingly inconsequential bit of banter, at the beginning of Chapter Six, revolving around the heaviness of her drum. Needless to say, after the scene which has just transpired in the previous chapter, we cannot take any reference to her 'drum' merely at face value, but the lightness with which the symbol is now treated forms a humourously ironic contrast to the previous instance, and reveals the narrator/protagonist's now greater detachment. But the 'message' is clear: in remarking that the drum is heavier than he thought, and heavier than his pack, the girl shows her awareness, perhaps still only half-conscious, of his naïveté about sexual relations, and his inability to bear the 'weight' of a mature, responsible relationship with a girl like herself.

If this seems to be reading too much into Kawabata's use of imagery, I would point out that there is an even more obvious example shortly afterwards, in Chapter Seven, of a symbolic usage which is also humourously ironical (though Kawabata is not often credited with humour) and which calls for much the same interpretation. One of the going-away presents which Eikichi buys the protagonist is a bottle of mouthwash called 'Kaoru' ('Fragrance'), which is also the dancer's name.[44] Whereas earlier she was reduced to or objectified as a drum, and thus made safely handable, now he is able to possess her pure essence as a mouthwash! (And we may also note the ironic contrast between the memento of the girl he had wanted – her comb, a poetic object – and the memento he is actually given.) Furthermore, when we consider the function of the mouthwash (in Japanese, literally a 'mouth-purifier'), it may occur to us that it corresponds ironically, on a physical level, to the 'purifying function' the protagonist wishes to assign the girl on a psychological level. Thus Kawabata here, in a manner reminiscent of his one-time mentor, James Joyce, seems to be gently satirizing his own idealizing, romanticizing tendencies as an artist – and perhaps even, at this early stage, what we might call the exploitative or narcissistic 'spirituality' of his male hero.

Shortly after the above banter about the drum, however, we are reminded that, although the narrator/protagonist may be able to take his relation with the dancer lightly, with a sense of detachment and even humourous irony, the girl herself is not so fortunate. She asks him again to take her to a movie, but this time she mumbles it, as if talking only to herself – thus seeming, again, at least half conscious of his disinterest. From this point on there occurs, intermittently, almost a change in the work's point-of-view, as the dancer's feelings, her sufferings at being parted from him, are emphasized above those of the young man, who now seems quite content to take his leave. Thus, when Ofukuro refuses permission for the dancer to accompany the protagonist to the movies, the girl is devastated, rendered speechless, but he calmly goes off to the movies by himself. His main reaction is to wonder why the older woman refused her permission. And indeed, we might ask, why did she?

Several critics have portrayed Ofukuro's role as that of opponent to the protagonist's advances and protectress of the dancer's virginity.[45] No doubt there is a strong element of this protectiveness in her, but on what is it based? It cannot be based merely on a desire to protect the innocence of a girl too young for sexual relations – a woman of her obvious perspicacity surely must have noticed that the protagonist no longer has any interest in the sexual conquest of the girl. Nor does it seem that she objects to him on social grounds – i.e., that his higher status would make a lasting relationship impossible. It is she, we must remember, who twice invites him – with some insistence – to visit their home on Ōshima. Thus it would seem that it must be something she perceives in the young man himself, some more personal factor, which causes her to 'cool' towards him, and explains her absence from the 'farewell' scene at the end. What this is may be hinted at on the two occasions when she invites him to visit them: both times no answer of his is recorded, perhaps indicating that he was non-committal – as, from what we know of his psychology, we would expect him to be. If this obviously discerning woman had perceived from this that he was not prepared for any deep or long-term commitment to the dancer, then perhaps she acted not so much to protect the girl's 'purity' as to forestall her heartbreak. If so, then the final events of *Izu* prove her circumspection to have been quite justified – although, by the time she intervenes, it is already too late to prevent the girl's suffering. And the protagonist's surprise at her refusal does not prove his 'innocence' only; it also reveals that he is blind to the consequences of his own egotism.

At any rate, the end of Chapter Six finds him again with an acute feeling of his aloneness; his 'union' with the group as a whole, at with the dancer, has proved illusory and short-lived. Staring out into the darkened town, he keeps thinking that he can hear a drum in the distance, and he weeps – a 'normal' reaction for anyone about to part from friends. There is an interesting contrast, however, between these 'normal' tears of sadness which close Chapter Six and the 'abnormal', blissful tears which close Chapter Seven and the work as a whole.

If *Izu* had ended at this point, the reader might have been permitted to assume that the young man does, after all, feel sad and lonely at parting from the dancer and her 'family', even though he now recognizes the inevitability of this parting – he would go away sadder but wiser. As an ending, this would have been quite conventional, and perhaps slightly sentimental: a note of gentle pathos in the orthodox lyric tradition – 'sadness at parting' being, after all, one of the most ancient (and well-worn) themes of Japanese as of other poetries. But the essential originality of *Izu* reveals itself here; its 'lyricism' is by no means of a conventional kind. What its final chapter makes plain, in fact, is that 'sadness at parting' is far from being the young man's predominant mood as he takes his leave. On the contrary, he is positively euphoric. But what is the meaning of this strange exaltation? We must address this question in a moment, but first I would like to point out that the final chapter does not simply serve the function of a ceremonious leavetaking – or, as one critic has said, a mere *cadenza*.[46] Without this chapter the whole character and structure of *Izu* would change, and quite drastically; it would become a far less interesting work and we would be without probably the most important of its hermeneutical clues: namely, the protagonist's elation at the end. The way we interpret this elation, of course, determines and is determined by our interpretation of the work as a whole. This becomes evident when we examine the views of another group of critics than those referred to above, a group not so obsessed with *Izu*'s autobiographical sources, but which tries rather to see the work in itself as an integral, autonomous whole.

Since Senuma Shigeki's pioneering study of 1957, these 'work-analysis' critics have generally agreed that, by his meeting with the dancer, the *Izu* protagonist is able to achieve self-knowledge and a kind of spiritual purification.[47] There is some disagreement, however, as to whether this leads to any ultimate liberation from his 'orphan psychology'. On the negative side, Kobayashi Ichirō argues that the work is structured around pendulum-like swings between 'reality' and 'unreality': the dream-world of the 'romance' between the protagonist and the dancer as opposed to the real world of Ofukuro's view of the impracticability of this 'union'. In the end it is Ofukuro's view, the reality principle, which triumphs, and the protagonist, his dreams dashed, remains separate and alone.[48] His elation at the end signifies that he is glad to escape from a reality in which he could not achieve union with the vagabond performers.[49]

At the opposite pole to this is the very positive view of Tsuruta Kinya: by his communion with the dancer, who is an innocent child rather than a sexually ripe girl, the protagonist is able to achieve a spiritual purgation – and this explains the 'refreshing sense of life' which pervades the work.[50] Even the final scene of parting is not a defeat for him, since he and the dancer achieve a kind of nonverbal union of souls, despite Ofukuro's opposition.[51] The fact that he progresses from being a warped, alienated orphan to being a gentle, sociable person is shown at the end by his kindness to an old lady and her grandchildren, which contrasts with his avoidance of the old man at the teahouse near the story's beginning.[52] His final euphoria is a kind of 'religious ecstasy' proving that he has indeed achieved 'salvation'.[53]

Generally, most critics are closer to Tsuruta's 'positive' end of the pole than Kobayashi's 'negative' one. Takeda Katsuhiko, for instance, sees *Izu* as the prototype of the many Kawabata works which deal with the spiritual salvation of a person deprived of the love of close relatives.[54] And, as in many of those later works, here too travel plays an important role: the *Izu* protagonist's spiritual search through travel is very much in the great Japanese tradition of artistic/religious pilgrimages, a tradition which produced such works as Bashō's *Narrow Road to the Interior* (*Oku no hosomichi*, 1702).[55]

Takada Kōda also places the spiritual dimension of *Izu* in a historical context, but contemporaneously and on a more grandiose scale. Pointing out that in his early literary manifestoes Kawabata expressed his vision of the 'salvational' function of literature, Takada offers *Izu* as a prime example of a literary work which can fulfill such an exalted purpose. Since, in this age of alienation, we are all victims of an 'orphan psychology', *Izu* is no mere personal confession; it is both a diagnosis of the spiritual malaise of our times and a prescription for its cure. In showing how the protagonist overcomes his own egotism, *Izu* teaches us how we may all achieve a warm and gentle society.[56]

Although not making such grandiose claims, Nakamura Mitsuo also views *Izu* as a product of its age in a significant way. It is a 'song of Shōwa youth' and its mood of 'self-negation' is very much in the spirit of the age, though it came naturally to Kawabata as an orphan.[57] But at the bottom of the work there is a desire to overcome this orphan's self-negation and to become someone, to affirm the self.[58] As in a Nō play, the protagonist achieves this 'salvation' by meeting a woman while on a journey.[59] Thus *Izu* is not merely a love story but, like other of Kawabata's major works, a 'drama of self-discovery'. This, claims Nakamura, is 'the most basic drama of life and art' and 'in the way it shows itself in this dramaless novella, it is the life of the whole work'.[60]

My own view of Izu's ultimate outcome lies somewhere between the majority positive view and the minority negative one. While it may well be true, as most critics claim, that the author <u>intended</u> the last scene to show his protagonist's final liberation – or salvation – from his 'orphan psychology', there is a legitimate distinction to be made between what an author <u>intends</u> (presuming that we can even know this) and what his text <u>reveals</u>. We must make allowance, after all, for what an author reveals <u>unconsciously</u> about himself or his characters, for such revelations are as much a part of the finished text as 'the author's intentions' and, indeed, cannot really be distinguished from them, since even the author himself, in the fever of creation, may not be aware of his deepest intentions. It may be noted in this connection that recent research on the two hemispheres of the brain has confirmed what many writers in the past have claimed: that their writing often seems to arise spontaneously from some pre-logical, intuitively integrating part of the mind (the right hemisphere) and that only on later reflection can they begin to comprehend (with the left hemisphere) the logical connections between the various images, metaphors and ideas thus produced – in other words, the overall thematic structure of the work.[61] Since, then, the writer himself may well be unaware of the full significance of what he has written, the purpose of critical analysis must be to determine not what the author (consciously) intended to write but what he has actually written. In the case of *Izu*, for instance, the young Kawabata, absorbed in the sweetness of his memories, may well have been unaware of a problem which was to rise to the surface in his later works: the problem of the male's egotism as an impediment to his real, long-term 'liberation'. But what does the text itself tell us?

As Chapter Seven opens, we encounter the protagonist again in a mood of loneliness, echoing his mood of the previous evening. The women of the group have not bothered to come see him off, and his resultant feeling of desolation seems intensified by the cold autumn wind that blows through the town. Eikichi soon cheers him up, however, by giving him, among other things, some mouthwash which, as we have seen, is a kind of 'objectification' of the dancer and an ironic symbol of her purifying function. And his mood picks up even more when, on approaching the dock, he finds the dancer waiting for him there: she has come, after all, to see him off, and all by herself, thus proving that she is still devoted to him.

The final scene between the dancer and the protagonist which now transpires is brief but all-important in what it tells us of their respective moods on parting. Firstly, the sudden 'lightening' of the young man's mood proves that the loneliness he has been feeling is no deep 'sadness at parting'. The mere fact that the dancer shows up is enough for him, since he is convinced by this that her devotion to him remains unabated. And he desires nothing more. Though their parting is still imminent, this obviously does not bother him in the slightest. Quite the contrary. Just like an infant in relation to its mother, all he wants is to <u>feel</u> loved; he feels neither the desire nor the obligation to give love in return. Thus his imminent parting from the girl makes her love for him all the more sweet, since he knows it will not encumber him with the burdens of a mutual relationship. It is rather as if he is able to 'have his cake and eat it too'. Thus his euphoria knows no bounds. And when we examine the actual psychological content of this euphoria, its narcissistic nature becomes even more apparent. Without a thought for the suffering of the girl left behind on the dock, he indulges himself in an 'oceanic' bath of *amae*, in the 'sweet pleasure' (*amai kokoroyosa*) of feeling that he is loved by all and is, indeed, the very centre of the universe.[62] Thus he eats the lunch of the other student as if it were his own and uses the other's cape to cover himself, feeling that 'no matter how kind people were to me, it was the most natural thing in the world for them to be so'.[63]

In other words, his 'orphan psychology' is still very much in operation here: he still looks to the world for the childhood he missed, the unconditional love of a mother. And he still remains incapable of returning love. How, then, can we claim that he has achieved any real 'liberation'? In finding a 'substitute mother' in the dancer, he no doubt has attained momentary relief from the suffering caused by his condition, but the root cause of that condition remains intact. His 'liberation' is therefore only momentary, illusory. For, we must ask, how long can he continue to relate to the world in his present unidirectional way without receiving a rude shock to his self-satisfaction? When, for instance, he cannot so conveniently bid adieu to the heartbroken girl as in the present instance, how will he respond to her pleas or demands for a more authentic relationship? We discover the answer to this question, of course, in some later Kawabata works.

For the present, although the girl's suffering is acutely obvious, the protagonist makes no attempt to come to terms with it. Indeed, to put it rather bluntly, his own happiness grows in direct proportion to her suffering, since, the more she suffers, the more he is assured of her love. Thus, in the final scene between them, the stress is on <u>her</u> feelings rather than on his. And the contrast between them could not be more obvious. The young man's 'aesthetic detachment' is made evident, again, by his 'objectifying' of the girl: noticing, as before, the traces of makeup still left on her face, which he always finds so appealing; significantly, the red at the corners of her eyes, in particular, makes her face seem 'angry' (and certainly she has reason to be angry), but, for him, this 'anger' of hers only seems to give her a cute 'childish gallantry' (*osanai ririshisa*).[64] An even more telling fact, though, is that, whereas the protagonist is able to attempt light conversation, the girl is incapable of response. She merely stares out to sea, as if unable to give voice to her sorrow. This is a sure sign of the greater depth of her feeling, because Kawabata, as one critic has pointed out, subscribed to the traditional Japanese view that taciturnity is a mark of sincerity, since words are inadequate to express emotions of real profundity.[65] This is exactly why, on the other hand, the protagonist must maintain his detachment: he is a writer and thus must be able to freely resort to words. The dancer, however, is unable even to say 'goodbye', though she makes an effort to do so; she can only nod and then, as his ship recedes into the distance, wave something white. In contrast again, the protagonist soon seems to 'get over' her once his ship is out at sea – indeed, with almost unseemly haste: 'I felt that my parting from the dancer was already in the distant past'.[66] And, as already noted, his final euphoric mood has no trace in it of 'sadness at parting'. The pathetic little dancer is no longer even thought of. As with his previous moments of elation, it is a strictly solipsistic pleasure, not to be shared with anyone. Though he weeps, these are the 'sweet' tears of a self-indulgent, even self-congratulatory contentment: 'as if I were resting in a soothing fulfillment'.[67] His condition, indeed, seems rather like that of someone whose nervous system has suddenly been 'put to sleep' by a large ingestation of some tranquilizer.

As if to ameliorate our sense of the young man's 'selfishness', however, we are told in this final scene of the help he provides to an old woman and her grandchildren who are also travelling on his ship. He agrees to take care of her until Tokyo and plans even to go out of his way to guide her to Ueno Station and buy her a ticket there for the train to her hometown. In his present expansive mood, he feels that his own kindness also is 'extremely natural'.[68] If, however, this was meant in some way to 'compensate for' the dancer's heartbreak (and one can think of no other reason for the scene's inclusion), the reader may feel it is 'too little too late'. And, from a literary-aesthetic point of view, there is something about this incident which seems unconvincing – as if it were an afterthought tagged on to the work for all too obvious reasons. Perhaps this has something to do with the inconsistency noted by one critic: namely, that in Chapter Six the narrator tells us that he was forced to return to Tokyo because he had run out of money, but now, in the next chapter, he is able so generously to pay for the old woman's train ticket.[69] More important, however, is our sense of this incident as being superfluous to the main action of the story (which is presumably why Edward Seidensticker deleted it from his English translation).

If the story was meant to end with a convincing act of kindness on the protagonist's part – enough, say, to make us change our minds about his 'selfishness' or 'narcissism' – then it would have had to have been directed towards the dancer, since it is she who has suffered most from her relationship with him, and since his way of relating to her is of central interest to the whole story and has formed, throughout, the principal basis for our judgements of his character. One need not go so far as to regard this incident with the old woman as an 'aesthetic flaw'; one could well argue, as we have already seen one critic do, that it neatly balances the episode with the paralytic old man at the beginning of the work, and thus, perhaps, shows that the protagonist has made some slight moral progress.[70] But the point is simply that it does not carry enough weight to reverse our impression of the 'callousness' of his behaviour towards the girl. Similarly, while it may be argued that there are other ways to spiritual liberation than by entering into human relationships – indeed, a traditional Japanese way would be by an inverse process, involving isolation and introversion – the fact is that this is the way attempted by the *Izu* protagonist, so that his ultimate progress must be judged in these terms.

Kawabata was supposedly inspired to write *Izu* by a Walt Whitman poem affirming the value of free, uninhibited relationships even between people who meet on a journey.[71] This may have been the ideal he had in mind in writing the work, but the end product is more reminiscent of another aspect of Whitman: the poet who, in *Song of Myself*, celebrated himself with an innocent, unabashed narcissism. At least, the *Izu* protagonist attempts such an unconditional self-celebration, albeit depending for support on the good opinion and love of others; and his final mood of self-satisfied euphoria is undeniably tinged by a Whitmanesque mysticism – a sense of 'all things in harmony' – as well as by a Whitmanesque narcissism. The one does not necessarily preclude the other. As Paul Zweig has amply documented in his excellent study, *The Heresy of Self-Love*, mysticism and narcissism are often, in fact, hard to distinguish from each other – which is why mysticism has always been suspect to the puritanical and moralistic mainstream of Western culture, from the medieval scholastics to the modern Freudians.[72] Eastern culture, of course, has been more tolerant of self-absorption in all its varieties, seeing it as the *sine qua non* of spiritual growth. And this may well include a healthy self-love. As *Izu* so convincingly shows, a man who loathes himself is incapable of loving others. Thus the protagonist's final 'narcissistic' rapture may legitimately be regarded, if not as proof of his ultimate liberation, at least as a promising sign of its future possibility. His progress beyond self-love to love of others may come too late to benefit the dancer, but at least her sufferings will not have been for nothing.

The protagonist's present euphoria, based so flimsily on his newfound sense of being loved, obviously will not survive his return to the 'real world'. The very structure of the work – tracing, as we have seen, a series of his emotional peaks and valleys – leads us to suspect that, once he finds himself alone again in the big city, he will soon descend from his present 'peak' to another dark 'valley'. But the fact that he will survive all such trials is also beyond doubt. For not only does he have his memories of the dancer to comfort him; like the boy of the *Diary*, the young man of *Izu* has a special weapon in his arsenal: he is a writer. He does not merely suffer adversities; he forges them into the material of his art. And herein lies his true act of transcendence in *Izu*: that he has gone on to write this very work. His final triumph does not consist in any ultimate liberation from his psychic problems; it consists rather in his attaining sufficient detachment to be able to write about them in a convincing and powerful way, and even with great beauty of style. If we come away from *Izu* with a sharp sense of the protagonist's human inadequacies and the suffering these cause the dancer, we must remember that it is his triumph as a writer which makes this balanced, even ironical, view possible. (And this applies whether we closely identify the protagonist with Kawabata himself, as traditional Japanese readers of *shishōsetsu* were accustomed to do, or whether, in the more 'postmodern' way, we make a strict distinction between the actual author and the author's 'persona' as narrator and protagonist of his own 'semi-autobiographical' fiction.)

What the two great 'autobiographical stories' of Kawabata's 'twenties finally leave us with, then, is an impression of a young writer discovering himself as an artist, and discovering the saving power of his art. Although he flirts with the ways of the lover and of the mystic, it is the lonely way of the artist which he finally chooses – which, perhaps, his destiny forces him to choose. It is not the way of ultimate peace or religious enlightenment, but a way full of suffering, of the conflicting tensions which give rise to art. The artist, unlike the mystic, cannot turn his back on the world of duality, of discriminative thinking, of aesthetic and moral judgements – in short, the

human world – because it is the very material of his art. But
certainly he can, as Kawabata did, keep the mystical vision in
mind as a distant ideal – because the more distant, the more
unrealizable it is, the more it will itself become, ironically, a
source of tension, the kind of creative tension which gives birth
to the *concordia discors* of art. Kawabata would never achieve the
spiritual tranquility of that most famous of *shishōsetsuka* or
writers of autobiographical fiction, Shiga Naoya – who, judging
by his *Dark Night's Passing* (*An'ya kōro*, 1919-37) was rather
more successful as a mystic.[73] On the other hand, neither
would Kawabata, like Shiga, stop writing mid-career. Until the
end of his days he would continue to grow as an artist, far
beyond the confines of the *shishōsetsu*, creating ever more
powerful and original works of art out of the contending forces
of his inner life.

CHAPTER THREE
EXPERIMENT AND EXPANSION

1. A Struggle for Growth (1926–1935)

Most of Kawabata's earliest writings, from the *Diary of a Sixteen-Year-Old* to the *Dancing Girl of Izu* – that is, from about 1914 to 1926 – easily fall within the mainstream Japanese literary tradition of autobiographical writing in a lyrical mode – though, as we have seen, some differ considerably from others in mood and style. Since these were the works which established him quickly as an important up-and-coming writer, no doubt it would have been expedient for him to go on indefinitely writing in this mode. At least one would not have expected him to break away from it immediately after scoring the stunning popular success of *Izu*. But one mark of Kawabata's stature as a writer is that he was never content merely to repeat his successes; even into his old age, he never lost his restless desire to grow as an artist – and he was always prepared for the struggle and the risk involved in developing a new mode of writing. Thus the bold experiments he attempted after *Izu* were not merely, as some seem to think, the product of youthful uncertainty or even foolhardiness; rather they were very much in character – and, as a matter of fact, he would repeat this kind of surprise 'change of course' several times again later in his career.

During the decade between the publication of *Izu* and the appearance of the first chapters of *Snow Country* in 1935, Kawabata would stray a long way indeed from the traditional mode of his 'virgin works', experimenting restlessly with new forms and expanding the scope of his work with new themes. Much of his writing now became less directly autobiographical, allowing for greater imaginative play. He began, for instance, to write stories from the point of view of his female characters. The example of European modernist writing of the 1920s (the 'golden age' of modernism) encouraged him to experiment with new techniques, such as 'stream-of-consciousness', and new styles, such as a language imitative of the quick, 'syncopated' rhythms of jazz. The tone or mood of many of his works became darker – we might even describe some of them as 'anti-lyrical'. And their implicit message too was often more cynical, even nihilistic. The 'innocent' young people who played at love in the idyllic surroundings of the Izu peninsula were now replaced by the jaded prostitutes and gangsters or, less sensationally, by the alienated married couples of the vast urban cacophony of modern Tokyo.

As with any writer or artist who takes risks by departing from the familiar, tried-and-true methods, the Kawabata of this period no doubt faltered at times. But, while perhaps none of his experimental writings may be regarded as masterpieces, many of them still seem remarkably successful in their own way, and, of course, they may interest us now not only as works in themselves but as representing a kind of growing stage in a great writer's career. Even to make this claim for them, however, we must be convinced that Kawabata learned something of lasting value from these 'modernist experiments', that these works were not merely short-lived anomalies in a long career devoted overwhelmingly to the creation of a more 'traditional-style' literature.

2. Kawabata's Modernism: a brief flirtation or a lasting affair?

Among the major Japanese fiction writers of the twentieth century, Kawabata is often perceived as one of those who were most deeply rooted in the native literary tradition – and therefore, one might think, most immune to Western influence. His exquisitely imagistic or impressionistic style reminds many of *haiku*. The associative leaps in his narrative structures are frequently said to resemble those of the medieval poetic form of *renga* or linked verse. The very images which recur as symbolic or thematic motifs throughout his major works often seem quite stereotypically traditional: cherry blossoms, *geisha*, Mount Fuji, tea bowls, *Nō* masks .... The general mood of these novels too seems redolent of a traditional elegiac pathos, a *mono no aware* nostalgia. Kawabata himself encouraged this impression – especially in the wake of Japan's defeat in the Pacific War, which, according to him, only deepened his elegiac mood and his single-minded dedication to the native tradition: 'The realization that I wrote in a Japanese style, and the determination to continue the traditions of Japanese beauty were not new for me, but perhaps I had to see the mountains and rivers of my country after it had been defeated before everything else could disappear'.[1]

No doubt he was also well aware, as his Nobel Prize acceptance speech suggests, that it was his 'traditionalism' which gave his work such great appeal to Western readers, who were, of course, delighted to find a writer who seemed so splendidly representative of the Japanese tradition – and who were also, perhaps, equally delighted not to be confronted by yet another Japanese clone of Kafka or Camus. Conversely, Kawabata's sometimes stereotypical 'Japaneseness' also accounts for his surprising (to us) unpopularity among some of the Japanese themselves, especially among the younger generation of *kokubungakusha* (scholars of Japanese literature). Perhaps Mishima Yukio, though an admirer of Kawabata, put his finger on the key objection when he claimed that Kawabata was totally lacking that *sine qua non* of the serious modern Japanese writer, a 'will to interpret the world' or, in the language preferred by the really serious-minded, a *Weltanschauung.*[2] What this really means, of course, is not that Kawabata was totally innocent of all philosophy but that, again like a good traditional writer and unlike Mishima himself, he was never, except in a few early stories such as 'Lyric Poem', overly obvious or explicit in giving expression to his world view, whether in his narrative passages or by the use of his characters as mouthpieces.

Given, then, all these factors which seem to make Kawabata such a dyed-in-the-wool traditionalist, what are we to make of his 'flirtation' with modernism in the 1920s and early '30s? Should we see it as an anomalous episode which had no lasting impact on the main body of his work? This seems to be the preferred approach of some of his Western interpreters: Donald Keene, for instance, claims that: 'For Tanizaki or Kawabata Modernism was only a passing phase in careers devoted to more traditional literature; to treat them as Modernists would be misleading, if only because their best works are not in this vein'.[3] Similarly, Gwenn Boardman Petersen categorically states that the 'true sources of Kawabata's delicate prose' are in the 'classical literature of Japan' rather than in 'supposed links with individual French writers or European movements, or the Scandinavian literature he is said to have read in high school'.[4]

Both of these statements, it seems to me, are based on a misconception and consequently underestimate the depth and persistence of Kawabata's modernism. The misconception is that modernism and traditionalism are necessarily mutually exclusive, that a writer must be essentially either a traditionalist or a modernist. I would argue that, in the context of Japanese literature in particular, in which many of the 'innovations' of the modernists seem to have been broadly anticipated by traditional writers, modernism and traditionalism are often mutually supportive. Thus it is sometimes difficult to discriminate between modernist and traditional elements in a given work of modern Japanese literature. Are Kawabata's freely associative interior monologues, for instance, in the tradition of the modernist writer James Joyce or of the medieval *renga* poet Sōgi and random essayist Kenkō? In a work of Kawabata's 'modernist period' such as *Crystal Fantasies* they are all too obviously, perhaps even crudely, Joycean. In a work such as *Snow Country*, written just a few years later in his 'traditionalist period', they seem to belong more to the native tradition – and thereby to benefit greatly in terms of aesthetic subtlety. And yet, can we assume that the fact that Kawabata experimented at one point with Joycean stream of consciousness has no relation whatsoever to the fact that, in writing *Snow Country* just a few years later, he developed his own form of this narrative technique, albeit in a more subtle and traditional way? This seems to me an extremely unconvincing assumption. What seems far more likely is that Kawabata did learn some lasting lessons from his encounter with modernism, not only in writing techniques but even in such fundamental matters as the role of the writer and the purpose of writing, but that, after a short period of raw influence, these lessons were adapted and absorbed into that native tradition which was still alive within him – in much the same way as, on a larger historical scale, foreign influences have always been absorbed and adapted by the Japanese.

Furthermore, if, as Keene argues, Kawabata's modernism was merely a 'passing phase' and his 'best works are not in this vein', then why did he continue to write the often very modernistic or surrealistic prose poems called 'palm-sized stories' (*tanagokoro shōsetsu*) for the rest of his career – works which Kawabata felt, as Keene himself notes, represented the very 'essence of his art?'[5] Certainly, by modernist standards, they are works of extremely high quality; though called 'stories', many are, in fact, pure poetry – or, at least, haunting surrealistic prose poems of the highest order, comparable to works in a similar vein by Breton, Reverdy or Michaux. Then again, if his modernism was merely a passing phase, we might ask why, very late in his career, Kawabata returned to an equally surrealist or modernist mode with works such as *Sleeping Beauties* (*Nemureru bijo*), 'One Arm' (*Kata ude*) and *Dandelions* (*Tanpopo*)? Are not these among his 'best works?'

71

Certainly they are among his most intriguing, and any reader with a taste for modernist writing would be loathe to rank them any lower than the more 'traditional' works.

To try to attain a clearer view of what Kawabata learned from his encounter with European modernism, I will first review the general outlines of that encounter and then focus in more depth on some of its creative products.

★　★　★

As we have seen, Kawabata began his career at a very early age in a very traditional mode: as a writer of autobiographical fiction or *shishōsetsu*. These works centre largely on the sorrows of his childhood, when all the members of his immediate family died off one after the other, and on his struggles to overcome the 'orphan psychology' which resulted from this. In some ways this apprenticeship as a traditional *shishōsetsuka* ('I-novelist') may be said to have predisposed him towards the European modernism of the 1920s. One of the main features of the modernist novel, after all, and certainly one of the features which distinguish it from the nineteenth-century European novel, is its extreme subjectivity, whether achieved by a Joycean stream-of-consciousness narrative or by the author simply focusing primarily on the contents of his own psyche. In fact, many of the Western novelists of this period also wrote fiction whose central characters could be closely identified with the authors themselves – Joyce, Proust, Lawrence, Woolf, Fitzgerald, Hemingway, to name just a few of the major examples.[6]

As for the young Kawabata's attraction to surrealism and expressionism, the reasons for this seem to have been more philosophic. Already by this time he had decided that the way to achieve salvation from his alienated existence as an orphan was by an embrace of traditional Buddhistic monism: the mother's love he had never experienced would be replaced by the universal love which comes when all sense of separateness between self and other or self and nature had been made to disappear by a radical transformation of consciousness. Rightly or wrongly, he felt that the surrealists and expressionists were in pursuit of the same monistic vision and, more importantly, that they had developed a style of writing which would help actualize that vision.

The 'twenties of this century, which were also Kawabata's twenties (he was born in 1899), were an exciting time for a young writer to be exploring the possibilities of his art, in Japan as in the West. It was an age conspicuous for its adventurous, experimental spirit, when all the old moral and aesthetic values

seemed discredited and a new aesthetic movement or 'ism'
seemed to be inaugurated almost every day: among the more
lasting ones, dadaism, surrealism, expressionism and futurism.
All these 'movements' had Japanese exponents, in literature as
in the visual arts. Whereas in the West it was primarily the
cataclysm of the First World War which had caused such a total
and radical break with the past, in Japan the devastation
wrought by the Great Kantō Earthquake of 1923 seemed to
accomplish much the same purpose – or, at least, to make the
younger writers more receptive to the Western avant-garde.[7] A
new radicalism arose in the Japanese literary world after the
earthquake, as if a cultural upheaval had followed the
geological one. This 'radicalism' formed itself naturally into
two main streams, one political, the Marxist-oriented 'prole-
tarian literature' movement, and the other aesthetic, the
modernism of the *'shin kankaku ha'* or 'neo-sensory school'.
These two dialectically opposed trends of early Shōwa
literature may be seen to have received their first significant
impetus in the late Taishō period from the founding in 1924,
the year after the earthquake, of two 'coterie magazines' which
served as their respective chief organs: the Marxist *Bungei
sensen* (*Literary Battlefront*, June 1924 to July 1932) and the
neo-sensory school's *Bungei jidai* (*Literary Age*, October 1924
to May 1927).

Besides the immediate 'stimulus' of the earthquake, however, there is another, more long-term historical factor which
should be taken into account. Kawabata's generation, those
writers born around the turn of the century and who came to
maturity in the 'twenties, were the 'third generation' of modern
Japanese novelists – that is, novelists who wrote, to some
extent, under the influence of Western literature. Writers of this
'generation of 1900', compared to previous generations, were
much less conversant with the Chinese classics and much more
familiar with the full range of Western literature, if only by way
of the many translations which had by then appeared. It is also
true, of course, that by their time the general 'Westernization'
or 'modernization' of Japanese culture had progressed apace,
so that cultural products of the West were bound to seem less
alien to them than they had seemed to earlier generations. Thus
they were able to absorb Western influences more naturally,
with less tension, than earlier writers, and also to turn these
influences more self-confidently to their own purposes – even
to the extent of adapting them more to native tastes.

Where does Kawabata himself fit within this overall context?
In many ways he is typical of his generation. Indeed, he soon

became one of its principal spokesmen: as a literary theorist and critic, writing manifestoes to justify the new techniques and new vision of himself and his fellow 'neo-sensory' writers, and writing more general essays on the 'new tendencies of the new writers', on the German expressionists, and so on. His contact with Western literature came early and was intimate: in 1920 he began his studies at the Tokyo Imperial University, in the English Department, although the following year he transferred to the Department of Japanese Literature, apparently to allow himself more time to write. His graduation thesis, *A Short Essay on the History of the Japanese Novel* (*Nihon shōsetsu-shi shōron*, 1924), is remarkable both for the broad sweep of its unorthodox concept of the novel and for its application of Western critical theory to the study of Japanese literature. To some extent, the young Kawabata seemed to anticipate the Anglo-American 'new critics' in his emphasis on work-analysis over the biographical or historical approach to literature – as perhaps was only natural for a creative writer. Furthermore, he also seemed to anticipate a later, mid-century view of what constitutes the novel. At the time he was writing, the 'orthodox' concept, in Japan as in the West, was a rather narrow one, defined mainly by the practice of the great nineteenth-century French 'realists', from Balzac to Zola. In his study of the Japanese novel, however, Kawabata finds novelistic elements not only in traditional romances such as the *Tale of Genji* (*Genji monogatari*, early eleventh century) but even in the myths of the *Record of Ancient Matters* (*Kojiki*, early eighth century), in a random essay (*zuihitsu*) such as the *Pillow Book of Sei Shōnagon* (*Makura no sōshi*, late tenth or early eleventh century), in a literary diary (*nikki*) such as the *Gossamer Diary* (*Kagerō nikki*, late tenth century) and in a historical romance such as the *Tale of Heike* (*Heike monogatari*, early thirteenth century). Thus he already seems to anticipate the freedom of his own later practice of the novel, a practice which often seems to transcend all generic limitations.

In general, the young Kawabata sees the novel more as an image of human consciousness than of an 'objective' reality – and in this also, of course, he is already very much in tune with modernism. And, just as he does not hesitate to compare Japanese with Western works of literature, he also freely mixes Western and Japanese critical theories. He derives his concept of the 'three main methods' of literary research, the historical, the biographical and the critical, from *Some Principles of Literary Criticism* (1899), the work of a now-forgotten American scholar, C.T. Winchester. On the other hand, he also makes good use of Bashō's principle of the harmony in art of 'the eternal and the current' (*fueki ryūkō*), a more impersonal version of T.S. Eliot's 'tradition and the individual talent'. The young Kawabata, perhaps naturally for a writer on the threshold of his career, emphasized more the *ryūkō* or 'current/individual talent' side of the equation, and it is on this basis that he attacks the older generation of Japanese naturalists, whose works he found unoriginal, pale imitations of Western models.

In this early essay, then, we may already detect some of the basic aesthetic stances which were to guide Kawabata's own practice as a novelist: a tolerant, expansive view of what constitutes a novel, with some preference shown for the twentieth-century notion of the novel as an image of human consciousness rather than of any 'objective' world; an easy, natural intermingling on equal terms of the classic and the contemporary, the Japanese and the Western – such interminglings were to be so well accomplished in Kawabata's own novels, as I have already pointed out, that often it is impossible for a reader to decide whether a particular narrative technique is traditional or modern, Japanese or Western.

Through his study of the English language, Kawabata also developed early on a more intimate acquaintance with particular works of Western literature, such as only the process of translation can confer. In 1922, for instance, he translated stories by Galsworthy, Lord Dunsany and Chekhov (all from English) for the January and February issues of the literary magazine, *Bunshō kurabu*. In September, 1924, he was one of the founding members of the seminal 'neo-sensory school' magazine mentioned above, *Bungei jidai (Literary Age)* – indeed, he chose its name, optimistically hoping to signify by it that the world was now passing from a 'religious age to a literary age', and that literature would now serve as an instrument of salvation as religion had done in the past. Though this may seem a typical case of youthful naïveté and over-enthusiasm, the idea, in fact, had a distinguished literary pedigree: Matthew Arnold had voiced it in the previous century, and, as we know from his graduation thesis, Kawabata was familiar with Arnold's views. He also wrote the magazine's first editorial, 'New Literature and a New Lifestyle', a rather impudent putdown of 'the literary establishment doing its legless dancer dance' as opposed to his own younger 'group', which he identifies as 'progressive writers'.

In January of the following year, 1925, he wrote a neo-sensory school manifesto for the same magazine, entitling it, quite grandly: 'An Explication of the New Tendencies of the Avant-Garde Writers', in which, calling for a new immediacy of expression in the language of novels, he draws for support on dadaist theories of free association (psychic automatism) and German expressionist theories of the primacy of the artist's subjectivity and the importance of subject/object union.[8] In another critical statement published in June of the same year (in *Bungei Nippon*) on 'New Tendencies of the Short Story' (*Tanpen shōsetsu no shin keikō*), Kawabata argues against the fallacies of nineteenth-century realism, with its pretensions to presenting an 'objective' view of the world, by simply pointing out that there is a literary equivalent of the Heisenberg effect in physics: whatever a writer touches is inevitably coloured by his own subjectivity, and even his choice of what to touch is determined by that subjectivity. Thus he should give up all pretensions to 'objectivity' and allow free creative expression to that very subjectivity.[9] This is not only a good summary of some of the theory behind modernist art but is also an interesting early justification of the increasingly 'anti-realistic' tendencies of Kawabata's own writing.

In the second half of the 'twenties, Kawabata continued in his critical role as apologist of modernism. This was the period in which Japanese readers were introduced to the really substantial achievements of the European avant-garde, as opposed to the many eccentric 'isms' of the immediate post-war years. After the demise of the *Bungei jidai* in 1927, Kawabata, besides writing a long series of reviews of current literature for the *Bungei shunjū* (*Literary Chronicle*), served on the editorial board of a new literary magazine, *Bungaku* (*Literature*, 1929–), which published translations of Proust, Joyce, Breton, Mann and other important contemporary European authors. In these first years of the Shōwa era, as I have mentioned, the Japanese literary world became sharply divided between a politically committed Marxist faction on the one side and an apolitical, 'aesthetic' faction on the other – both of them, of course, influenced by current trends in the West. In his association with the 'Avant-garde Art Group' (*shinkō geijutsu ha*), the 'Club of Thirteen' (*jū-san no kurabu*) and other such groups, Kawabata became something of a militant 'aesthete'. Nevertheless, although he was relatively apolitical, this should not be taken to mean that he was an advocate of 'art for art's sake' in its narrowest sense. On the contrary, as we have seen, he held to a grand vision of literature's ultimate purpose as a vehicle to replace religion in leading mankind on to spiritual salvation. No doubt these grand ambitions were tempered with time, but it must be said that Kawabata seems never to have completely abandoned them: in one form or another, the theme of 'spiritual salvation', especially the spiritual salvation of his male protagonists, would remain central to his work until the very end of his career.

Apart from the many specific instances of modernist practice which could be pinpointed, perhaps the most important and lasting thing Kawabata inherited from his early encounter with European modernism was a certain spirit of adventure, a willingness to take aesthetic risks, to venture forth into new areas of expression – especially in the dark terrain of the unconscious. Thus, unlike many other Japanese writers of his time, he did not confine himself to the autobiographical story or *shishōsetsu*, despite his early successes in this form. Having proved his mastery of what was then the dominant genre of the Japanese literary world, he soon struck out in new directions, allowing his imagination more free reign. Considering the preeminent status of the *shishōsetsu* in the Japan of that day, this was a bold departure. And certainly it was not the last time Kawabata would risk such an adventurous change of course. In this sense the example of European modernism remained an important inspiration for him throughout the rest of his career.

3. The Artist as Narcissus

> This Narcissus of yours
> Cannot look in the mirror now
> Because he is the mirror himself.
> Antonio Machado[10]

In November of 1927, for instance, only about two years after the publication of *The Dancing Girl of Izu*, Kawabata published a short story, 'Narcissus' (*Nāshissasu*), which is as distinctly modernist in flavour as the former work is traditional, though in some ways it strangely echoes that work as a kind of reverse mirror image – albeit with some nightmarish distortions. The general problem of egotism or narcissism as an impediment to a transcendent monistic vision is already present in Kawabata's early autobiographical works, from the *Diary of a Sixteen-Year-Old* to *The Dancing Girl of Izu*. Whereas in those earlier works the theme of narcissism is only implicit, however, here it is dealt with quite explicitly, although with enough ambiguities to avoid any over-obviousness. One 'twist' is immediately apparent though: here Narcissus is not male but female. A hostile critic might surmise that this is the author's devious way of deflecting any charge of narcissism from himself. But, in a Kawabata story, things are not necessarily as they first appear.

'Narcissus' is a psychological story *par excellence*, being filtered almost entirely through the consciousness of a single female character, a consciousness we come not only to know but to suspect. By this use of a possibly 'unreliable' narrator the author is able to create some interesting effects of irony and ambiguity – which save the story from becoming a mere diatribe against the woman accused of being a 'Narcissus'.

The story consists almost entirely of accusatory 'letters' written by the younger sister of this woman to the man who introduces them (briefly, at the story's beginning) as 'letters which came to me from Mieko'.[11] This is the last we hear from him directly, although he is referred to again later by the letter-writer. One can think of at least three reasons why Kawabata here adopts the epistolary format. Firstly, by doing so he is able to directly and accurately reproduce the young woman's rather catty tone of voice; the letters are written in that feminine conversational style of Japanese which is so inimitably expressive of female sentiment and sensibility. Secondly, the letter format allows the author to directly represent the woman's sometimes highly digressive 'stream of consciousness' in a more natural way than would be possible in 'straight' narration. And, finally, the format also enables Kawabata to indulge his penchant for the 'framed story', the 'story within a story', and for complex games in the manipulation of point of view. No doubt he learned something about this from his readings of contemporary Western novelists and theorists of the novel. For instance, we might recall that this was the period (the 1920s) in which the critic Percy Lubbock, under the sway of Henry James, was vaunting the proper aesthetic uses of point of view as an essential ingredient in the art of fiction.[12] At any rate, by the simple expedient of having the younger sister address letters complaining about her older sister to the man who, it turns out, is supposed to marry that older sister, the author is able to neatly delineate, from the very opening of the story, a complex triangular relationship – and in an unobtrusive, indirect way, with some fine touches of irony.

Having decided on this epistolary format, the author's next choice – as to which of the three characters should be the letter writer – was in this case no doubt an easy one. Mieko is, of course, the 'complainant', and thus has both the motive to write and much to write about. But, more than that, she is also quite obviously a 'natural' writer: she is a highly literate young woman with an already well-stocked mind. She quotes from Shelley and Tennyson to set the mood and illustrate her points and, of course, in her detailed comparison of her sister with Narcissus, she proves her familiarity with Western mythology. Indeed, in her supercilious, catty tone, her disapproving view of others and even in her penchant for making lists ('Things the Same Here as Last Year', etc.), she is strongly reminiscent of Sei Shōnagon, the archly aristocratic court lady of the eleventh century whose 'poison pen' caused many of her rivals to weep. Is Mieko, then, to be taken symbolically as 'the Writer', in much the same way as she would have us take her sister as 'Narcissus'? And, if so, is there any significance in the fact that the Writer and Narcissus are sisters? In other words, is the 'older sister' merely a personification of the narcissism which, as Kawabata's early autobiographical works seem to argue, is an inherent and necessary part of the writer's make-up?

Mieko's first letter opens: 'This is the fairy tale of a girl who had an older sister who, because she was too beautiful, would not get married'.[13] The words 'fairy tale' (*otogibanashi*) are curious. Already they jolt one with that sense of 'confusion of genres' which seems a hallmark of much of Kawabata's writing. One does not expect a 'fairy tale' to be told in letters – this seems to bespeak an odd mixture of the realistic and the romantic. But, of course, that is exactly the point: like many of his contemporary modernist counterparts in the West, Kawabata is here adding a larger dimension to his psychological realism by raising it to the timeless level of symbol and myth. Just as, for instance, Joyce's Bloom in his *Ulysses* is at the same time both the mythic figure Odysseus and a mediocre and troubled Irish Jew, an *homme moyen sensuel* of turn-of-the-century Dublin – and an ironic counterpoint is set up between these two 'dimensions' of his character – so Mieko's older sister is presented as 'Narcissus', though with equally ironic overtones. We may already see here, then, Kawabata putting into practice Bashō's principle of *fueki ryūkō* – but in a Western modernist manner never envisioned by Bashō. Furthermore, in the particular context of this story, by referring to what is to follow as a 'fairy tale' Mieko warns the reader against accepting her words at face value or in a too literal way.

Nevertheless, the long list of complaints she proceeds to voice against her 'narcissistic' sister are convincing, detailed and certainly 'realistic'. The two sisters are staying at a hotel at a seaside resort near Kamakura and, besides her general complaint that her sister's 'narcissism' prevents her from getting married (and thus, because of Japanese custom, the younger sister too), Mieko's complaints revolve mainly around her older sister's behaviour at the resort: for instance, how arrogantly she acted in the hotel lobby, puffing out her chest 'like a Westerner' (a supreme offense!) as if giving orders to the manager with the very impudence of her demeanour. And acting with such immodest, unbecoming self-confidence in spite of the fact that she is well aware that, as she signs the hotel registry, her handwriting is very poor![14] (A criticism Sei Shōnagon might well have voiced.) Furthermore, Mieko complains that her sister refused to accompany her to the beach because, she claimed, she would be too embarrassed by the stark contrast between her own white skin and the sun-tanned bodies of the other bathers. Here we are given the first real evidence of the sister's 'narcissism': since white skin is highly prized as a feature of beauty among Japanese women, her protestation hides a disguised compliment to herself, and also leads us to suspect that the real reason she does not want to venture out onto the beach is to protect this precious possession. Still another of Mieko's complaints concerns how her older sister waved from her room to 'a man in a bathing suit on the hotel lawn', forcing Mieko to break off her letter-writing, since that man began to approach them. Thus, it seems, the older sister, though supposedly unwilling to give herself to any man, enjoys playing the siren or temptress.

The moment when Mieko actually accuses her older sister of being a Narcissus is led up to in a subtle and unobtrusive way, by a combination of external chance and internal associations of thought. Opening a drawer to get some hotel letter-writing paper, she finds a book entitled *Flowers and the Language of Flowers* which, she surmises, has been left behind by some small girl. She discovers in this book a simple system of floral symbology: the iris means good news, the geranium means tears, a triplet lily means a girl's confession, and so on. And this reminds her of the more complex, mythic symbology associated with the flower called 'narcissus' in the West. She proceeds to give a beautiful account of this myth of the handsome youth who, always cool to others' advances, finally fell in love with his own image reflected in the pure water of a forest spring, and ended up being metamorphosed (to use Ovid's word) into a beautiful flower. After recounting this story, she blurts out loud: "'Now I understand why my older sister hasn't got married.'"[15] But when she accuses the older sister directly of being a Narcissus, the latter remains unruffled:

'I don't like narcissus'.
'I mean the beautiful youth Narcissus'.
'I don't like myths either'.[16]

To support her case, however, Mieko next reports what a French woman supposedly said to her in the hotel lobby: '"Your sister is as beautiful as a Japanese myth."'[17] Using her newly acquired 'flower language', Mieko now accuses her sister of being Janus-faced in her dealings with the two sexes: 'She talks to women as gently as a blue iris, but in front of men she is, as always, as stuck-up as a narcissus'.[18] This is perhaps a veiled reference to the theme of homosexuality which is also a definite component of the Narcissus myth: the young man unwittingly in love with his own image is, after all, a male in love with 'another' male. Kawabata seems to have agreed with Freud (and with his own 'disciple', Mishima) that there is in homosexuality an unmistakable element of narcissism, of an inability to go beyond self-love to love of the truly 'other'.[19] This emerges clearly in the sexual experiences (or, rather, non-experiences) of Kawabata's *alter ego* in his autobiographical works: on the one hand, his avoidance of and even escape from any real intimacy with females, as typified by the episode recounted in *The Dancing Girl of Izu*; and, on the other hand, the fact, as revealed in the later autobiographical novella, *The Boy* (*Shōnen*, 1948–49), that the most satisfying of his early 'love affairs' was with a young man.

After firmly establishing her older sister as a Narcissus figure, Mieko introduces a new element of tension, in the form of her anxiety for the future:

> It's certain that sister, like the youth Narcissus, is in love with her own too-beautiful form. Somehow, just as the youth Narcissus fell into the spring and drowned, so sister has fallen into her own beauty, and I feel uneasy, as if something unfortunate is about to happen.[20]

This note of anxiety will recur at the story's very end but, as we shall see, only after itself having undergone an interesting Narcissus-like metamorphosis.

In her third letter, Mieko complains still more that her sister has gone off with some 'foreigners' (*ketō*, an extremely disparaging term for Westerners; the older sister, we note, has been identified with Westerners and accused of acting like a Westerner from the beginning – more proof, presumably, of her narcissism). The older sister has gone with these foreigners to a dance at a Kamakura hotel and left her younger sister behind feeling bored and lonely. At this point the reader may begin to feel some qualms about accepting Mieko's version of the truth. Firstly, there is an obvious overtone of jealousy in her remarks here, the jealousy of a 'wall-flower' towards her more beautiful and popular older sister. Secondly, the older sister's behaviour does not quite jibe with her supposed character as a Narcissus. No doubt she has her fair share of the small-scale vanity common to beautiful women (or handsome men), but she seems to have none of the in-grown moroseness, the claustrophobic solipsism, of the true narcissist; on the contrary, judging from the younger sister's own portrait of her, she is a lively, out-going girl, popular with all, possibly even a social butterfly. While she goes off gaily to the dance, it is the younger sister who stays behind, brooding morosely on her sister's 'narcissism'. And, contrary to Mieko's previous claims, she now reports that her older sister had assured her that she would gladly marry anyone Mieko recommends, 'even if he's a one-eyed crippled beggar'.[21] Furthermore, in an effort to convince the man the letters are addressed to that he should 'come visit Narcissus',[22] she reveals that she was awakened one night by her older sister's crying – the implication being that she misses him desperately. This is hardly the sort of behaviour expected of a remote, self-absorbed 'Narcissus'.

If, however, the reader were to ask at this point who is the 'true Narcissus', suspicions would likely turn not only to Mieko but to the man to whom she is writing. It now becomes clear that Mieko's motive in writing the letters is not merely to complain about her older sister but also to persuade the man to come visit that sister – and ultimately to marry her. Is, then, her portrayal of her sister as 'Narcissus', besides being the natural 'complaint' of a younger about an older sibling, merely a perverse attempt to make her seem a more 'romantic', alluring figure to the reluctant, standoffish male? And is there not even a sly suggestion here that it is the man himself who is the actual Narcissus, since he seems strangely reluctant to visit even such a beautiful, vivacious and popular girl as Mieko's older sister? A further piece of evidence may be furnished by the introductory 'frame' which precedes the letters: it seems a strangely detached man who would offer for public inspection such highly personal letters addressed to him – as if they were the laboratory specimen of a young girl's heart – and one may surmise, from this fact alone, that, like other Kawabata males, he has no intention of ever entering into an intimate relation with the girl in question. And now we might also surmise that it was no coincidence when, in defining narcissism near the end of her third letter, Mieko included a male as well as a female variety: 'A too-beautiful woman falls in love with her own beauty and dies of it, a too-intelligent man falls in love with his own intelligence and dies of it'.[23] But, of course, an excessive fondness for one's own intelligence is not confined to men alone – Mieko herself, who demonstrates her cleverness quite convincingly in these letters, seems in danger also of succumbing to this form of narcissism. And the consequences of this become painfully clear in her fifth and final letter.

In her fifth letter Mieko (and Kawabata) turns the Narcissus myth more to her (or his) own purposes by raising the problem of narcissism from the purely physical level of what we might call petty vanity to the moral and even metaphysical level of a more profound self-obsession. Her starting-point is an ingenious meditation on mirrors and on the fact that, compared to the mythic age of Narcissus, our own age suffers from a vast proliferation of mirrors (one is reminded, in an anachronistic Borgesian kind of way, of Borges' famous horror of mirrors). Thus, she reasons, whereas the ancient Narcissus was able to enjoy life until early manhood, when at last he came across his own image reflected in a forest spring, the modern Narcissus, living in an age 'in which any woman can carry a mirror in her *obi* or pocket',[24] will begin to suffer from a very early age. And Mieko confesses that, thinking such gloomy thoughts, she stared long and hard at her own image in a hotel mirror. But, perhaps because she is more of an intellectual than a beauty, she does not succumb to the fascinating, hypnotic pull of her own physical image: 'The mirror which reflects one's appearance is still tolerable'.[25] She admits, though, that what does terrify her is the possibility that one day she may have to confront 'a mirror which reflects my heart'.[26] As the story ends, then, Mieko seems in imminent danger of succumbing to a more serious form of 'narcissism' than afflicts her sister. And the contrast between them is further enforced by the older sister's light-hearted reaction when Mieko tells her of her gloomy reflections on the problem of mirrors: '"All kinds of things happen because I don't get married, don't they? It's begun to turn you into a philosopher . . . ."'[27]

Thus, when Mieko makes her final heart-felt appeal to the man to come visit them, it seems more on her own account than on her sister's: 'Please come just once to visit the unfortunate Narcissus of the age in which there are too many mirrors. And also, so as to prevent me from acquiring another unfortunate mirror, soon . . . . '[28] The reader is naturally left wondering as to the significance of this ambiguous close, this final enigmatic twist in the story's thematic thread.

If, however, Mieko now views the man's 'coming' to be as much for her own sake as for her sister's, this is not, as some readers might suspect, because she herself is secretly in love with him. She makes it clear that she still wants him to come for the 'unfortunate Narcissus'. But what her final unfinished statement makes clear is that she now realizes that her need to 'be rid of' her sister is even more desperate than she had previously realized. During the course of writing these letters she has undergone an important psychological 'metamorphosis' herself, a transformation which may be seen as the story's central 'dramatic action': namely, in meditating on the myth of Narcissus and on her older sister's supposed narcissism, she has come to realize that her own narcissism is of a far more subtle and dangerous variety. Her older sister has thus begun to serve as the 'unfortunate mirror' which reflects her own heart with all its pettiness, jealousy and vindictiveness – the reader has already seen all these qualities made manifest in her letters. Thus her desperate appeal to the man for 'salvation', for him to rid her of the 'unfortunate mirror'. But since the man himself, from what we know of him, is also apparently something of a narcissist, it seems unlikely that he will ever come to her rescue. Perhaps Mieko's half-awareness of this fact is what gives her letters, especially towards the end, such a despairing tone.

On a more general level, the story may be read as an allegory of the dangers inherent in the vocation of the artist. What was only implied in earlier Kawabata works here becomes explicit: the necessary self-absorption of the artist leaves him or her open to the danger – or at least to the charge – of narcissism. Thus Mieko, the writer, presents herself as the younger sister of Narcissus, and the more she contemplates her older sister's image the more she perceives her own image – or her own narcissism – reflected back, but in an even more ominous form. Since the artist as narcissist is an alienated, solipsistic figure, he or she would seem to stand at the opposite pole to the artist as mystic or monist, united in harmony with man and nature, the Whitmanesque ideal which the young Kawabata, at times, yearned to embrace, for his own 'salvation' as much as for his reader's. In this early story, then, he has used a Western myth to objectify and universalize the 'negative' side of what we might call the 'dialectics of salvation' which were to preoccupy him to the end of his career.

The use of mythic figures in this way (i.e., their 'redressing' in modern form) was an extremely common feature also of the

Western literature of this period, whether modernist or not. Besides the example I have already mentioned – Joyce's Ulysses – there are innumerable others: Shaw's Pygmalion, Eliot's Tiresias, Woolf's Orlando, Cocteau's Orpheus, O'Neil's Electra and so on. Like the best of these writers, Kawabata does not merely 'update' the mythic figure by fitting it out in modern dress. As we have seen, he turns it very much to his own uses. In the first place, of course, much is revealed by his choice of this particular myth. In the same way as his 'disciple' Mishima would later be (in, for instance, a novel such as *The Sound of Waves*), Kawabata seems very much at home in the world of Greek mythology in general: its atmosphere of gentle melancholy, of 'beauty and sadness', its sharp, clean images with their powerful symbolic overtones. But the Narcissus myth in particular – if one may speak so anachronistically – seems 'tailor-made' for Kawabata (and, need one add, for Mishima even more so). Certainly one can easily imagine why he felt so strongly attracted to this myth: not only because it so powerfully and succinctly expresses certain tensions which, as his autobiographical works show, existed from the beginning at the very core of Kawabata's creative process, but also because it does so in such an aesthetically pleasing way, using imagery that one is almost tempted to call 'Kawabataesque'[29] – the 'pure', beautiful youth, untouched by women and who is cold towards them, the crystal-clear spring water which serves as his mirror, the lovely white flower he is metamorphosed into after he pines away for love.

Of course, in retelling the myth Kawabata emphasizes certain features of it which particularly appeal to him and even adds some of his own details. This becomes evident if one compares his version with, say, that given in the most famous treatment of the myth in Western literature, in Ovid's *Metamorphoses*. Kawabata emphasizes more the aesthetic than the moral aspects of the myth: whereas, for instance, Ovid lays stress on the youth's hubris leading to his downfall, Kawabata dwells lovingly on the beautiful image of the youth, emphasizing especially his virginal purity: he is like a 'pure fragrance', his heart 'had the purity of a crystal', and, when finally he sees his image reflected, it is in 'pure water'.[30] Thus, ironically, Narcissus comes to seem not so much a moral reprobate as an ideal Kawabata hero or heroine, a symbol of untouched beauty. Kawabata also emphasizes the young man's innocence. Whereas Ovid portrays his Narcissus as fully aware of the nature of his folly ('"Alas! I am myself the boy I see"'.), Kawabata insists that, up to the end, 'he did not suspect in the least that the beauty in the water was his own mirror-image'.[31] And, indeed, Narcissus' ultimate fate – being turned into a lovely white flower (again, a perfect symbol of purity) – no doubt appeared as quite an attractive one to Kawabata, judging by the heroine of another of his early stories, 'Lyric Poem' (*Jojōka*, 1932), who ardently expresses the wish that she and her lover may be reborn as flowers.[32] Kawabata the monist, in fact, was at this time strongly attracted to the idea of the transmigration of souls, for aesthetic as much as for philosophic reasons.

If, however, Kawabata throws new light on the Narcissus myth, the Narcissus myth also throws new light on Kawabata. By the placement of some of his familiar images and themes in the novel context of this Western myth, our eyes are opened to deeper and more universal levels of their significance. We can now see more clearly, for instance, the intimate relation between the theme of purity, so central to Kawabata's work, and the theme of narcissism. As we have already observed, Kawabata obviously finds the Narcissus figure attractive because of his 'purity', his self-contained, hermetic solipsism which preserves his beauty from the 'corruptions' of the world (including woman). But, as the myth teaches us, there is a price to be paid for such 'purity'. In Kawabata's own works, this price may be seen in terms of the general inability of his heroes and heroines to overcome their mutual alienation.

Kawabata's life-long fascination with 'mirror-images', from the train window of *Snow Country* to the hand-mirror of 'Moon in the Water', (*Suigetsu*, 1953) also takes on new significance in the light of the Narcissus myth. But this is not simply a matter of the theme of 'self-love'. As Sir James Fraser pointed out in his *Golden Bough*, the Narcissus myth itself probably has more primitive origins in ancient taboos, in both Greece and India, against looking at one's own reflection in water, lest one's 'soul', thought to be present in the reflection, be stolen by the water-spirits.[33] Similarly, mirrors were often covered up after someone had died in a house, for fear that the dead person's ghost would steal the souls of those reflected in the mirror.[34] Such superstitions, if such they may be called, are, indeed, still very much alive in East Asia, as I myself had occasion to experience some years ago, in a small town in South Korea, when I narrowly escaped attack by a group of irate elderly chess players, convinced that I had captured their 'souls' with my camera. At any rate, it is hardly surprising that Kawabata, raised by a grandfather who practiced the occult arts, and himself keenly interested in 'spiritualism' and psychic phenomena, should possess a strong sense of the primal psychic power – and danger – as well as of the eerie, other-worldly beauty, of reflections, whether in water, window or mirror. And his encounter with the myth of Narcissus no doubt helped him to focus the fear and fascination he felt towards their 'terrible beauty'.

Narcissism and Mysticism

> Sin of self-love possesseth all mine eye,
> And all my soul, and all my every part;
> And for this sin there is no remedy,
> It is so grounded inward in my heart.
> > Shakespeare, Sonnet LXII.

> Who sees all beings in his own Self, and his own Self in all beings, loses all fear.
> When a sage sees this great Unity and his Self has become all beings, what delusion and what sorrow can ever be near him?
> > Isa Upanishad[35]

K awabata's invocation of the ancient myth also seems highly fortuitous in another sense – and this is really the main reason why I introduce this little-known story here: by culturally enriching our understanding of one of the core problems addressed by his work – narcissism – the myth makes it harder for anyone to adopt a dismissive or simplistic attitude towards that problem. Especially since Freudian ideas have percolated down to popular culture, often in distorted form, the term 'narcissist' has become an emotionally loaded, pejorative epithet, a new way supposedly sanctioned by modern science of quickly passing judgement upon and dismissing anyone who seems overly self-absorbed or 'anti-social' – or even, in the worst-case scenario, a new way of categorizing such a person as abherrent or mentally ill. The myth reminds us in a clear and powerful way that narcissism is, in fact, an inherent part of the human condition – and thus not so easily judged or dismissed. When approached in this more broadly humanistic way, the problem of narcissism reveals itself as intimately related to some of the deepest mysteries of the human mind, and to have profound and universal ramifications not only for psychology but also for philosophy, religion, literature, social criticism and even aesthetics. To explore all of these would require, of course, another book than this, but, since the problem is so central to Kawabata's work, I would like at least to tentatively suggest some of these wide-ranging ramifications – especially those which emerge from Kawabata's own treatment of the theme.

Perhaps I had best begin with a question which has often preoccupied me in reading Kawabata: what is the relation between the narcissism of his protagonists and those 'mystical experiences' which often seem to come as a kind of climax to their struggles?[36] Is it an antithetical relationship: the mystical experience representing a genuine way of escape from the impasse of their self-absorption? Or is it more a relationship of collusion: the self-absorbed ecstasy of the mystical experience being merely the positive emotional side of the protagonists' narcissism, perhaps a spontaneous psychological compensation for the feelings of loneliness and alienation which oppress them on the negative side? The answer to this question is by no means clear, perhaps because Kawabata, for aesthetic reasons, preferred to keep it ambiguous, or perhaps simply because he himself was not sure. Also, the likelihood of the answer being one way or the other varies with each work or period of Kawabata's career: generally, as we shall see, he seems to have grown more pessimistic about the possibility of the 'salvation through mystical experience' of his narcissist heroes as he grew older – although the hint of this possibility is never completely absent from his work.

Of course, Kawabata is not alone in his ambiguity: it is a common problem of modern Japanese literature in particular, and an age-old problem of both Eastern and Western culture in general. Paul Zweig has explored this ambiguity at great length and in fascinating detail in *The Heresy of Self-Love*, his groundbreaking study of 'the West's millennia-long fascination with Narcissus: deploring his inhuman solitude, admiring him as a figure of fulfillment and transcendence'.[37] Zweig too laments the fact that narcissism in our own times has been clinicized, narrowed down to a psychiatric case history, so that 'a precious dimension of cultural adventure' has been reduced to a mere 'diagnosis'.[38] And he succeeds brilliantly in restoring our vision of the problem to its proper cultural and historical dimensions, which are very wide indeed, encompassing writers from the ancient Gnostics to modern philosophers and poets such as Kierkegaard and Baudelaire. As Zweig writes:

> The language of self-love has served often in the West to characterize our deepest experience. The isolated, inwardly regarding self stands at the heart of our spiritual life: in the strained elevation of the

mystic, in the 'grace' of the courtly lover, in the insistent reasoning of the philosopher.[39]

However, it seems to me that Zweig's vision does not extend quite far enough: not merely because he does not include Asian culture – an oversight which could easily be excused by lack of time or knowledge – but because he purposely excludes it. Following a suggestion made by the great historian of the Renaissance, Jacob Burckhardt, he claims that these cultural tensions – between narcissism or what he calls 'subversive individualism' on the one hand and the forces of socialization on the other – are unique to Western culture, which thus suffers from an 'anxiety and spiritual restlessness which makes it so different from the great civilizations of the East'.[40] In other words, Zweig offers us yet another version of the 'individualistic West versus group-oriented East' stereotype. And hidden behind that stereotype is another: 'creative West versus conformist East', because central to Zweig's argument is the idea that the tension between narcissism and social conscience has been an endless source of creative energy in the West. The West's 'restlessness' is a sure token of its creativity, whereas, by implication, the East's supposed 'spiritual tranquility' equally betokens an uncreative culture.

The truth is, of course, that, while 'spiritual tranquility' may be a cultural ideal of the East, it is all too rarely a reality, and the conflicting demands of self and society have been a creative irritant as powerful in the East as in the West. In the religious and philosophical realms, for instance, we can see this 'cultural dialectic' at work in the age-old confrontation between the Buddhist and Daoist emphasis on self-cultivation and mystical experience and the Confucian emphasis on social action and responsibility. In the literary realm, Japanese literature is, in fact, particularly rich in self-exploratory or confessional writings, works which record, with great sensitivity, the inner life of a self withdrawn from and often in conflict with society. Already by the eleventh century such works had attained a depth of psychological realism which would not be seen in the West until Montaigne and Rousseau. Indeed, these Japanese *nikki* and *zuihitsu* exhibit exactly that quality of 'public privacy' which Zweig regards as a uniquely Western creation, and which he claims as the source of 'our most powerful cultural values'.[41]

Thus it is perhaps no surprise that the greatest Japanese literary critic, the eighteenth-century 'nativist' scholar Motoori Norinaga, based his theory of literature on the view that literary works appeal to us by revealing our innermost self, not the transcendent Self of the Buddhists but the small, vulnerable, sentimental, self-indulgent self – exactly what we might call today the narcissistic self – which we must usually keep hidden from society's disapproving gaze.[42] (By the kind of interesting coincidence which almost convinces one of the reality of a universal *Zeitgeist*, at about the same time in Europe Rousseau, with his confessional writings, was expounding and practicing – with all due allowance for cultural differences – a remarkably similar literary theory.)

In modern Japanese literature the confessional tradition has again become part of the mainstream with the *shishōsetsu* writers, whose acts of 'public privacy' have often quite purposely scandalized society at large. With Kawabata, of course, we have a Japanese writer who is as fully aware as Zweig himself of the religious, cultural and historical ramifications of the myth of Narcissus and the 'heresy of self-love', and in an Eastern as well as a Western context. Furthermore, and more importantly, we have a writer who drew much creative energy out of his own struggle with that 'cultural dialectic'. What this means, after all, is that Narcissus is a figure of even more universal human and cultural significance than Zweig envisions – as Kawabata, long before Zweig's study appeared, was prescient enough to recognize.

On the relation between narcissism and mysticism, Zweig illuminates the question from a historical perspective, showing how Western mystics since the Gnostics of the late Roman Empire have been fascinated, even obsessed, with the figure of Narcissus, as a symbol both of their inner quest and of the dangers of that quest. Already the Gnostics distinguished between a 'good Narcissus' and a 'bad Narcissus', a distinction which Zweig likens to that between self and Self in Buddhism.[43] To an unsympathetic outsider, of course, the self-absorption of the mystic may seem indistinguishable from that of the narcissist, but the mystic insists that the inner quality of his experience is radically different, and that he goes beyond egoistic self-absorption to union with an ego-transcending inner divinity. As an Arab mystic put it: 'To mount to God is to enter into oneself. For he who inwardly entereth and intimately penetrateth into himself, gets above and beyond himself and truly mounts up to God'.[44]

The fact that Kawabata too was fully aware of this mystical paradox – that one achieves self-transcendence through extreme self-absorption – and that he related this to his own preoccupations as a writer, was made clear when he tried to sum up his life's work and thought in the short but beautiful literary/philosophic credo which he gave as his Nobel Prize acceptance speech. Expressing this insight, naturally, in the context of his own cultural tradition, he describes how the Zen practitioner, through long hours of silent, motionless sitting, achieves a state of egolessness and, significantly for the student of Kawabata, monistic consciousness of an all-embracing unity:

> He departs from the self and enters the realm of nothingness. This is not the nothingness or the emptiness of the West. It is rather the reverse, a universe of the spirit in which everything communicates freely with everything, transcending bounds, limitless.[45]

(When Kawabata says: 'This is not the nothingness or the emptiness of the West', he means, of course, that it is not the nothingness or emptiness of Western nihilism, the despairing negation of all meaning and value. It is an interesting fact, however, that Western mystics too, like their Buddhist counterparts, sometimes used the term 'nothingness' to signify the Godhead or absolute ground of reality, which is 'no thing'.)

Different ages and cultures have responded to this teaching in different ways but, generally speaking, one of the fundamental and defining distinctions between Eastern and Western culture is surely that, whereas Eastern culture has incorporated versions of this teaching into some of its mainstream religious doctrines and practices, Western culture since the age of the Gnostics – ironically in view of its much-vaunted individualism – has been deeply suspicious of individual mystical experience and has tended to marginalize it: first as a threat to religious orthodoxy, and later as a threat to scientific rationalism.[46] Cardinal Newman expressed the common church attitude, albeit with uncommon wit, when he remarked that 'mysticism begins in mist and ends in schism'.[47] The popularization of a science-based, materialistic world view after the industrial revolution of the early nineteenth century made Western society even less friendly to the mystic and more likely to view him as a madman or a narcissist. As Søren Kierkegaard, a great inner explorer himself and one of the most prescient early critics of the advancing despiritualization of Western culture, put it at about this time:

> The relationship of the Isolated One to God is, in the eyes of the world, only egotism. Since the world, deep down, does not believe in God, the one who fears God must, in the final analysis, love only

> himself – the one who fears God does not, in fact,
> love what the world loves; then what is there left?
> God and himself: but the world eliminates God: thus
> the one who fears God loves only himself.[48]

By the end of the nineteenth century a presumptive 'science of the mind' had appeared to make the charge official: according to Freudian theory, the mystic was engaged in a process of regression back from a mature, ego-based, socially responsible individual identity to the infantile, non-individuated, escapist and ecstatic 'oceanic feeling' of Primary Narcissism. Did this mean, then, that all of the great spiritual and cultural achievements of the mystics of all times and places – from the poems of St. John of the Cross to the Zen rock gardens of Kyoto – were merely expressions of an infantile self-love? If so, one might say, then we could use a few more narcissists!

But by no means has there been unanimity on this point, even among psychoanalysts. One of the most interesting of recent Freudian revisionists is Jacques Lacan, who so much differs with his master on this point that he has been moved to declare that his own writings should be added to those of the mystics, because they are 'of the same order'.[49] What justifies this claim more than anything else, it seems to me, is the distinction he makes between the ego and the subject, so reminiscent of the traditional mystical distinction between self and Self. The purpose of Lacanian psychoanalysis is the liberation of the subject from the ego – not the strengthening of the ego, as Anglo-American 'ego psychology' requires.[50] The ego, for Lacan, is a falsely limited self-image based on the child's sense of its own body, and thus creates an 'imaginary alienation'; narcissism, which is a fixation on this false self-image rather than on the true self, generates aggression and a death drive as an expression of the will to break out of the false self-image.[51] The resemblance of these theories to traditional mysticism is obvious.

Among Japanese psychoanalysts who have written on these issues Doi Takeo has probably been the most influential. In his view Japanese culture differs from Western culture precisely in its attitude towards narcissism: rather than attempt to socialize the child by weaning it away from its narcissistic dependency on its mother, Japanese society encourages the prolongation of that sense of loving dependency (*amae*) not only towards the mother but also towards a variety of 'mother substitutes' which society provides – wife, company boss, Emperor, etc. Japanese mystical traditions such as Zen, according to Doi, also reinforce this tendency, enabling their practitioners to regress to a primary state of *amae*. Unlike Freud, however, Doi regards this as a healthy tendency both for the individual and for society.[52]

As was already evident in his early short story, 'Narcissus', Kawabata's own understanding of narcissism was a profound one in both psychological and cultural/historical terms. Unlike his most famous 'disciple', Mishima Yukio, Kawabata had little interest in or taste for narcissism in the most popular sense of the word: as mere vanity about one's good looks or as vulgar self-display. As the 'sister of Narcissus' tells us in the above-mentioned story, the mirror which reflects one's heart can be far more terrifying and dangerous than the mirror which merely reflects one's physical appearance.[53] More dangerous no doubt, but also potentially more illuminating and thus more conducive to spiritual growth. In his painful self-absorption, his feelings of self-hate as well as self-love – which make him so receptive to any experience of ego-transcendence – in his longing for purity, innocence and beauty, and his concomitant reluctance to become involved in any intimate relationship, in his romantic idealism and its accompanying misanthropy, the Kawabata hero is a classic narcissist of this more 'spiritual' variety.

The question then arises: if the Kawabata hero is a narcissist, and thus by definition solipsistic, is he an appropriate subject for a novel, which is by definition a social art form, dealing primarily with human relationships? Would not Kawabata have done better, after all, to write poetry?

One may answer this question in the first place by saying that Kawabata, like some of his contemporaries in the West, wrote a new kind of novel, what has been called a 'lyrical novel', the kind of novel which does focus largely on the psyche of the central character. This is true enough, but it is not the whole truth: however reluctantly, however awkwardly, Kawabata's narcissist hero does enter into relationships with others, and clearly needs to do so. To understand why, perhaps we could do no better than consult perhaps the greatest authority on narcissism (and greatest narcissist?) Western culture has yet produced: Jean Jacques Rousseau.

Rousseau, the 'father of Romanticism', was the first major artist of modern times to discover and exploit the paradoxical fact that one person can not only tolerate but actually revel in another person's display of narcissism (given a sufficient 'aesthetic distance', of course). In this sense he was the rock star of the eighteenth-century European élite: just as the modern rock star prances and preens and works himself into an autoerotic frenzy onstage – a primal narcissistic display which, judging by their gasps and squeals, obviously delights the crowd – so Rousseau thrilled eighteenth-century readers with his shameless self-revelations. (But, apparently, only when they could read him in private; judging by the embarrassed response to a public reading he gave, as described by Rousseau himself, the eighteenth-century aristocratic sensibility found this 'too close for comfort'[54]). Obviously we are attracted by such blatant displays of primal narcissism because they mirror a side of our own natures which social convention usually obliges us to conceal; they allow us a kind of surreptitious or surrogate outlet.

But Rousseau was also keenly aware of the tragic problem of the narcissist: his loneliness. Rousseau valued self-love as a primal, natural virtue, and even believed, as Zweig writes, that if 'man were more perfectly conceived', he would be 'autonomous and self-delighting, like God Himself'.[55] But man's basic imperfection reveals itself in the dawning loneliness of the primally narcissistic everyman, who thus surrenders the autonomy of 'natural man' and becomes 'social man', with a desperate need to be seen by others and even to be approved of by them. If looked at in this Rousseavian perspective, the unwonted elation of the *Izu* protagonist on hearing himself praised as a 'good person' by the vagabond performers certainly becomes more explicable. At any rate, what is even more pertinent is that for Rousseau the narcissist's ultimate dilemma, the conflict between his natural self-love and his social ego, remains forever tragically unresolved. It is the ongoing dialectic of his life, as summarized ably by Zweig, with some quotes from Rousseau's *Confessions*:

> On one side of the line is the 'sad prison' of his loneliness, a life of stifled recognition, closer to death than to life; for 'someone who gathers all his emotions inside him, finally loves nothing but his own self ... his frozen heart no longer trembles with joy ... he is already dead'. On the other side of the line, however, lie the corrupt energies of society, where the natural self has been sacrificed to the passion for appearances, for comparison, and finally for vain pretense. Here, the natural *amour de soi* has been twisted into a simulacrum; it has become *amour propre*, vanity, which for Rousseau was the source of all 'negative sensibility' and all 'aggressiveness'.[56]

In Kawabata's work too this dialectical struggle is never finally resolved; indeed, as we shall see, in his very last works it seems all the more painfully irresolvable. This distinguishes him sharply from another major Japanese writer who was much concerned with male narcissism and the 'dialectics of salvation:' Shiga Naoya. Shiga seemed to resolve the issue once and for all in his only novel, *A Dark Night's Passing* (*An'ya Kōro*, 1937), with his hero Kensaku's culminating mystical experience on Mount Daisen, and consequently he did not write very much thereafter.[57] Though Kawabata's failure to achieve any ultimate resolution was no doubt painful for him on a personal level, the fact that he struggled with the issue into old age also meant that he never exhausted a prime source of his creative energy.

4. A Mirror of the Heart

> Look in thy glass, and tell the face thou viewest,
> Now is the time that face should form another . . . .
> For where is she so fair whose unear'd womb
> Disdains the tillage of thy husbandry?
> Or who is he so fond will be the tomb
> Of his self-love, to stop posterity?
>
> Shakespeare, Sonnet III

*C*rystal Fantasies (*Suishō gensō*, 1931) is generally regarded as the most notable product of Kawabata's 'modernist' or 'experimental' period. Indeed, Japanese literary historians have emphasized the work's general historical importance as a uniquely successful adaptation of a Western modernist technique – Joyce's 'stream-of-consciousness' – by a Japanese writer of the 'experimental' age of the late 'twenties and early 'thirties. Apart from its obvious interest as an experiment in literary technique, however, the novella is also important as one of Kawabata's most successful early attempts at presenting a woman's psychology, especially as that psychology reveals itself in response to the problematic nature of male/female relations. It achieves this impressive level of success despite its occasional gaucheries and despite also its incompleteness (it is another of Kawabata's 'unfinished' works). If, as Malcolm Cowley has said, the 'talent of a great novelist is in large part a talent for creating passionately living women',[58] then in *Crystal Fantasies* and some other early stories Kawabata was well on his way to developing this quintessential novelistic talent. The culmination would come a few years later with the creation of Komako, the 'passionately living woman' who is the heroine of *Snow Country*, the masterpiece of Kawabata's middle period.

In *Crystal Fantasies* Kawabata's presentation of the goings-on in the mind of the viewpoint character, the unnamed wife – the memories, thoughts and reactions which reveal her personal history and her inner nature – is not as unremittingly direct as Joyce's presentation of Molly Bloom's mental activity in the long interior monologue which concludes *Ulysses*. To some extent this is merely a difference in scale, but also, by intermingling passages of pure stream of consciousness with passages of more conventional third-person narrative and dialogue, Kawabata is able to present more objectively certain external stimuli which set in motion the interior monologues. There are mainly four of these: a mirror, a dog, her husband and a young lady visitor, each of which takes on a particular symbolic significance in the woman's mind. Roughly speaking: the mirror – often, as we know from 'Narcissus', a complex symbol in Kawabata – represents luxury and narcissistic self-indulgence but also art and self-knowledge (and it is significant that here again, in a Kawabata story, the protagonist's narcissism is shown to lead to an uncomfortable level of self-knowledge); the dog embodies a healthy sex instinct but also sex in the raw, rather ugly to look upon; the husband represents the alienating and dehumanizing power of science, and the young lady visitor represents glamour and the possibility of love. The story is structured in an almost fugue-like manner as a contrapuntal interplay between external stimuli and interior monologue.

Because of the life they take on in the woman's mind, the two non-human stimuli, the mirror and the dog, seem to function as 'characters' in the story as much as do the two human ones. That even an inanimate object such as a mirror should take on a 'character-like' life is not actually a rare phenomenon in a Kawabata story. One thinks, for instance, of the tea bowls in a much later work, *A Thousand Cranes*. Indeed, this 'animation' of objects is a unique and important feature of Kawabata's art. Moreover, as we have seen, the image of the mirror in particular has an enormous presence, a central symbolic significance, in many of Kawabata's works.

In the first of the story's three 'scenes' or 'movements', the mirror is the main stimulus both of the wife's thoughts and of her dialogue with her husband. It is the 'crystal' reflecting her thoughts and fantasies, a true 'mirror of the heart' – to borrow a phrase from Kawabata's earlier story, 'Narcissus' – and it also protects her against reality, especially reality in the form of her husband – since, as we are told, she often talks to his reflection in the mirror rather than to the 'real man'.[59] Indeed, what is reflected in the mirror is also the major topic of their conversation to begin with. The mirror has three sides, and the left-hand side reflects the glass roof of a cage for small animals used in experiments by her husband, an embryologist. Their dialogue begins with the wife's claim that their purchase of the mirror is not at all 'extravagant' because it will enable her to constantly contemplate 'the garden's sperms and eggs' (i.e., in the embryological cage) reflected therein – implying that this might help her to become fertile.[60] The narrator comments on the 'tragedy implicit' in these 'sweet words' (*amai kotoba*) betraying a Freudian influence on Kawabata here: the idea that even in our jokes we unconsciously reveal our deepest anxieties.[61] Whatever we might think of it now, Freudian theory was, of course, very much part of the intellectual background of modernism, and *Crystal Fantasies* is one of Kawabata's most obviously 'Freudian' stories. At any rate, through the agency of the mirror, we are quickly introduced to this couple's 'tragedy', the main irritant and alienating force between them: their infertility.

The narrator then tells us that the wife 'did not notice the slight strangeness of her own words', partly because she had become absorbed in another reflection in the mirror: that of the blue sky.[62] This beautiful reflection precipitates her first stream of consciousness:

> (Small birds which fall like silver stones thrown through the blue sky. Sailboats which speed like silver arrows released from the sea. Fish which swim like silver needles through a lake.)[63]

This rather *renga*-like stream of images may first seem to have no relation whatsoever to the previously mentioned 'tragedy', but on closer inspection one notices that each of the images suggests the sudden, darting movement of ejaculated sperm. Kawabata, following Freud, shows how even a seemingly random stream of images arising spontaneously from the depths of the woman's mind betrays what troubles and obsesses her. Thus, the narrator tells us, the images give her feelings of 'coldness', 'loneliness', and 'sadness' – because, of course, they remind her of her childlessness and of her consequent alienation from her husband.[64]

Although the wife may have desired the mirror as an 'extravagant' indulgence of her narcissism, it turns out, then, to function also as a kind of Freudian 'reality principle', reflecting certain uncomfortable truths about her condition – including the husband whose presence so obviously disturbs her. But the husband objects to the mirror's placement: after all, he had bought this vanity item, so 'uncharacteristic of a scientist, in order to banish science from the family bedroom'.[65] He argues that there is no need to have '"the cage for animals used in scientific experiments reflected along with my wife's profile while she's applying her makeup"'.[66] He goes so far as to suggest that she close the side of the mirror with the '"unpleasant reflection"'.[67] He obviously fears that the reflection of the embryological test cage will encourage his wife to dwell morbidly on her own infertility and thus make it even less likely that she will ever become fertile. And, generally, he seems to feel that this unsavory bit of reality will spoil the 'romantic' mood of their bedroom.

The wife mocks his concern, joking that the mirror threatens to turn him into a psychologist. And she questions his ability, as a scientist, to understand her feminine sensibility: '"What relation can there be between a woman's heart and your science?"'[68] No doubt stung by this insult to his intelligence or sensitivity, the husband retorts – with a cruelty which, ironically, proves the validity of his wife's accusation – that science tells us of the '"necessity of psychological joy for a woman's orgasm"'.[69] Since he obviously associates his wife's frigidity, implied here, with her infertility, he seems to imply that she remains infertile because of her lack of enjoyment in their sex life. Looking into the mirror to discover her own reaction to these words (the mirror functioning here, quite literally, as a 'mirror of the heart'), she finds that her cheeks have paled rather than flushed, as she had expected, and takes this as a sign of her sadness (caused, presumably, by her husband's reminding her of her infertility).

Though a scientist himself – engaged in research in, of all things, embryology – the husband has no desire to adopt a scientific attitude towards his own sex life. Like the stereotypical Japanese husband, he wants to keep his work and his domestic life – which in this case means science and romance – strictly separate. He wants his wife to live in a protective cocoon, insulated from reality, and always ready to shower him with attention when he returns home from a hard day at the lab. Though in a somewhat unusual form – because of his identity as a scientist – the husband thus shows the typical Kawabata male hero's romantic and narcissistic longing for 'purification' from the 'dirt' of the world (*yo no yogore*) through the medium of a pure, unearthly, almost unreal woman.

It soon becomes obvious, however, that his wife has already been irredeemably 'sullied' by the reality of science – both through her contact with him and through her contact with her own father, who also took a scientific approach to sex and the process of birth, as a gynecologist. We may recall here the strange euphoria felt by the young protagonist of *The Dancing Girl of Izu* when he discovered that the girl he was pursuing was too young for any intimacy with him. Now we may understand something more of the reason for that euphoria, because here, as in many later Kawabata works, we discover what happens when the male actually manages to attain his goal. This is what might be called the 'double bind' of the Kawabata male, the trap he lays for himself with his romantic/narcissistic – or, seen from the woman's point of view, vampirish/exploitative – longing to be 'purified' by a beautiful and 'innocent' young woman: the moment such a woman has intimate contact with him, she begins to lose her innocence in his eyes (partly, no doubt, because of the self-loathing which is the reverse side of his narcissism) and thus is no longer 'usable' by him as an agent of purification. At best, his sense of being purified by her can only be a highly transient thing. Kawabata would remain obsessed with this fundamental paradox and conundrum throughout the rest of his career. Indeed, it is hardly too much to say that it is the central problem of his literature – at least to the extent (which is considerable) that his literature deals with male/female relations.

But it seems to me that it would be extremely short-sighted if, for this reason, we labelled Kawabata a 'male chauvinist', as some of the more doctrinaire feminists have done. Kawabata's aesthetic sensibility would not permit him to adopt an overtly moralistic, 'sledgehammer' approach to the issue. And most of his works are, of course, written from the viewpoint of a male character. But perhaps for this very reason the point ultimately is made all the more tellingly. Few writers, male or female, have exposed so convincingly both male egotism and the female suffering which results from it, and few have aroused such sympathy for their female characters, who, even when they are not the viewpoint character, are generally presented in a far more 'sympathetic' way than the male protagonists. Also, there was a definite progression in Kawabata's work in this respect, as we shall see: his later works evince a much more extreme sense of the potential for evil in male egotism.

In *Crystal Fantasies*, however, the unhappy male only lurks in the background, a mere reflection in the mirror. It is the woman's unhappiness we are concerned with here. As the scientist's wife looks at her own pale cheeks in the mirror, a series of images arises in her mind which clearly point to the cause of the repulsion she feels towards sex and the process of birth – and thus to the cause of her infertility. The images are of things she witnessed in both her father's and her husband's laboratories, mixed in, significantly, with images of her own wedding night:

> (The pipette attached to the artificial insemination device. French letter. A white mosquito net, looking like an entomologist's net, draped over the bed. Her myopic husband's eyeglasses, which she stepped on and crushed on their wedding night. Herself as an infant and her gynecologist father's examination room.) She shook her head, as if shattering apart the glass chains within. (The sound of microscope specimen glass slides and glass covers smashing to pieces as the egg and sperm specimens of many different animal species fall to the laboratory floor. Glass slivers which glint like sunlight.)[70]

All these images of breaking glass, of course, brilliantly convey the wife's nervous tension when confronted by any form of sex. And the scientific/sexual paraphernalia suggest the inhumanity and sterility of the scientific approach to sex – cerebral, discriminative, anti-monistic – the consequences of which may be seen in the ironic situation of the woman herself: despite being an embryologist's wife and a gynecologist's daughter, she is infertile. In other words, her infertility is both caused by and symbolical of the life-destroying sterility of modern science and technology.

The husband/wife exchange continues with her suggestion that, since she wants nothing more to do with 'pipettes' – that is, with artificial insemination – he had better hurry up and discover a method of 'ectogenesis' (using the Aristotlean term) or, to use the modern term, a method of producing test-tube babies. He might thus be able to produce a child entirely from his own sperm, a modern scientific version of the mythical 'virgin birth', what she calls 'this dream of chaste reproduction, of being able to produce a child who was purely the father's offspring, without any admixture of the mother's blood'.[71] Thus modern science, at least as viewed ironically by the woman, seems to promise an ultimate expression of male solipsistic narcissism and female alienation.

The husband accuses her of being anti-scientific, and points out that nowadays even her rouges and powders, those favourite materials of feminine art, are regarded as part of 'cosmetic science'.[72] She counters by accusing him of trying to 'force your wife to bear a child' and comments that this is a 'sad retreat for embryology'.[73]

He then claims that 'our love was born in an embryology lab'.[74] But her feelings for him, he now realizes, were more like loathing than love – a complex of fascination and repulsion towards the 'terrible powers' of science he represents as an embryologist. 'The mother inside the woman resisted embryology'.[75] He claims, though, that now she is coming to see things from an embryologist's point of view – reinforcing our suspicion that she has been 'corrupted by science' – whereas he himself is coming to see things as a mother.

Perhaps because this rather aggressive banter back and forth with her husband is becoming too much for her, the wife now escapes again into her 'mirror world'. Ignoring her husband completely, she becomes lost, first, in admiration of 'the beautiful rose colour' of her own cheeks, and then in various erotic reveries ('The buttocks of a beautiful youth afloat in transparent water', etc.) and more troubling memories of her father and husband and the nightmare of science they represent for her.[76] Seeing her become so distant and self-absorbed, her husband wisely withdraws from the room.

There now ensues the longest of the wife's interior monologues, arising spontaneously in her mind as she sits, Narcissus-like, dangerously absorbed by her own image in the mirror. Her obsessions emerge clearly now through certain recurrent motifs: her father the gynecologist's cold, antiseptic examination room, all white enamel; remembered sexual longings, including homosexual longings for a former classmate; fertility and reproduction of all kinds, including parthenogenesis or (to translate literally the original Greek of this word) 'virgin birth'; her own marriage, ill-omened from the start – she stepped on her husband's glasses for myopia on their wedding night, an accident which seems as symbolic of the 'myopic' state of their marriage as the glasses are of the scientist's own psychological as well as physical 'myopia'; various scientific apparati and the scientific way of thinking; Freud and Christ and what these archetypal 'wise men' mean to her; various images, again, which suggest the ejaculation of sperm. Ultimately, though, her thoughts are directed back to her own infertility, what she calls her 'shame', and she closes the left side of the mirror, which reflects that constant reminder of her infertility, her husband's embryological 'mating-pen'.[77]

The second 'movement' of the story revolves around the wife's fascination/repulsion towards her stud dog, the wire-haired terrier 'Playboy'. We are told that, since the fancy three-sided mirror did not bring her the happiness (and fertility) her husband had hoped for, he decided to get her a dog. It made the wife 'shiver', though, to realize that the dog was intended, as it obviously was, as a substitute child. Nevertheless, the fact is undeniable that, like the hero in 'Of Birds and Beasts' (*Kinjū*, 1933), another Kawabata story of this period (and also, to some extent, like Kawabata himself at this time) she does relate better with the dogs than with the humans in her life. Also, the dog provides her with some salutary activity, since she uses it to start a stud service in her own home. The central scene of the second movement depicts one such canine 'assignation'.

There is a delicious irony in the whole situation: two refined, upper-class ladies watching a pair of well-manicured dogs mate lustily in a well-appointed living room. Even more ironic, of course, is the contrast between the riotous sexuality of the dogs and the human couple's infertility – and also between the consequent 'rapture' of the dogs and the misery of the humans. There can be no doubt as to with which side Kawabata's sympathies lie, and *Crystal Fantasies* certainly could be seen as yet another expression of the misanthropy which was often said to underlie his love of animals in the early 1930s. But he handles the irony and humour of the scene with a restrained, delicately satiric touch: for instance, suggesting the male dog's passion by the 'frantic' tinkling of his silver collar bell – which, with equal effect, suddenly stops after he achieves orgasm – and observing the wife's reaction to 'this ugly act, which she had seen but pretended not to see' – which, nonetheless, in its raw power and reality, its perfect consonance with the elemental rhythms of life, makes her realize the falsity and unreality of her own life.[78]

The young lady who brings her female dog to be impregnated also serves an important catalytic function: her boyish good looks arouse the wife's homoerotic fantasies – and this reinforces again our sense of the intimate relation between narcissism and homosexuality in Kawabata. Once she recognizes these feelings in herself, there ensues an interesting psychological interchange or dialectic between the two women. The wife purposely stays in the room watching the dogs mate because it gives her a pleasurable feeling of sexual power over the young lady, as if, using the dogs as proxies of their respective owners, she were vicariously possessing her. The dog-mating thus becomes a symbolic as well as a literal sex act. The wife searches the young lady's face, trying to decipher her feelings, perhaps her embarrassment, but she remains impassive. This lack of response makes the wife feel again her own isolation. Although sitting together with the young lady, she feels alone – and she recognizes this as 'the kind of solitude I feel when I'm in my husband's arms'.[79] In this way, Kawabata's use of the stream-of-consciousness technique allows us to be privy to the woman's innermost thoughts simultaneously as we listen to the rather trivial chat she carries on with the young lady, and an effective counterpoint is made again between outer and inner realities – or, perhaps we should say, between an outer falsity and an inner reality.

In her mind, for instance, she takes revenge on her husband by scornfully comparing his impotence with Playboy's sexual prowess – all the while chatting with the young lady. She revenges herself further by making sarcastic remarks about her husband to the lady: for instance, telling her that, in his book on embryology, he makes no distinction between humans, plants and animals – thus evoking, again, the theme of the dehumanization of sex by science. One of her more significant remarks quotes her husband as saying that women should revenge themselves on nature by refusing to bear children. Ironically, of course, it seems that she has faithfully followed her husband's advice – whether he intended her to or not. But then she also seems to try to justify herself by insisting that art and religion prove that we are not on earth merely to reproduce ourselves.[80] She also articulates here a theme previously implied: that science, with its artificial methods of reproduction, is nostalgic for 'the world as it existed before Creation, without any living things', and thus is leading us to the 'glacier of death'.[81]

In the end, however, the wife herself realizes, as the narrator tells us, that all this 'chatter' is mendacious and merely serves as a kind of surreptitious substitute for her real heart-felt complaints.[82] Again, we find that contrast between outer falsity and inner reality which is one of Kawabata's main dramatic themes in this work, and one very well served by his use of the stream of consciousness.

When her dog is finished performing, the wife receives money for his services – proving that she is every bit as ready as her husband to exploit sex, albeit for commercial rather than scientific purposes. In parting from the young lady she asks her to come alone next time, without the dog-dealer, further strengthening our impression that she wants to turn this dog-mating into an 'affair' of her own.

The third and final scene or movement of the story, like the first one, depicts the wife again before her mirror and in reluctant conversation with her husband. Her solipsism and narcissism here reach a kind of climax. After the young lady leaves she returns to her mirror as to her most trusted companion. Even when her husband arrives home late that night, she is still sitting there, so absorbed by her own image that she fails to notice his return. Irritated at being ignored in this way, her husband shakes her by the shoulders and remarks sarcastically: "'It's a happy man whose wife is so absorbed in her vanity mirror that she doesn't even notice his arrival home! That sounds like something from one of those novels you're always reading, doesn't it?"'[83] His words, of course, have more impact in the context of prewar Japanese culture: a proper middle-class wife was expected to rush to the door and welcome her husband home with humble prostrations and affectionate greetings. It is hardly surprising, then, that, with even sharper sarcasm, he goes on to suggest that perhaps she might attain Buddhahood through make-up, or enlightenment by gazing into the mirror![84] (On a deeper level, though, the husband's remark may be regarded as quite perspicacious, since it implies the link between narcissism and mysticism which I discussed earlier.)

His wife hits back hard by claiming that he returns home with such eagerness not because he misses her in particular but because he longs for 'the thing called a human female', something which he feels might relieve his loneliness after a long day of dehumanizing activity in the lab.[85] He replies that not only he but she too suffers from loneliness. And this, of course, is true enough: both lead lonely, alienated lives, he spending his days staring into a microscope, she staring into a mirror. But the crucial question is: are they capable of the love for each other which would enable them to break out of their mutual isolation?

As if to confirm the wife's accusation as to why he misses her, the husband then suggests that they immediately go to bed. She meekly obeys, although all the while thinking to herself how stupid he looks, like a clown. And her stream of consciousness here also betrays her feeling that she has already deceived her husband, in planning a kind of 'affair' with the young lady with the dog. She wonders 'how beautiful is the happiness a woman feels when, for the first time, she receives from a stranger the joy she could never feel with her husband?'[86] And again she recalls the solipsistic ideal of 'virgin birth', without the agency of any human husband. In one of the many Christian and Biblical references in this story, she reflects that, whereas Mary was impregnated by the Holy Ghost, she longs for an 'evil spirit' – no doubt considering herself unworthy of a divine one.[87]

Her thoughts are suddenly interrupted by her husband's discovery of the money paid her by the young lady. It becomes obvious at this point that, despite this couple's extreme modernity in other respects, in terms of the balance of power their relations are still quite traditionally Japanese. Having caused a loss of face to her husband by accepting money for her dog's stud service, the wife anticipates his anger and passively waits to be 'slapped or kicked' by him.[88] Soon, however, her self-protective 'feminine wiles' come into play: she suggests that her husband might take the pretty young lady as his mistress, reminding him that they had once agreed that he could take a mistress if they failed to produce a child in three years.

Her strategy seems to work: rather than flying into a rage her husband merely suggests that she try seeing a doctor again about her infertility – automatically assuming, of course, that the problem must be her infertility rather than his own impotence. She suppresses her anger at his words and merely answers sarcastically that she would rather wait for him to make a test-tube baby in his lab, which she promises to love 'like a true embryologist's wife'.[89]

Her husband gullibly swallows this bait and talks on happily about recent advances in robot technology – science seems on the verge of creating an artificial man – and she is relieved that he seems afraid to confront her uneasiness about being tested again for infertility. Of course, we know by now that she has no real desire to bear his child. This is confirmed by her penultimate stream of consciousness, in which she fully reveals her strategy for taking a 'secret revenge' on her husband: 'By smelling the hematoxylin [on his hands] and by thinking of the mirror's reflection of the hothouse-style glass roof in the garden, I can destroy the rhythms of my orgasms'.[90] In other words, she will use his science against him, against his longing for progeny, by using the anti-natural, life-negating power of science to render herself infertile.

We must remember that these thoughts pass through her mind as her husband is about to have sex with her (given the clinical coldness of their relationship, one cannot say 'make love with her'). Her final thought before submitting to him, a thought which seems to give her considerable satisfaction, is that her husband may be driven to suicide by his obsession with his research.[91] Thus he too would become, as she already seems to be, a 'sacrificial victim' of science.

Although Kawabata never 'officially' finished this story, its conclusion, as often with his 'unfinished' stories, seems entirely appropriate. Certainly we are left in no doubt as to the wife's true feelings towards her husband or the true cause of her infertility. Nor can we possibly entertain any illusions as to the possibility of this couple's ever overcoming their mutual alienation, that excess of narcissism and solipsism they both seem to suffer from. This is true despite the wife's reference near the end to her 'childish' dream of a 'fairytale world in which baby peacocks were born to dogs', a dream symbolizing her pathetic longing to break out of her isolation and live in a world in which all boundaries between living beings would be dissolved – a monistic state of grace.[92]

Unlike many of Kawabata's later works, *Crystal Fantasies* does not end with any comforting monistic resolution. It remains an uncompromising and highly sophisticated study of the psychology of alienation. Alienation, of course, was probably the modernist theme *par excellence*, and readers by now may be tired of it. But in *Crystal Fantasies* Kawabata handles the theme already in his own distinctive manner, with his own considerable delicacy of touch. The skill and subtlety with which the painful interactions of husband and wife and wife and young lady are depicted, with all the complex nuances of their mutual dislikes, the powerfully convincing evocation of the wife's psychic turmoil, and the brilliant interplay of a whole range of still-urgent contemporary themes – scientific, psychological, philosophical and even religious – which touch upon the central theme of alienation, make this relatively short work seem a marvel of compressed modernist writing at its best. In other words, it is not only impressively modernist in technique but also startlingly up-to-date in its imagery and themes – it almost seems to belong more to our own time than to the early 1930s, dealing, in its brief compass, with topics such as artificial insemination, test-tube babies, the dehumanization of life by science and even, less directly, male oppression and exploitation of women. Looking back at it from our present perspective, it seems to take on an almost prophetic air.

Because *Crystal Fantasies* is Kawabata's most obviously or even startlingly 'modernistic' work, and also because it is so successful in its own way, it may give rise to certain doubts about the direction his career took thereafter. Given the fact that he made such a very good showing as a modernist, one might ask why he did not pursue this line of development further rather than 'retreat' so soon (by the mid-1930s) back to a more traditional style of writing. One might even suspect that he no longer wished to confront the challenges and problems of the contemporary world, seeking rather to retire into the comforting cocoon of the Japanese past, with its long-established themes and conventions and its general mood of nature-loving serenity. In literary terms, this could be described as a 'retreat' back from modernism to a traditional kind of Japanese romanticism – a 'retreat' which has led some critics to charge Kawabata with escapism. From this perspective, the dilettante Shimamura, the hero of *Snow Country*, the first major work of this new 'conservative' period, might be seen as an apt symbol of such retreat and escapism.

If one were politically or historically minded, one might even see Kawabata's 'retreat' as part of the general conservative nationalism, the anti-foreign 'back to Japan' movement, of the late Thirties. But Kawabata, of course, was the most apolitical of writers – and, even in the heat of the China conquests and the Pacific War, he was never a drum-beating nationalist. If one must place it in a social/historical context, it would perhaps be more convincing to regard his 'retreat' as a manifestation of a phenomenon typical of his generation (Tanizaki would be another good example): the 'return to Japan' of middle-aged Japanese males who as young men had experimented, often in wildly extreme ways, with the very latest, most new-fangled Western fads and fashions in everything from art to food to sex to philosophy. In other words, yet another example of the ultimate victory of the overwhelming conservatism of Japanese society, which opens itself to new and foreign trends only to thoroughly adapt and 'Japanize' them. Though there may be some truth in this latter view, nevertheless it still presents the case in an altogether too negative way. After all, one might also ask: what did Kawabata gain by his return to tradition?

I shall address this question in subsequent chapters, but an important point for the present is that, when Kawabata did return to a more traditional style of writing, he did not forget what he had learned from modernism. In this sense his modernism was by no means merely a 'brief flirtation'. One could point, of course, to his startling 'return to modernism' in old age, but even more significant, it seems to me, is the fact that, on closer analysis, his 'modernist' works and his 'traditional' works actually have a great deal more in common than one might suspect from a first glance at their surface differences: in their central themes, certainly, but also, to a surprising extent, in their narrative techniques. What this means, surely, is that Kawabata never really abandoned or rejected modernism – that is why he could return to it later with such effortless mastery. But in his 'middle period', the period of those works usually regarded as his masterpieces, from *Snow*

Country to *The Sound of the Mountain*, he devised a new union between modernity and tradition. Thus, for instance, the modern 'in-depth' psychology of 'Narcissus' and *Crystal Fantasies* is still very much present in such a 'traditional' work as *Snow Country*, as is the modernist narrative technique of presenting that psychology by mimesis of a random-seeming 'stream of consciousness', but all of this is as if 'filtered' through a traditional sensibility. Some modernist 'purists' may regret the admixture of the traditional with the modern, but if Kawabata had remained strictly a modernist – say, an earlier version of Abe Kōbō – I doubt that his writings would still possess such great appeal, especially to Western readers. More than that, he would have missed his destiny as one of the great twentieth-century revitalizers of Japanese tradition.

5. Monism and Poetry

'Lyric Poem' (*Jojōka*, 1932), written about a year after *Crystal Fantasies*, is, like that work and also like 'Narcissus', *a shinkyō shōsetsu* ('state-of-mind story') narrated from a female point of view. Indeed, this is even more true of 'Lyric Poem', since it has no 'objective' narration at all, but consists of a long soliloquy the female protagonist addresses to her dead lover. This, of course, allows for even more play of 'free association' than in *Crystal Fantasies*, but in 'Lyric Poem' the 'free associations' are no longer Joycean in style: that is, they do not attempt such a strict mimesis of the actual flow of thoughts in a human mind, which is often completely random or disjointed, and rarely forms itself into orderly, grammatical sentences. Here the thought-flow is more formally controlled, not only in the sense that it is formed into complete and comprehensible sentences but in the sense that it flows along certain well-defined 'channels'. In the formal perfection of its style, which <u>suggests</u> but does not strictly imitate the random flow of thoughts, it is closer to the traditional *zuihitsu* (random essay) and *nikki* (diary) than to Joyce. Ultimately, of course, this is a matter of degree: the Joycean stream-of-consciousness too is not really as random or as 'disorderly' as actual human thought-processes often are; here too the author is exercising his selecting and ordering powers towards a certain semantic or symbolic end. But Joyce does come much closer to giving the illusion, at least, of presenting a thought-flow 'in the raw'. And to achieve this effect he writes in a somewhat 'disjointed' style: that is, he defies all the logical and grammatical conventions of the traditional 'correct' or 'elegant' prose style. In 'Lyric Poem' Kawabata no longer follows him in this.

Indeed, his 'classical' perfection of form extends beyond individual sentences to the structure of the story as a whole, which has a 'finished' perfection rare in Kawabata (he actually completed it), a circular structure which ends where it begins: 'Speaking to the dead – what a sad human custom!'[93] (On this structural level, in fact, the story is quite Joycean.) Just as this theme recurs, so the story's other themes also are interwoven throughout like motifs in a piece of music – or, indeed, in a lyric poem – so that ultimately the apparent 'free associations' come together in a kind of formal perfection which is something entirely different to the formal perfection of a 'well-made' plot. Of course, this does not mean that the story fulfills the Flaubertian fantasy of being entirely plotless. There are, in fact, a few – a very few – plot-like elements which can be pieced together from the woman's 'ramblings': she was once very much in love with the dead man she soliloquizes, so much so that she could read his thoughts, so much so that she defied her parents's wishes and went to live with him, but their love ultimately played itself out and he abandoned her for another woman – after which, she implies, she used her psychic powers to murder him.

What makes this rather rudimentary plot come alive in an original way, however, and what makes the story work on one level as, indeed, a strangely moving 'lyric poem', is the quality of the woman's 'free associations', especially her use of various elements of monistic lore, philosophy and imagery culled from both Eastern and Western traditions: Buddhism, Christianity, European and Asian literature, 'occult' spiritualism, and Greek mythology. Her invocation of all these diverse traditions is motivated by a single purpose: her desire to be reunited with her dead lover. But since, when they loved each other in human form, he ended up betraying her, she cherishes the rather misanthropic hope, based on the various esoteric lore she refers to, that next time they will meet in non-human form, perhaps as flowers.

But the work obviously has significance beyond this strange if interesting story of one somewhat bitter woman's exploitation of the doctrine of reincarnation: in fact, it is Kawabata's most explicit statement in fictional form of a monistic world-view, and of the importance this world view had for him not only in philosophical but in emotional terms, as a kind of means of psychic salvation. As the story's title suggests, it also clarifies Kawabata's view of the literary importance of monism: in short, he identifies the monistic vision with the poetic vision, which is why his narrator is able to claim, as Kawabata himself also did, that the Buddhist sutras are 'lyric poems without parallel . . . .'[94]

Monism in this story, because of the woman's peculiar obsessions, takes the form primarily of the doctrine of reincarnation, which is associated not only with various religious traditions but with poetry. The narrator quotes an unnamed philosopher to the effect that: '"The feeling that men and plants share a common fate is the perennial theme of lyric poetry"'.[95] What attracts her so much to the doctrine of reincarnation is its dissolution of rigid divisions between human beings and other life-forms – since one may be reborn as the other. As we know from some of Kawabata's non-fictional writings, he shared her view that it is the loss of this 'primitive' sense of the unity of all forms of life, present in the ancient traditions of both East and West, that had produced the psychic malaise of modern man:

> The soul which must be reborn again and again is a confused and pitiable thing. Still, it seems to me that there is no fairy tale more splendid or richer in suggestion than this one of the transmigration of souls. It is the most beautiful love lyric that man has ever composed. In India this belief is as ancient as the Vedas, and it is an expression of the essential soul of the East. But even in the West, there are the colourful flower myths of Greece [such as the Narcissus myth!] and the song of Gretchen in her prison cell in *Faust*. Indeed, legends of men changing into animals and plants are very plentiful even there.
>
> The saints of old, as well as the spiritualists of today, people who have thought long and deeply about the human soul, have been wont to exalt it at the expense of the souls of other animals and plants, which they have completely ignored. Over a period of thousands of years men have run ever more precipitately in this direction, making ever sharper distinction between themselves and the other phenomena of nature. Isn't it this very self-complacency, which is finally so futile, that accounts for the deep sense of solitude of the human soul today?[96]

From a literary/aesthetic point of view, this and other statements of the narrator's (or Kawabata's) monistic faith may seem altogether too baldly explicit, too essayistic, even perhaps a little preachy, but this impression may be somewhat ameliorated when one looks at the overall context in which these statements are 'imbedded': in fact, the fictional context provided by the female narrator gives them all an ironic, ambiguous and paradoxical flavour. For the truth is that even in this most philosophically direct of his stories, Kawabata could not present what we might call his nostalgia for a simple monistic faith in a straightforward, unproblematical way. If he had done so, the story really might have been a 'lyric poem', a hearty Whitmanesque celebration of the joys of togetherness. But the woman and her lover, despite their almost painful intimacy – indeed, perhaps because of it (there is something oppressive, after all, about lovers being able to read each other's minds) – eventually become alienated from one another, as lovers in modern realistic prose fiction are almost obliged to become, and her resultant mood is far from lyrical.

The essentially ironic, ambiguous and paradoxical nature of the work is evident even in the title: it is a modern psychological story of a woman's bitter and jealous obsession with her dead lover – nothing could be more anti-lyrical. Nevertheless, it aspires to be a lyric poem, just as the woman aspires to transcend the anguish of her ego by awakening in herself a 'primitive' animistic, world-embracing consciousness, and just as Kawabata himself, a modern Japanese writer 'disinherited' from his own cultural and spiritual traditions and suffering also the more personal anguish of an 'orphan psychology', longed to be a lyric poet in the great Buddhist tradition of Saigyō and Bashō, and longed also for the ego-transcending monistic consciousness which he believed such poets possessed. The important difference between Kawabata and his female narrator, of course, is that, whereas she seems blissfully unaware of her self-contradictions – in particular, the fact that her 'mystic quest' is so obviously motivated at least as much by bitterness and hatred as by love – Kawabata himself is all too painfully aware of the contradictory nature of his ambitions: as an artist, to write modern prose fiction with something of the quality of traditional lyric poetry; as a man, to attain to a 'primitive' monistic consciousness without giving up the sophisticated analytical, Western-influenced mind of the modern Japanese intellectual. But a great writer is defined in large part by the challenges he sets himself, and Kawabata was, in fact, remarkably successful in realizing and reconciling these 'contradictory' goals. As we shall see, the masterworks of his 'middle period', beginning with *Snow Country*, the works in which he perfected his '*haiku* style' and in which he gave a powerful new expression to lyrical monism, these works, undoubtedly, were born out of the conflicting ambitions first clearly articulated in 'Lyric Poem'.

6. The Beauty of the Beasts

If the female narrator of 'Lyric Poem' hopes to escape from human relationships by being reborn as a flower, the male narrator in 'Of Birds and Beasts' expresses an even more pronounced misanthropy in a more direct and immediate way: by choosing to live with a whole menagerie of animals, fish and birds rather than with his fellow humans. Perhaps the fact that this protagonist is male, and obviously quite closely modelled on Kawabata himself at this period, goes a long way to explain why, of the four *shinkyō shōsetsu* of the early 1930s studied in this chapter, this one is the darkest in tone and gives the most extreme expression of a narcissistic, misanthropic and even nihilistic state of mind. (Kawabata himself once confessed that it was written out of 'unbearable feelings of self-hatred'.[97]) But even this story is not unrelieved by lyricism and a promise of monistic transcendence – although the protagonist's aestheticism and 'spirituality' may seem still more perverted by an exploitative egotism than were those of the heroine of 'Lyric Poem'. And, on a literary/aesthetic level, it is undoubtedly the most successful of the four stories. Written in 1933, 'Of Birds and Beasts' may be regarded as a culminating expression of Kawabata's development as a writer of a new style of psychological fiction, which combined modernist themes and techniques seamlessly with some of the aesthetic qualities of the Japanese poetic tradition. Indeed, with this story Kawabata may be said to have found his mature style. It is already the style he would use shortly to write such major works as *Snow Country* and *The Sound of the Mountain*.

The narrative unfolds entirely within the mind of the central character, moving freely and effortlessly, by association of image or idea, back and forth between the present and the past. As the story opens we find the protagonist in a taxi on his way to a dance recital to be performed by a woman named Chikako. His taxi gets stalled in a funeral procession, behind a truck carrying caged birds which are to be released at the funeral. The birds and the thought of the funeral naturally occasion his first flashback, which begins with the thought that he has left two dead birds at home without the benefit of a funeral. (The naturalness, the seeming 'inevitability', of the associative leaps in this story is certainly one of its greatest virtues; they have none of the 'forced' feeling of some of the associations in *Crystal Fantasies*, for instance.) In the lengthy flashback which follows, we learn of this man's unusual lifestyle: a bachelor, he lives with a whole houseful of 'pets', preferring their company to that of human beings. And yet, although he takes aesthetic pleasure in these creatures and sometimes waxes sentimental about them, he also betrays, in the way he treats them, the ruthlessness of an artist towards his 'raw materials': those which do not measure up to his high aesthetic ideals are promptly discarded. Indeed, his behaviour towards his 'pets' is also reminiscent of the vampirish behaviour of the usual Kawabata male towards young females: he treasures them at first for the feeling of 'freshness', of innocent life-force, which they give him; he feeds upon them, so to speak, and sucks the life-blood out of them; but once their 'innocence' has been corrupted by contact with him, he does not hesitate to discard them. (In this context his 'over-washing' of his favourite birds, which eventually causes their death – proving again that 'each man kills the thing he loves' – seems appropriately symbolic: a desperate, futile attempt to preserve the very 'freshness' which they soon will lose as his captives.) As with John Fowles' 'collector', albeit with birds rather than with women, the cycle will then be repeated all over again: the animal dealer is always happy to supply him with a fresh stock of pets.

This impression of the pets serving for this Kawabata male as 'surrogate women' – who are, of course, more easy to dispose of than real women – is further strengthened and confirmed as the story progresses and we learn more of his relationship with Chikako (the erstwhile prostitute and dancer whose performance he is on his way to see). First of all, he himself makes the association between Chikako and one of his pets: the naïve, unknowing expression on a female dog's face as she is giving birth to puppies reminds him of the expression on Chikako's face when she first sold herself to him, ten years earlier. Again, when he sees this dog scampering joyously about, totally indifferent to the fact that she has just squashed to death her own puppies, this also reminds him of Chikako: both because of the animal 'wildness' of her dancing and because of her insouciance about her own baby.

Both these examples point to an important fact about the peculiar nature of the need this Kawabata aesthete finds to be satisfied both by his animals and by his woman: it is not merely an aesthetic need, a need to look at beautiful objects; his need also has a strong moral and psychological or even spiritual component. The negative expression of this is his misanthropy:

> All alone, he came to his arbitrary conclusion: he did
> not like people. Husbands and wives, parents and
> children, brothers and sisters: the bonds were not
> easily cut even with the most unsatisfactory of
> people. One had to be resigned to living with them.
> And everyone possessed what is called an ego.[98]

Conversely and more positively, what this means, of course, is
that he loves animals for their 'egolessness', their innocent
quality of pure being, which enables him to live with them
without any loss of his own freedom, without forming any
uncutable 'bonds'. His life of what might be called 'oneness
without ego-bondage' seems to a certain extent the fulfillment
of a monistic ideal:

> ... for him life was filled with a young freshness for
> several days after a new bird came. He felt in it the
> blessings of the universe. Perhaps it was a failing on
> his part, but he was unable to feel anything of the
> sort in a human being.[99]

This last statement, however, is not completely accurate. As we
presently discover, there is, in fact, one human being who did
once give him the same sense of wild animal 'freshness' and
unselfconsciousness as his pets: Chikako, the very woman he is
reminded of by his dog. Her dancing expressed this, but also
her whole way of being. His most powerful memory of her
concerns the time they had decided to commit 'lovers' suicide'
together, for 'no special reason'. She is as innocent and
unselfconscious in this as in all her actions:

> She lay with her back to him, her eyes calmly closed,
> her head up. Then she brought her hands together in
> prayer. He was struck, as by lightning, by the joy of
> emptiness.[100]

Although the protagonist of this story has often been
described as a nihilist, the 'emptiness' (*kyomu*) he experiences
here obviously has a Buddhist rather than a nihilist tenor (in
this case, at least, one must agree with what Kawabata himself
said in his Nobel speech about the experience of emptiness in
his works, as quoted above[101]). 'Emptiness' in this sense, in
fact, is merely a synonym for 'egolessness', because the
experience is awakened in the protagonist's mind as he
witnesses the innocent, unselfconscious (*mushin*, a favourite
Zen term) way in which the teenaged Chikako prepares to
embrace death. Thus the experience gives rise to a feeling of joy
or blessedness (*arigatasa*) quite opposite to the despair

associated with the Western nihilist experience of nothing-ness.[102] And the lasting and profound spiritual meaning of this experience for the protagonist is obvious:

> Quite taken by surprise, he neither spoke nor thought again of suicide. The knowledge echoed deep in his heart that whatever happened he must treasure this woman.[103]

Or, at least, treasure her as she was at that moment, before time had had a chance to work its evil, before she began to lose that animal-like vitality and innocence which was what he really treasured. For the problem with Chikako, as with other teenaged girls in Kawabata, is that she is not immune to time, which brings temptations as well as depredations, and, once she has begun to age, the protagonist finds that he cannot replace her as easily as one of his pets. As a whore, of course, she is theoretically easier to dispose of than other women – which is why, no doubt, he first allowed himself to become involved with her. Nevertheless, she is the one who awakened in him such a profound experience of 'the joy of emptiness', which caused him to vow that he would always treasure her. Thus, in reality, he finds that his bond with her is not so easy to cut – which is exactly why, after so many years and so many changes for the worse, she is still so much on his mind and he still feels compelled to attend her concert.

But we are left with the strong impression that this will be the last of her concerts he will attend. In Chikako's case, unlike other of Kawabata's young women, her 'deterioration' is not simply a matter of aging: she is an artist, and, as we have seen, Kawabata regarded loneliness, even alienation, as a necessary part of the artist's condition. Chikako proves unable to endure this, she gives in to the temptation to become a 'normal' woman, to settle down with a husband and bear his child. (In sharp contrast, the protagonist himself, even though he is a kind of frustrated artist, a dilettante with a keen aesthetic sensibility but without any adequate means of expression – he fails even as a bird-breeder – nonetheless understands the price an artist must pay and is quite willing to pay it).[104] Because of her betrayal of her artistic destiny and her surrender to life, Chikako's dancing and her very being entirely lose that wild, animal quality, that innocent, unconscious *joie de vivre*, which attracted the protagonist to her in the first place. In the story's climax, no longer enacted in memory but in the present tense, we witness this deterioration along with the protagonist:

> Her dancing had so degenerated that he had to look
> away. All that was left of the savage strength was a
> common coquettishness. Form had gone to pieces
> with the decay of her body.[105]

The protagonist desires now only to escape, but Chikako sends a message that she wants to talk with him. When he goes backstage, the impression of her total degeneration is only reinforced in a startling and absolute way: as she lies stretched out like a corpse having a heavy white makeup applied, her face seems to him 'the face of a lifeless doll, a dead face'.[106] Her death-like pose reminds him of the time when they had decided to commit suicide together. But, ironically, this was a much happier time, because the upshot had been his experience of the 'joy of emptiness', which had restored his will to live. Now her 'degenerate' dance performance gives him quite the opposite impulse. He quickly escapes, without even uttering a word. Unhappily, though, he runs into her ex-husband, a stupid philistine, whose praise of Chikako's dancing only reinforces the protagonist's sense of her fallen state. Now thoroughly depressed, he tells himself that he must 'think of something sweet'.[107]

He seeks immediate relief by purposely calling to mind (as opposed to all his previous trains of thought, which seemed to proceed by 'free association') the pure memory of a girl who had died at fifteen, and whose mother had applied makeup to her dead face, so that at her funeral she looked 'like a bride'.[108] In ironic contrast to the aging Chikako, then, whose makeup face, although still alive, looks dead, the makeup face of this innocent young girl, although dead, looks like that of a living bride. Indeed, having died at fifteen, she will remain forever young. In the story's eerie, vaguely necrophilic final passage (which sounds a note Kawabata would return to many years later, at much greater length, in those two late masterworks, *Sleeping Beauties* and 'One Arm'), the protagonist seems to have found his ideal bride at last, one who is not only eternally young and virginal but who does not impose upon him any of the usual bonds of an ego-bound human relationship.

★   ★   ★

This technically brilliant and psychologically profound and disturbing short story marks the culminating point of Kawabata's period of 'experiment and expansion' (circa 1926–1933). With this story he may be said to have found his true voice and his true subject. First of all, on a purely technical level, all the main elements of his mature style are already present: a freely associative structure in which imagery plays a major role in advancing the plot (and the quality of that imagery too is bold and striking, often approaching what we might describe as a 'borderline surrealism' – something Kawabata obviously had absorbed from his study of the European modernists); an interior or subjective focus on the state of mind of the central character – in other words, a narrative method preeminently suited to psychological fiction. On the thematic, psychological and philosophical levels too, the basic dialectical tensions or interplays which would structure his major works – his 'dialectics of salvation' – are also already clearly defined: egotism, alienation and nihilism in contest with lyricism and monistic transcendence. All that really changes in the more 'traditional' works, compared to his 'modernist' works of the late '20s and early '30s, is that the balance slants a little more towards the monistic side, the mood lightens somewhat, and this allows for the use of a more lyrical, 'traditional' imagery – especially the kind of imagery which celebrates the beauties of nature. But, as we shall see, the negative side of the equation, especially the egotism of the Kawabata male, is certainly never entirely absent from the more 'traditional' works. And the balance could just as easily tip back the other way – as, in fact, ultimately it did.

CHAPTER FOUR

BETWEEN TRADITION AND MODERNITY

*S*now Country (*Yukiguni*, 1935–47) is often regarded as the first major work marking Kawabata's return to a more traditionally Japanese style of writing after his experiments with a Western-style modernism in the late 1920s and early 1930s. Certainly, if we compare it to a radically experimental work like *Crystal Fantasies*, that study of impotence and alienation among the urban intelligentsia, written partly in a stream-of-consciousness style and replete with up-to-the-minute scientific terminology, then *Snow Country*'s more traditional Japanese flavour is obvious: with its setting in the mountainous 'snow country', far away from any modern urban centre – an area redolent of fairy tales, folk arts and traditional country lifestyles, the beauty of the scenery lending itself well to lyrical descriptions using *haiku*-like imagery – and with its ostensibly traditional story of the tragic love affair between a wealthy Tokyo dilettante and a poor hotspring *geisha*, the work seems to revive the timeless world of traditional Japanese poetry, romantic fiction and *kabuki* theatre. Coming after such eccentric and even misanthropic works as *Of Birds and Beasts*, *Snow Country* seems determinedly designed to ingratiate itself with the Japanese reading public at large, to achieve the same kind of popularity and even mass cultural icon status as *The Dancing Girl of Izu*. If that was its purpose, it succeeded brilliantly: like *Izu*, it has become a standard fixture of modern Japanese popular culture, inspiring films, songs, tourist booms in the snow country, and other such epiphenomena.

An historical and political factor should also perhaps be taken into account here: Kawabata's 'return to tradition' was as characteristic of the 1930s as his experimentalism and openness to Western modernism was of the 1920s. The demise of 'Taishō liberalism' and the rise of militarism and nationalism made Japanese society generally more conservative and traditional, even reactionary, in its tastes in the 1930s. Indeed, even Kawabata himself once noted with pride that, during the years when the Japanese Imperial Army was deployed all over Asia and the South Pacific, he often received letters from frontline soldiers who told him how much reading *Snow Country* meant to them. This may seem surprising to us now: the effete Shimamura, the novel's hero, hardly seems a fit model for frontline warriors, and the novel as a whole has nothing of the gung-ho militarist spirit in it. But its traditional Japanese ambience and gentle, lyrical melancholy no doubt satisfied the soldiers' nostalgic longing for their homeland – as also, one surmises, Komako's charming and vivacious femininity spoke to another kind of longing.

In any case, Kawabata should not be faulted for his talent for mass appeal – at least he will not be by me – so long as he did not allow this to interfere with his genius for writing serious literature. In *Snow Country* he did not – although he did, it must be admitted, in the numerous 'potboilers' he wrote for womens' magazines. But the question which really interests me here is: how deep a matter was his 'return to tradition'? Was it merely a surface affair of a few cosmetic 'adjustments' to make his 'face' more appealing to the public? Or did it involve some really fundamental changes in the way he wrote or the things he wrote about? To put this in another way: what if any are the continuities between his 'modernist' and his 'traditionalist' works?

1. The Art of Juxtaposition

The style Kawabata uses in *Snow Country* has often been described as a '*haiku* style'. This does indeed seem a fitting description, and on both the microcosmic level of individual sentences and the macrocosmic level of the structure of the narrative as a whole. That is, many individual sentences read like *haiku* poems, a juxtaposition of images, often natural or seasonal, which, by their sudden conjunction, create a deep reverberation of mood or meaning. To take a beautiful example from late in the novel: 'On the worn floor of the hallway, polished to a dark glow, a *geisha* had left behind a samisen box, the very embodiment of quiet in the late autumn night'.[1] This single sentence movingly encapsulates the increasingly elegiac, autumnal mood of the latter part of the novel, and does so by bringing together two simple images: an old polished floor and a *samisen* box.

Much of the most beautiful and powerful imagery in the novel is achieved by such juxtapositions: the whole opening scene, for instance, which plays upon images reflected in the 'evening mirror' of the moving train window, culminates in the most celebrated juxtaposition in the entire novel: of a girl's eye reflected in the train window and a light on the dark mountains outside:

> It was a distant, cold light. As it sent its small ray through the pupil of the girl's eye, as the eye and the light were superimposed one on the other, the eye became a weirdly beautiful bit of phosphorescence on the sea of evening mountains.[2]

A mirror of a more ordinary kind is used later in the novel to achieve another beautiful effect of superimposition, when Shimamura notices Komako's face reflected along with some snow. Her cheeks are particularly red because of the cold:

> The white in the depths of the mirror was the snow, and floating in the middle of it were the woman's bright red cheeks. There was an indescribably fresh beauty in the contrast.[3]

Finally, to intensify the effect even more, these two imagistic juxtapositions are themselves juxtaposed a few pages later, when Shimamura encounters Yōko again and she looks at him with a 'quick, piercing glance':

> Even when he had left the house, Shimamura was haunted by that glance, burning just in front of his forehead. It was cold as a very distant light, for the inexpressible beauty of it had made his heart rise when, the night before, that light off in the mountains had passed across the girl's face in the train window and lighted her eye for a moment. The impression came back to Shimamura, and with it the memory of the mirror filled with snow, and Komako's red cheeks floating in the middle of it.[4]

But Kawabata is so insistent on these juxtaposed images not exclusively for their aesthetic effect – or, rather, the aesthetic effect includes a philosophic nuance, which I shall discuss in some detail presently. Furthermore, this *haiku*-like technique of juxtaposition is not confined to single sentences or image clusters. A similar principle underlies much of the novel's narrative structure, often replacing more conventional techniques of narrative progression. To take an example from early in the novel: when Shimamura tries to prove his 'seriousness' to Komako by boasting that he has come back to see her even in

December, out of the usual season for snow country tourism, there follows a discussion of Komako's habit of keeping a diary, and then of Shimamura's own interest in Western ballet.[5] At first glance the latter two topics may seem to have nothing to do with the first one – and a reader unaccustomed to this narrative method may feel irritated by what seems to be the disjointed, irrelevant, *non sequitur* advance of the narrative, its lack of 'smooth progress'. But Kawabata has, in fact, placed these three topics together with a definite semantic purpose in mind, and this becomes evident with a little more reflection. The function of the two latter topics is first of all to undermine Shimamura's smug boast about his 'seriousness': Komako's industrious diary-keeping, which she admits is a 'complete waste of effort', reminds him of his own futile efforts as a dilettantish critic of Western ballet, an art form he has never even beheld with his own eyes. The reader is left to complete the argument: is it likely, then, that this dilettante who takes nothing seriously, who does not even have to work seriously for a living, will suddenly turn serious in his relationship with a mere hotspring *geisha*? Our suspicions are confirmed, of course, as the novel progresses and Shimamura turns out to be as uncommitted to Komako as he is to his artistic 'avocation'.

The question arises then: why indeed does Shimamura, the dilettante in love as in life, bother to come back several times over a period of about two years to visit this woman? The answer to this more difficult question is also hinted at in the above juxtaposition: in the way she takes pleasure in her own 'wasted efforts' and wasted life, he sees himself strangely reflected in her – a powerful enough attraction for any narcissist. At any rate, we may see in this way that Kawabata's novels begin to yield their full meaning only when they are read with an alert sensitivity to the significance of their juxtapositions.

One may note here also the interesting fact that, although the novel is narrated largely from Shimamura's point of view, Kawabata is not restricted to that point of view, as some critics have claimed: by his use of such meaningful juxtapositions, he is able to introduce a deeper, implicit authorial viewpoint, as an ironic counterpoint to the explicitly expressed views of his central character.[6]

On a somewhat wider level, whole scenes are also juxtaposed against each other for meaningful effect. For example, the closing scene of Part One echoes the opening scene, but with significant differences. Shimamura is again riding on a train, and, as the narrator says:

> The window began to steam over. The landscape
> outside was dusky, and the figures of the passengers
> floated up half-transparent. It was the play of that
> evening mirror again.[7]

But now he is on his way out of the snow country, away from
Komako, and that makes all the difference. There are no
beautiful eyes reflected in this train window. Whereas in the
initial scene the train's passage through the tunnel into the
snow country marked a moment of high lyricism, expressed by
the celebrated *haiku*-like sentences which open the novel, now
passage back through the tunnel represents a 'come-down' in a
psychological as much as a geographical sense. Like Alice
passing back through her mirror out of a fantasy land,
Shimamura passes back through the tunnel into the 'real
world' of his everyday life. Since there is no snow on this side,
immediately the whole world darkens – and even the train
seems to have lost its lustre: 'The dim brightness of the winter
afternoon seemed to have been sucked into the earth, and the
battered old train had shed its bright shell in the tunnel'.[8] The
only bright object in the 'withered' landscape is 'a stark white
building, a hydroelectric plant perhaps' – a fitting symbol of the
anti-aesthetic, alienating power of modern scientific civilization, which is encroaching into the mountains even this close to
the snow country.[9] In a similar vein, a little later he notices 'the
chimneys of spinning-factories' – not a pleasing sight to an
aesthete and nature-lover like Shimamura.[10]

There is another echo of the earlier train scene when
Shimamura notices a man and girl travelling together, talking
happily and intimately with each other, their relationship
apparently like that of Yōko and Yukio in the first scene. But it
turns out to be a false echo: the man soon gets off, and bids
farewell to the girl in a way that shows they have only just met.
Shimamura is strangely affected by this – almost to the point of
tears – because it reminds him suddenly that he too has just
said farewell to Komako and to the snow country and 'was on
his way home' – in other words, on his way back to a world he
obviously finds much harder to live in. Thus, although we are
shown nothing of his life in Tokyo, we are left in no doubt as to
how he feels about it – by virtue of a kind of 'negative
definition' which emerges from the skillful use of juxtaposition.

Yet another major use of juxtaposition is in what we might call
the definition of the main characters. Just as the red of Komako's
cheeks stands out more vividly against the white of the snow in
the above-mentioned scene, so too one character is more clearly

defined by being sharply juxtaposed against another. Many novelists, of course, have used this technique; certainly it is not as unusual as some of Kawabata's other techniques of juxtaposition. But he relies on it to a degree that is unusual. Shimamura, for instance, is undoubtedly Kawabata's most convincing portrait of a narcissistic male, a man who is aesthetically highly sensitive but is incapable of love – or any other form of passion. But, as is perfectly in keeping with the man's passivity, this portrait derives its power not so much from any depiction of Shimamura in himself as from the contrast between him and Komako: we feel what he lacks so strongly because we are made to feel so strongly what she possesses. In other words, he emerges so clearly by virtue again of a kind of negative definition – a technique which reminds one of the play of empty space against strong calligraphic line in the East Asian art of ink painting (*sumi-e*). We feel his emptiness by her fullness, his coldness by her passion, his passivity by her dynamism, his effeteness by her vitality. Thus we realize that his first intuition about her – that she had something deeply in common with him – was little more than his own narcissistic illusion. But still she retains a fascination for him, and a dangerous one: as a kind of negative mirror, showing him everything that he is not, but still thus enabling him to learn about himself in a way he has never done before: the same way that we learn about him, by his contrast with her. Though he is flattered by her love he is also discomforted by it, because, as Komako makes all too clear, it demands reciprocity. What ultimately he most values about her is her mirroring quality. Even such a negative mirror is an object of fascination for Narcissus, because it gives him what he most craves: the self-knowledge that promises a more complete self-possession. Komako's function may thus be compared with that of the mirrors in the earlier stories, 'Narcissus' and *Crystal Fantasies*. She too is a 'mirror of the heart' – or, rather, of Shimamura's heartlessness.

2. Juxtaposition in Western Modernism

> '. . . the world cannot be expressed, it can perhaps be indicated by a mosaics of juxtaposition'.
> William Burroughs[11]

It seems safe to say, then, that the art of juxtaposition, in a wide variety of forms, is central to Kawabata's practice as a novelist in *Snow Country*. But does this necessarily mean that it is basically a traditional work with affinities more with pre-modern *haiku* and *renga* (linked verse) than with modern novels, at least as written in the West? When this question is addressed in its full literary/historical context, it seems to require something more nuanced or even equivocal than a simple 'either/or' kind of answer.

The fact is that, for a Japanese writer of 1935, the 'return to tradition' need not have entailed anything like a complete rejection of modernity; indeed, in some cases, any clear-cut antithesis between tradition and modernity would have been very difficult to establish. Kawabata's use of juxtaposition is an excellent example of this fact, both because of a complex story of East/West intercultural relations and also, it seems, because of the pure coincidence that a favourite technique of traditional Japanese writers was 'rediscovered' by Western modernists.

The first fruitful exposure of Western artists to Japanese modes of juxtaposition was not in literature but in the visual arts: Impressionist and Postimpressionist painters like Monet and Van Gogh learned much about colour, line and composition by studying the kind of startling juxtapositions found in Japanese wood-block prints, the bold, dramatic counterpositioning not only of disproportionate images – such as Hokusai's famous wave against Mount Fuji – but also of large areas of flat, bright and sometimes discordant colours against each other. The resultant vogue of *Japonisme* became one of the major artistic trends of late nineteenth-century Europe.

In English literature the first significant modernist literary use of *haiku*-style juxtapositions was by Ezra Pound and his fellow Imagists. Pound himself recorded that he first used the technique in his celebrated mini-poem of 1912, 'In a Station of the Metro', which he described as a '*hokku*-like sentence':

> The apparition of these faces in a crowd;
> Petals on a wet, black bough.[12]

Pound described this kind of imagery as 'a form of superposition; that is to say it is one idea set on top of another'.[13] And he went on to expand his use of the technique vastly, as a structural principle even of his huge poem series, *The Cantos*. As Earl Miner says in his seminal study of this kind of Japanese influence on British and American literature:

> After devising the technique for 'In a Station of the Metro', Pound used the super-pository method, as it may be called, as a very flexible technique which provides the basic structure for many passages and many poems'.[14]

But when one surveys the whole history of modernism in the West, one may question whether this was a case of simple 'influence' – in the straightforward sense of one artist imitating another – or whether rather, as seems so often the case, it was more a matter of the foreign model encouraging and perhaps helping to refine a tendency that was already very much present. This seems even more so when we look at Western modernist fiction – an area more directly relevant to Kawabata.

In a celebrated and seminal essay on the modernist novel, Joseph Frank has pointed out how central to the practice of these novelists too were techniques of juxtaposition, or what he calls 'spatial form'. But Frank traces the origins of this technique back to Flaubert in the 1850s – interestingly enough, just on the eve of *Japonisme*. In the country fair scene of *Madame Bovary*, Flaubert, working against the chronological order of the narrative, tried to attain effects of simultaneity by juxtaposing words and sounds heard in several different places at the same time. As Flaubert himself said: 'Everything should sound simultaneously; one should hear the bellowing of the cattle, the whisperings of the lovers and the rhetoric of the officials all at the same time'.[15] Of course, given the sequential nature of language, this is a practical impossibility, but Flaubert attempts at least to approach this effect by interrupting the time-flow of the narrative and juxtaposing simultaneous events. The method depends, as Frank says, on the 'continual reference and cross-reference of images and symbols which must be referred to each other spatially throughout the time-act of reading'.[16]

Frank goes on to demonstrate how this method was taken up later by modernist writers, both poets and novelists, who were also interested in overcoming the limitations of chronological narrative. Joyce, for instance, applied it on a massive scale in *Ulysses* to try to represent all the simultaneous goings-on in a single Dublin day. Proust, however, offers the closest parallel to Kawabata, because he found the perfect theme to fit this innovative form: like many of Kawabata's central characters, Marcel, in *A la Recherche du temps perdu* (*In Search of Lost Time*, translated as *Remembrance of Things Past*), is obsessed with a longing somehow to transcend everyday chronological time, to escape into the timeless realm with its promise of complete spiritual freedom. I will discuss several interesting affinities between these two writers in more depth in Chapter 6, but for now there is just one that seems particularly relevant: what Frank points to as one of Proust's major uses of juxtaposition –

the same character at different ages juxtaposed in Marcel's mind – is also used to the same effect by Kawabata in *Snow Country*. Shimamura visits the snow country three times over the course of a couple of years, and each time he notices that Komako has aged slightly. It is mainly by the juxtaposition of the images of these three 'different' Kamakos that Shimamura – and the reader – is made to feel the *mono no aware* pathos of the young *geisha*'s gradual aging.

Finally, one might also note that these spatializing techniques meant to achieve effects of anti-narrative or supra-narrative simultaneity: juxtaposition, superimposition, montage, etc., are characteristically cinematic, and, of course, the new art of cinema was another major influence on modernist writing. Kawabata too undoubtedly felt this influence, as his work clearly shows. Indeed, during his modernist twenties, he even wrote the scenario of a surrealistic film called *A Mad Page* (*Kurutta ichi pēji*, 1926) which depicts the delusions of mental patients – a theme he would return to many years later in his very last work, *Dandelions* (*Tanpopo*, left unfinished at his death). *A Mad Page* itself is now celebrated as Japan's first avant-garde film and is all the more significant because it was not only scripted by Kawabata but directed by Kinugasa Teinosuke (1896–1982), a leading figure of the Japanese cinema, at the beginning of his long career.[17]

What all this seems to argue, then, is that there was a definite continuity between Kawabata's 'modernist' '20s and 'traditionalist' '30s, that we should view these two phases of his career not as radically separate but as organically related – that, paradoxical as this may seem, his traditionalism was a natural outgrowth of his modernism. More specifically, we might conclude that it was no coincidence that, shortly after being exposed to Western modernism, and making his own quite successful versions of modernist writing – in which typically modernist techniques of juxtaposition are also much in evidence – he continued to use the same techniques of juxtaposition and spatial form even in his more 'traditional' novels.

3. Monism, Aestheticism and Narcissism in Snow Country

But the continuities are not confined to the realm of technique alone: more fundamentally, there was no basic change either in the nature of the themes and issues Kawabata continued to address – as even a cursory analysis of the main lines of thematic development in *Snow Country* will reveal. Furthermore, the central character of the novel, Shimamura, is recognizably akin to many previous Kawabata protagonists, female as well as male, in his narcissism, alienation, aestheticism and longing for monistic or mystical transcendence. In this case in particular, to say that he is the 'central character' is not to say that he is the most powerful presence in the novel – as I've already pointed out, Komako is far more dynamic and alive. But Shimamura is the focal point around which the novel's basic themes are worked out, especially the typically Kawabataesque 'dialectics of salvation' whose main contending forces are narcissism, aestheticism and monism; in this sense *Snow Country* is his 'story', not Komako's. In short, Kawabata is ultimately more interested in Shimamura's inability to love than in Komako's love. The 'snow country' stands as the perfect metaphor for Shimamura's psychological condition, which is the 'lifelong psychic cold' typical of the narcissist.[18] Since there are some real affinities between this novel and a traditional Gothic romance, perhaps we might even allow ourselves a more melodramatic mode of expression, and say that 'the true snow country is in his heart'.

At any rate, to try to 'reread' the novel from Komako's point of view, as certain feminist critics have recently attempted, is to 'read' a different novel than the one Kawabata wrote. In her valiant attempt to rewrite the novel in this way, Tajima Yōko admits as much: 'It is surprisingly difficult ... to adopt Komako's point of view'.[19] But she justifies this artificial reconstruction of the novel on the grounds that it enables us to perceive the full extent of Komako's victimization by Shimamura. However, it hardly seems necessary to resort to such distortions in order to make this elementary deduction – as I hope to demonstrate, the novel provides ample grounds for this as it is written. No doubt one reason why Tajima feels obliged to resort to this artificial reading is that, like many other critics, she fails to recognize that the novel is not, in fact, limited to Shimamura's point of view, that there is, as I have already pointed out, a second, authorial viewpoint strongly present, both directly, in the form of narrative statement (e.g., 'It did not occur to Shimamura that it was improper to stare at the girl so long and stealthily'.[20]) and indirectly, in the form, for instance, of those ironic juxtapositions I have already referred to. I hasten to add, however, that, although *Snow Country* is unalterably male-centred, this does not mean that Kawabata, being a male author, was incapable of writing in any other way. As we saw with his earlier stories, 'Narcissus', *Crystal Fantasies* and 'Lyric Poem', he was eminently capable also of writing convincing female-centred fiction.

★ ★ ★

Although, given the nature of our language and logic, one must analyse the above-mentioned 'three themes' – narcissism, aestheticism and monism – sequentially, as if they were neatly discrete elements, we should not forget that one of the great strengths of Kawabata's novel is the way he presents them as closely interwoven within the fabric of his narrative – we are constantly made aware, to use a Buddhist philosophical term, of their 'dependent coorigination'. Thus, while analyzing them 'discretely', I shall also try to point out some of the main ways in which they are interrelated: for instance, how his narcissism leads into both his aestheticism and his monism.

Our first important hint as to the way Shimamura relates with women comes in the novel's opening scene: he seems strangely fixated on body parts. He is, of course, entranced by the reflection of Yōko's eye in the train window, but immediately before this (another significant juxtaposition) we are told:

> In his boredom, Shimamura stared at his left hand as the forefinger bent and unbent. Only this hand seemed to have a vital and immediate memory of the woman he was going to see. The more he tried to call up a clear picture of her, the more his memory failed him, the farther she faded away, leaving him nothing to catch and hold. In the midst of this uncertainty only the one hand, and in particular the forefinger, which even now seemed damp from her touch, seemed to be pulling him back to her from afar.[21]

Shimamura himself is so struck by the truth and strangeness of this 'epiphany' that as soon as he meets Komako he extends his forefinger and says: 'This remembered you best of all' – a rather perverse and cold way to greet her, considering, as the narrative tells us: 'In spite of what had passed between them, he had not written to her, or come to see her, or sent her the dance instructions he had promised'.[22] The erotic implications of the gesture are obvious but, since only his finger remembers her, what it seems to mean on a deeper psychological level is that he is incapable of relating with women in a wholehearted way but only in a kind of fragmented way, as erotic or aesthetic objects. Although to do so is to read anachronistically, one cannot help recalling here a much later work, 'One Arm', the surrealistic short story in which Kawabata takes his male hero's 'fragmentation' of women and fixation on body parts to an extreme: the protagonist borrows a woman's detached arm for the night. At any rate, Shimamura's realization of his own 'finger fixation' marks the dawning of his awareness of certain uncomfortable truths about himself, including his 'coldness' or human inadequacy.

It is, in fact, only the first in a series of self-revelatory epiphanies which he will experience in his relationship with Komako throughout the novel. Again, if we were to ask what it is of lasting value that he derives from his two-year affair with this hotspring *geisha*, it is precisely this: self-knowledge.

If the 'finger' episode made us think he was a typical playboy visitor on a 'sex tour' to a hotspring town, the next self-revelatory incident quickly disabuses us of that notion. At first, though, he tries to act that unsavory part to the hilt. Flaunting his 'masculine shamelessness', he asks Komako to call a *geisha* for him. After some conventional protests, she does so. But the moment Shimamura sees the *geisha* Komako has chosen, a rather lumpen, aesthetically unappealing country girl, he immediately loses interest. And, with a flash of insight into his own psychology, he realizes that it was Komako he had wanted all along: 'As it became clear to Shimamura that he had from the start wanted only this woman, and that he had taken his usual roundabout way of saying so, he began to see himself as rather repulsive and the woman as all the more beautiful'.[23]

But even then he does not exactly become the most active or eager of lovers. Komako is far more aggressive: that night she barges into his room, almost forcing herself on him, and Shimamura is shocked by the violence of her passion: 'It was, with no attempt at covering herself, the naked heart of a woman calling out to her man'.[24] Clearly he himself would never be able to open himself or give himself to his lover in such a spontaneous, unrestrained and wholehearted way. As the narration has already informed us, he has come to hide himself away in the snow country, with an 'idler's bent for protective colouring'.[25] Although he is the most sexually active of Kawabata's major protagonists, and has the most attractive of Kawabata's female characters as his partner, still he betrays that resistance to intimacy typical of the narcissistic Kawabata male.

What confirms us even more in this impression is that, when finally Shimamura does become physically intimate with Komako, his first thought is that there is 'something a little motherly in her'.[26] This is an oft-repeated theme. Whenever Shimamura feels particularly attracted to either of the two females who catch his eye in the snow country, Komako or Yōko, there are two qualities which are unfailingly emphasized: the woman's 'purity' and her 'motherliness'. Neither of these may seem high on the list of feminine charms for the 'average' male, but for the narcissist their appeal is obvious.

Looking back at the original Greek myth, we remember that the beautiful youth, Narcissus, was in love not only with his own beauty but with his own purity, and was afraid that any contact with females would pollute that purity (a fear which seems to have very deep roots in the male psyche, since it finds expression not only in ancient myths but in many religious traditions, both 'primitive' and 'advanced'). Thus the girl who loved him, Echo, was condemned to call out to him in vain forever, her voice echoing plaintively through the woods – rather like Komako's, 'calling out to her man'. The Kawabata male's obsession with purity is a slight variation on this: because he already feels somewhat polluted by his life in the world, he seeks a 'pure' female who will refresh his spirit. Although his motives may thus seem more 'spiritual' than those of the usual womanizing sensualist, the relationship which results is equally one-sided and narcissistic, the male exploiting the female, albeit for 'spiritual' purposes.

As for his attraction to 'motherly' women: we may agree with Freud that narcissism represents an infantile stage of psycho-logical development, and that a man whose psychic growth has been arrested in this stage is incapable of a mature, mutually giving love relationship.[27] Thus he naturally seeks a woman who will love him like his mother, with an unconditional love that will pamper his ego to an infinite extent but demand nothing in return. Up close to any woman, Shimamura wants her to function in this way, not as a lover but as a mother.

Thus it is also understandable that, as Komako begins to make demands for at least some reciprocation of her passion and commitment, Shimamura begins to turn away from her and look towards Yōko, a more remote and mysterious girl who seems to him both purer and more motherly than Komako.

That Shimamura is thus willing to ruthlessly discard Komako and add another girl to his 'collection', that he has thus been exploiting her in his peculiar 'spiritual' way as mercilessly as any more sensual Don Juan, becomes obvious to both of them in what may be regarded as the climax to his series of self-revelatory experiences. The way this 'climax' is brought about is also an admirable example of Kawabata's economy of means, his artistic minimalism. Shimamura betrays all by a careless slip of the tongue, the change of a single word: after calling Komako 'a good girl', he changes this to 'a good woman'. She reacts furiously, accuses him of laughing at her, then breaks down into tears and tells him that she hates him. Shimamura is stunned, not realizing at first the nature of his *faux pas*. Or perhaps we should call it a 'Freudian slip', because this seems to be a good example of something Kawabata learned from Freud during his modernist period: that one false word can betray a vast amount about unconscious motives or desires.

But the true fascination of this scene is that we actually watch Shimamura achieve a profound and painful enlightenment about himself through the catalyst of Komako's anger and sorrow. If he had not made that 'fortuitous' slip of the tongue, and if Komako had not been a passionate woman and reacted in the way she did, he might have gone on forever thinking that his treatment of her was basically blameless. After all, by the standards of his time and place, he has not done any particular wrong. She is a low-class *geisha* and he is her high-class customer; the socio-economic gap between them precludes the possibility of any serious commitment on his part – which is why, of course, this 'dilettante' allowed himself to become involved with her in the first place. In social or legalistic terms, she has no right to expect anything more than fair payment for a night's services. And Komako herself shows that she is well aware of this. But her heart is at war with her head, and she must suffer the age-old tragedy of the *geisha* who makes the mistake of falling in love with her customer. This is an all-too-familiar story, a story that has been told in both verse and prose – as the saying goes – 'for as long as stories have been told'.

But, as I have said, *Snow Country* is not really Komako's story; it is Shimamura's. And what makes it a recognizably 'modern' story is his irresolvable psychological conflict – or resolvable, as we shall see, only by a form of 'escape'. On the one hand, regardless of the unassailable 'legality' of his position, when he is finally confronted by the raw human fact of Komako's suffering, Shimamura seems to experience at long last the dawn of something like a moral intelligence: 'Shimamura felt a stabbing in his chest as he saw what the mistake had been. He lay silent, his eyes closed'.[28] And: 'Shimamura could not bring himself to follow her. She had reason to feel hurt'.[29] One cannot imagine any self-respecting womanizer in a Tokugawa *kabuki* play or a Heian romance responding with even this minimal degree of introspective guilt. But it is Shimamura's budding moral sensitivity, however tentative and fragile, his dawning ability to see the problem in its full human reality and to realize that, although his society may exonerate him, he stands condemned by the laws of a kind of Rousseauvian natural morality – the 'laws of the heart' – this is what raises the novel above its particular time and place and gives it a fair bid at universality.

Shortly after the scene of Komako's 'breakdown' and Shimamura's resultant shock there ensues his fullest 'confession' (albeit only to himself) of his own emotional sterility and narcissism, as well as of the real reason why he has allowed their relationship to continue so long: she serves as a kind of 'reverse mirror' in which this Narcissus gazes with both fascination and horror, making discoveries about himself which are obviously as new to him as they are to her. Thus he finds it hard to 'look away':

> He had stayed so long that one might wonder whether he had forgotten his wife and children. He stayed not because he could not leave Komako nor because he did not want to. He had simply fallen into the habit of waiting for those frequent visits. And the more continuous the assault became, the more he began to wonder what was lacking in him, what kept him from living as completely. He stood gazing at his own coldness, so to speak. He could not understand how she had so lost herself. All of Komako came to him, but it seemed that nothing went out from him to her. He heard in his chest, like snow piling up, the sound of Komako, an echo beating against empty walls. And he knew that he could not go on pampering himself forever.[30]

But what does he end up doing? Nothing much, of course. Because his mental state remains the alienated one all too familiar among modern intellectuals – he is the very model of what Nietzsche called a 'passive nihilist' or what nineteenth-century Russian novelists called a 'superfluous man' – he is unable to act on his new-found moral insight in any way that would be helpful to Komako. Though it may not have occurred to the 'playboys' of traditional Japanese literature to pity their women or to feel that they had wronged them, they were at least capable of loving them. Indeed, if *Snow Country* were a *kabuki* play, Shimamura, confronted by an irresolvable conflict between *giri*, the obedience he owed to the implacable laws of society, and *ninjō*, his love for Komako, might well have opted to die with her in a splendid act of *shinjū* or 'lovers' suicide'. But our modern anti-hero is incapable of that kind of total commitment – or that kind of love. He can only stand aside and watch helplessly as Komako stages her own spectacular *Götterdammerung*, all fire and madness – melodramatic perhaps, and reminiscent of grand opera and gothic romance, but the perfectly appropriate expression of her level of frustration. And, then, as if unable to bear any longer this spectacle of female passion and courage – Komako not only recklessly acting out her frustration but bravely taking up the burden of the 'mad' Yōko – he escapes 'to the stars', or, as the very last words of the novel tell us: '... the Milky Way flowed down inside him with a roar'.[31] It is a disappointing way, of course, for Shimamura to respond to the pain of his new 'moral awakening', but a way that is completely consistent with his passive character.

Nevertheless, this final scene reveals the positive as well as the negative side of Shimamura's passivity, and thereby neatly ties together in an 'end-knot' the novel's various thematic strands – especially those related to the protagonist's narcissism, aestheticism and monism – and resolves the psychological and philosophical – if not the moral – tensions which had been engendered by these. Indeed, if we look back over the novel from this perspective, we realize that the ambivalent value of Shimamura's passivity has been shown to us from the very beginning.

He is first presented to us as a voyeur, invading Yōko's privacy by stealing secret looks at her reflections in the train window, but he is a *voyeur esthétique*, with a profound capacity for being moved and even overwhelmed by beauty. On this first encounter with his aesthetic voyeurism, when the series of train-window reflections culminate in the sudden superimposition of a fire on Yōko's eye, we are told: '... Shimamura felt his chest rise at the inexpressible beauty of it'.[32]

There is, of course, something cold, detached, almost inhuman about this kind of aesthetic delectation of the human body – especially in the form of a 'disembodied' eye – and there is an ironic contrast between Shimamura's openness to beauty and his imperviousness to love. In Kierkegaard's terms, he is definitely a man who has chosen an aesthetic over an ethical lifestyle, a man who lives 'an existence in thought' rather than in reality – and, indeed, Shimamura conforms perfectly to Kierkegaard's portrait of the aesthete in *Either/Or*: narcissistic, melancholy, indolent and passive (which we may regard as one more token of the psychological truth of Kawabata's portrait).[33] Apparently he also enjoys the means which allow him to lead this self-indulgent lifestyle (as usual in Kawabata, we are never told the source of his income, but he seems to be independently wealthy). And Kawabata himself seemed to enjoy adopting, in public at least, the Wildean stance of the complete aesthete. In a talk he gave at the University of Hawaii in 1969, entitled 'The Existence and Discovery of Beauty', he begins with a long disquisition on the beauty of glasses shining in the brilliant Hawaiian sun one morning at a terrace restaurant in his hotel. Finally he remarks:

> I encountered this beauty for the first time. I thought
> that I had never seen it anywhere until then. Is not
> precisely this kind of encounter the very essence of
> literature and also of human life itself?[34]

But perhaps Kawabata was able to make what seem such exaggerated claims for aestheticism precisely because he was well aware of its latent monistic and even ethical potential. To take an obvious example, his famous ideal of 'purity', after all, has strong ethical as well as aesthetic implications. More generally, the cultivation of aesthetic experience may be regarded as one effective way of developing a monistic world view.

Perhaps the most appropriate symbol of this process, in *Snow Country* and in Kawabata's work as a whole, is found in one of his favourite images: the mirror. Like framed paintings, mirrors capture and heighten the beauty of objects or people, but, like paintings too, they also sometimes bring things together in unexpected and aesthetically pleasing juxtapositions. The mirror may thus function as an intermediary device between the monistic and aesthetic realms of experience – or as an apt symbol of their interrelationship. Remembering the way the train window had brought together Yōko's eye and a fire on the mountainside, and the way another mirror had juxtaposed Komako's red cheeks against a field of white snow, Shimamura is awed by this mysterious power of the mirror, which he regards as both natural and other-worldly:

> Always ready to give himself up to reverie, he could
> not believe that the mirror floating over the evening
> scenery and the other snowy mirror were really
> works of man. They were part of nature, and part of
> some distant world.[35]

More specifically, mirrors are 'part of nature' in that they capture and heighten nature's beauty, and 'part of some distant world' in that they reveal the transcendental realm beyond our everyday discriminative intellect, the realm of absolute unity. In Shimamura's mind, even Komako and Yōko are blended together through the power of the mirror.

Shimamura's fascination with mirrors may seem a natural concomitant of his narcissism. But this Narcissus sees far more in mirrors than his own image. Of course it is true that, like the female protagonist of *Crystal Fantasies*, who cannot bear to look at her husband directly but only at his reflection in her mirror, Shimamura too seems more comfortable with mirror-reflections than with real people. Certainly he enjoys the aesthetic distance this allows him. At the same time, though, the aesthetic experience becomes a monistic experience when, entranced by the beauty, he forgets himself for a moment and becomes one with the object of beauty. In other words, the power of the mirror is such that it enables even this narcissistic aesthete to achieve a degree of unity with the other which he could never achieve through direct relationship. In this sense Kawabata's mirrors have a psychological or spiritual as much as an aesthetic function – rather like Tantric Buddhist ritual implements. Through their almost magical agency, Shimamura's aesthetic sensitivity is heightened to a self-transcending monistic consciousness.

Kawabata's 'haiku style' itself is also an exemplary demonstration of how monism and aestheticism may work together in a close symbiotic relationship. The original haiku poets, writing under the influence of Zen Buddhist monism, realized that juxtaposition was the perfect technique for suggesting the underlying unity of all phenomena, and they exploited this potential to the full, even using such 'modernistic' devices as synesthesia, in which the unexpected blending of different orders of sensory impression produces a heightened intuition of all-encompassing unity. To take a celebrated example from the greatest haiku poet of all, Bashō:

Umi kurete	The sea darkens
Kamo no koe	And a wild duck's call
Honokani shiroshi	Is faintly white.[36]

Not surprisingly, Kawabata also uses this most 'monistic' of juxtaposing techniques throughout his work. He seemed to have a particular penchant for linking visual with auditory experiences: for instance, when Komako plays the *samisen* for Shimamura, the notes go out into the clear mountain air and seem to define 'the far, snowy peaks'.[37] And, of course, in the very final scene, the sense of Shimamura's suddenly being overwhelmed by his vision of the Milky Way is heightened by the statement that it enters him 'with a roar'.[38] But probably the most celebrated example in *Snow Country* comes when the sound of a teakettle causes Shimamura to have a vision of Komako's dancing feet, and thus convinces him that he is becoming too obsessed with her – or possessed by her (Kawabata did once describe her as a 'ghost') – and so must break free. In this passage the synesthetic impressions are quite elaborately multiplied:

> The innkeeper had lent him an old Kyoto teakettle, skillfully inlaid in silver with flowers and birds, and from it came the sound of wind in the pines. He could make out two pine breezes, as a matter of fact, a near one and a far one. Just beyond the far breeze he heard faintly the tinkling of a bell. He put his ear to the kettle and listened. Far away, where the bell tinkled on, he suddenly saw Komako's feet, tripping in time with the bell. He drew back. The time had come to leave.[39]

The monistic world view implicit in synesthesia and other techniques of juxtaposition was 'rediscovered' by Western modernists, especially the French symbolists and surrealists, for whom Baudelaire provided the credo in his seminal poem, *Correspondences*:

> Nature is a temple whose living pillars
> Speak at times a mingled language;
> Man travels there through forests of symbols
> Which watch him with a familiar look.
>
> As faraway echoes blend together
> In a dark and profound unity,
> Vast as the night and as the daylight,
> Scents, colours and sounds correspond.

As Makoto Ueda has pointed out, it was the Japanese followers of the French Symbolists who first emphasized the affinities between this 'modern' form of Western verse and the traditional Japanese *haiku* – especially as represented by Bashō – both in terms of a shared monistic vision and a common use of juxtaposing techniques to express that vision:

> According to the modern Japanese Symbolist poets, Bashō ventured deep into the forest of nature and had mystic 'correspondences' with it. He was aware, they said, of the interrelatedness of all things in the universe and tried to suggest it by Symbolist means such as synesthesia.[40]

As Ueda also points out: 'The Symbolist movement in Japanese poetry had its counterpart in the novel, in the so-called Neo-Sensualist movement that flourished in the 1920s'.[41] As I mentioned earlier, Kawabata was a leading member of this 'movement', the *Shinkankaku-ha*. Thus, here again, we must place him somewhere 'between tradition and modernity', since he seems to have imbibed his 'monistic style' as much from Western modernism as from his own literary tradition.

At any rate, whichever poetic tradition was the paramount influence in shaping Kawabata's style, whenever that style is described as 'lyrical' or 'poetic', it is important to understand the deepest sense of what this means. The usual tendency of language is to discriminate one thing from another by naming each thing as a separate entity. In this sense language is 'anti-monistic' – which is why mystics often favour silence. The language of poetry, however, tries to overcome the discriminative tendency of ordinary language through the use of such 'unitive' devices as metaphor, simile, synecdoche, synesthesia and juxtaposition. Thus, even when Kawabata writes prose, his monism leads him naturally to write in a 'poetic' style.

To return now to the particular case of Shimamura: it is important to note that his 'aesthetic moments' are the only time he achieves anything like self-transcendence, or escapes from his narcissistic ego. Thus they must be regarded as the only possible avenue of his ultimate 'salvation' – something with which Kawabata as a writer was always centrally preoccupied. It is also important to note, in this context, the close psychological affinity between aesthetic and monistic experience. Although the enjoyment of beauty may seem a completely passive process, it involves at least an act of self-surrender: one 'opens' oneself or 'gives' oneself to the object of beauty and finally 'becomes one' with it. At the deepest level, sometimes attained by artists or mystics, the subject is literally 'entranced' by the object, losing for a while all sense of separate identity in a form of ecstatic union which can only be compared to love. One can understand, then, why a 'love-starved' narcissist such as Shimamura would want to cultivate these monistic/aesthetic experiences: they afford him some of the psychological benefits of love while allowing him to maintain his 'purity' – that is, to avoid the threats to self-esteem involved in human intimacy.

At the same time, though, one should also recognize – especially since *Snow Country* is a Japanese novel – that Japanese, like other Asian, religious, philosophical and literary traditions, have long sanctioned the cultivation of this state of 'passive receptivity' to monistic/aesthetic experience as a way to encourage spiritual and even moral growth. The idea is that even the most inveterate narcissist will develop an expanded capacity for openness and self-transcendence by experiencing 'all as one', and that ultimately he or she may even extend this to other human beings.

Kawabata's taste for subtlety and ambiguity no doubt would prevent him from being very explicit about this final 'promise', but another novel inspired by a traditional monistic vision published about the same time as *Snow Country* and with an ending in some ways quite similar, spells it out quite clearly. Shiga Naoya's *A Dark Night's Passing* also ends with the monistic experience of its protagonist, Kensaku – indeed, one far more intense and elaborated than Shimamura's. But the significant fact here is that, after Kensaku has had his final experience of ecstatic union with nature on Mount Daisen, the novel's final scene shows that this erstwhile narcissist, who formerly treated his wife with coldness and even cruelty, now has developed a capacity for love which overawes even his wife:

> His gaze was like a caress. She thought she had never seen such gentleness, such love, in anyone's eyes before. She was about to say, 'Everything is all right now', but she refrained, for in the presence of such contentment and quiet, the words seemed hollow.[42]

Obviously Shimamura has not yet gone this far – in Shiga's terms, he is still at the same stage as Kensaku in his earlier experiences of union with nature, when the feeling was 'more that of being sucked in by nature than that of merging into it; and though there had been some pleasure attached to it, he had at the same time always tried to resist it, and on finding such resistance difficult, he had felt a distinct uneasiness'.[43] This sounds like a perfectly apt description of Shimamura's experience: 'being sucked in by nature', as if nature has to conspire to overcome his resistances. It is still an entirely passive experience but, nonetheless, for the Milky Way to flow 'down inside him with a roar', he must be at least an incipient monist, unusually open to experiences of this monistic/aesthetic kind.

Although it may be tempting to conclude, then, that the high monistic ideals Kawabata had once cultivated in order to confer a redemptive power upon literature have now been reduced to a mere form of escapism, it seems to me that this would be a rather simplistic reading, and one perhaps that was based too much on Western cultural values. What we might call the 'retreat to nature' has long been sanctioned by Japanese tradition, religious as well as literary, as a way of dealing with psychological suffering or seemingly irresolvable psychic problems. It is hardly surprising, then, that Kawabata uses this strategy again and again, especially in his more 'traditional' works, as a kind of *deus ex machina* to rescue his troubled male characters from their moments of duress. Furthermore, he undoubtedly means these moments of self-transcendence in nature to carry some promise of ultimate 'salvation' – although, as I have said, his aesthetic taste for subtlety and ambiguity would preclude his being overly explicit about this. Nevertheless, Shimamura's moment of 'access to the stars' is placed at the very end of the novel for a definite purpose, and I doubt that it is simply that we should label him an 'escapist'. Although his final solitary, monistic experience does nothing to resolve Komako's tragic problem, it does promise a kind of spiritual progress for Shimamura himself – along with his dawning moral awareness – and, again, we must remember that *Snow Country* is ultimately his story rather than Komako's.

CHAPTER FIVE

ELEGIES FOR A DYING TRADITION

In the wake of Japan's total and catastrophic defeat in the Pacific War, with most of the major cities levelled, the populace facing starvation and the country occupied by a foreign army for the first time in its history, the general mood of the nation seemed to favour a wholesale rejection of Japanese values and traditions. Not since the early Meiji period had there been such a general enthusiasm for Westernization and modernization and such a corresponding lack of enthusiasm for all that belonged to the country's own past. Despite his 'modernist phase' in the 1920s and early '30s, in the public mind Kawabata was by now thoroughly identified with those traditional values which seemed slated for early extinction. Though he was by no means an old man (he was still in his forties), and though he was still to write some of his greatest works, to many of the younger, more 'realistic' postwar writers, he already seemed to belong to the past. Fortunately, however, Kawabata did not succumb easily to the fashions or pressures of the moment. Perhaps we may regard this as the compensating positive aspect of his 'solipsism'. Or perhaps we should simply say that he had the confidence and maturity to go his own way.

In the literary realm, a work which may be regarded as a representative 'manifesto' of the new, iconoclastic mood was Kuwabara Takeo's essay of 1946 'debunking' the *haiku* as a 'secondary art' without any reliable standards of critical judgement, and arguing that: 'as we keep on working to rebuild our culture as well as our nation, now committed to peace, we will have to reappraise the entire tradition of haiku, going back to Matsuo Bashō'.[1] Indeed, Kuwabara had begun his essay with a sweeping condemnation not just of *haiku* but of the whole of modern Japanese literature:

> The quality of Japanese creative writing since the Meiji era is mediocre. It may be that inadequate intellectual and social awareness on the part of the writers accounts for this, but a distinctly casual attitude toward creative writing prevails among Japanese, and haiku is a prime example.[2]

Obviously Kawabata, the writer famous for his 'haiku style', would not have found such sentiments congenial. Indeed, his response to the disaster of his country's defeat was quite the opposite of an iconoclastic, anti-traditional one. Rather it may be described as gently elegiac, sorrowing over what, in that immediate postwar period, seemed to be the imminent demise of his native culture – Bashō's aesthetics along with Tōjō's militarism. No doubt he felt the sorrow of this all the more keenly because, during the war, he had reimmersed himself deeply in the Japanese classics as a consoling spiritual refuge from the drabness and misery of the life going on around him. Speaking of his feelings in the immediate postwar period, he expressed his renewed commitment to tradition in eloquent language that is itself evocative of the classics: 'The realization that I wrote in a Japanese style, and the determination to continue the traditions of Japanese beauty were not new for me, but perhaps I had to see the mountains and rivers of my country after it had been defeated before everything else could disappear'.[3]

A few years after making this determined if melancholy pronouncement, Kawabata would publish two works which, each in its different way, was a fine expression of his elegiac mood: *Thousand Cranes* (*Sembazuru*, 1950), in which the decline of the tea ceremony becomes a metaphor for a general decline of the moral atmosphere of postwar Japan, and *The Master of Go* (*Meijin*, 1954), in which the defeat of an old-style master of this traditional game becomes a metaphor for the general defeat of Japanese tradition. (One must hasten to add, however, that it would be reductive to treat either of these works as *nothing but* a cultural metaphor; they are both also complex psychological studies of particular human beings, in Kawabata's best *shinkyō shōsetsu* manner.)

From our present perspective we can readily recognize that these and other of Kawabata's postwar works performed a salutary service by reasserting, both for the Japanese themselves and for an increasingly wide international readership, the continuing value and beauty of the aesthetic, 'chrysanthemum' side of Japanese culture – now that the 'sword' side seemed so ignominiously discredited.[4] By quietly going his own way, and by refusing to follow the postwar fad of 'tradition-bashing', Kawabata achieved an impressive new stature in the postwar era, eventually becoming accepted as one of the most 'representative' Japanese writers of the period, as well as a worthy heir to the classical Japanese tradition – a distinction internationally recognized when he was awarded the Nobel Prize in 1968.

1. A Study in Ambiguity

On examining the narrative style of *Thousand Cranes* (*Sembazuru*, 1950) perhaps the first thing to strike one as distinctive is the number of sentences in the interrogative form. The narrative seems to proceed not so much from statement to statement as from question to question. These questions may be asked either by the narrative voice itself: e.g., 'Chikako did not marry. Had the birthmark then governed her whole life?'[5]; or by the characters in dialogue, as when Fumiko asks Kikuji: "why should Miss Kurimoto tell such lies?"[6]

Few of these questions are answered in any explicit or conclusive way by the text itself. This is, in fact, one thing that distinguishes this and other of Kawabata's works from the conventional Western novel. All novels raise questions – though usually not with such persistence as *Thousand Cranes*. As Roland Barthes pointed out in his study of Balzac, *S/Z*, the raising of questions is an essential part of the dynamic of any fictional narrative (or what structuralists call the 'narrative syntax'). But, as Barthes also points out, stories traditionally have always provided clear answers to the questions they raise – after keeping the reader in suspense for a certain time, of course. By not doing so, *Thousand Cranes* creates a level of ambiguity unparalleled in the conventional novel.

The first task of the novelist, after all, is to convince us of the reality of the world he invents – using all those devices which constitute what Wayne Booth called the 'rhetoric of fiction'. Thus most novelists establish a narrative voice that is authoritative and affirmative, stating their fabrications as if they were well-established facts. A good example of the power of this device may be seen in fantastic stories such as Kafka's 'Metamorphosis', which convince us of the reality of even the most surreal events because of the authority and matter-of-factness of their narrative voice. In an age, however, in which everyday reality itself seems difficult to fathom, in which there are no certainties, perhaps a more questioning or even perplexed narrative voice, uncertain of the true nature of the facts it is recounting, seems more convincingly real.

The *nouveau roman* of Robbe-Grillet and other contemporary French writers, for instance, frequently presents an incident from several different angles, and even with the introduction of contradictory data. Although this is a recent development in the West, it seems that Japanese writers have always evinced a strong sense of the ambiguous nature of reality – deriving in part, perhaps, from the Buddhist teaching of the illusoriness of the phenomenal world. Certainly the *Tale of Genji* is pervaded by this sense.

And a conspicuous example of its presence in a modern work would be Akutagawa's 'In a Grove' (*Yabu no naka*, 1922), the story on which Kurosawa Akira based his celebrated film, *Rashōmon*, a story which graphically demonstrates a 'perspectivist' view of reality, to use Nietzsche's term, by showing how the same incident may be interpreted by different people in very different, even contrary ways.

The sense of ambiguity which Kawabata creates in *Thousand Cranes*, however, does not serve merely to heighten the sense of reality. It is not merely a rhetorical device; it pervades the novel to its thematic core. To begin with, this ambiguity reflects the state of mind of the central character, Kikuji. The novel opens with a depiction of his indecisiveness: he cannot make up his mind whether or not to attend Kurimoto's *chakai* (tea ceremony). The impression of Kikuji as an irresolute, even neurotic young man emerges more clearly as the novel progresses: he seems to be more the seduced than the seducer in his relations with Mrs. Ōta, and similarly he allows himself to be dictated to by Kurimoto. Throughout the novel he is in a continual state of puzzlement over the behaviour of the three main female characters and, more seriously, he seems to find difficulty even in understanding his own behaviour – for instance, when he finds himself acting in a rather cruel fashion towards Mrs. Ōta.

Although *Thousand Cranes* is written in the third person and is not explicitly autobiographical, like most other Kawabata novels it resembles a *shishōsetsu* (literally, 'I-novel') in that the whole reality of its world seems to be filtered through the consciousness of its central character. Thus the ambiguity at the core of his consciousness pervades this entire world.

With the possible exception of Kurimoto, for instance, none of the characters in this novel has a clear-cut identity of his or her own. For the three main female characters, Kikuji serves as a kind of substitute for his late father, who had played an important role in all their lives – and even Kikuji admits that there is much of his father in him. For Kikuji himself, Fumiko serves as a substitute for her dead mother. Even Kurimoto and Mrs. Ōta seem to be more archetypes than individual human beings: Kurimoto the archetypal jilted woman, full of venom, ambiguous even in her sexuality; and Mrs. Ōta, by way of contrast, the equally archetypal woman as pure sexual being, totally passive and unresisting. For Kikuji, in fact, Mrs. Ōta seems to belong to some primeval world predating Creation in which everything is ambiguously mixed and all boundaries are blurred:

> He could ask himself if she was human. If she was
> prehuman, or again if she was the last woman in the
> human race. He could imagine her in this other
> world, making no distinction between her dead
> husband and Kikuji's father and Kikuji.[7]

But Mrs. Ōta's world is not 'other' than the world of the novel itself, where even the boundaries between the human and the nonhuman are blurred: in the final chapter, the Shino and the Karatsu tea bowls vividly and eerily take on the presence of Fumiko's mother and Kikuji's father. So much so, in fact, that Kikuji concludes that there could have been nothing 'unclean' in Mrs. Ōta, because she was as much an aesthetic 'master-piece' as the tea bowl.[8] In a typically Kawabataesque way, this ambiguous 'blurring of boundaries' is given its objective correlative even in the natural world of the novel, as in this scene from the last chapter:

> He looked out toward the cottage. In front of it there
> was a large oleander, heavy with blossoms, a vague
> white blur. For the rest, the night was so dark that he
> had trouble following the line between trees and
> sky.[9]

Of course, it is not enough to explain away a novel's ambiguity merely by saying that it reflects the state of mind of the central character. Whenever questions are raised, our minds naturally seek answers to them. This, in fact, may be seen as another major function of the ambiguity in *Thousand Cranes*: that it invites us to delve beneath the surface of the action to try to understand the seemingly inexplicable behaviour of the characters. Kawabata is, after all, the least explicit of writers – he works more by vague hints and ambiguous symbols than by direct statement. Like Hemingway, he believes in the power of 'the thing left out'. What meaning, then, are we to extract from the tangle of ambiguities that forms the world of *Thousand Cranes*?

Like many of the protagonists in Kawabata's other novels, Kikuji has not only an indistinct self-image, he also has a very unflattering one. According to the narrator, in fact, Kurimoto appealed to the masochistic streak in him because everything she said 'went with the self-loathing that had become a part of Kikuji's nature'.[10] From the *Dancing Girl of Izu* on, Kawabata's self-loathing heroes are usually 'purified' by coming into contact with a beautiful and innocent young girl. *Thousand Cranes* is interesting within the context of Kawabata's works in that the woman who performs this 'purifying' role is neither young nor innocent. Although the familiar Kawabata heroine does appear peripherally in the figure of Yukiko, it is the jaded Mrs. Ōta that Kikuji gravitates towards. It is as if Kikuji has chosen to cleanse himself with dirt, as certain animals do. Or, as the narrator remarks after Kikuji has made love to Mrs. Ōta's daughter: 'It was as if an addict had been freed of his addiction by taking the ultimate dose of a drug'.[11] Kikuji must be 'purified' in this peculiar way because of the peculiar nature of his 'defilement'.

To understand this more fully perhaps we should consult the father of psychoanalysis, since *Thousand Cranes*, along with *Crystal Fantasies* though in quite a different way, is one of Kawabata's most convincingly 'Freudian' stories: Freud himself, in fact, movingly described how his own psychic crisis was resolved only when he could bring himself to 'forgive' and to accept his own father. Kikuji's complex is not necessarily Oedipal – the principal woman involved is his father's mistress (who, nonetheless, could be regarded as a 'substitute' mother) – but the childhood memory that is given a key place in the novel clearly indicates that Kikuji too finds it difficult to forgive and to accept his father. Kikuji's resentment seems to be based as much on aesthetic as on moral grounds: he is horrified that his father could have made love to such a physically repulsive woman as Kurimoto, with the hairy birthmark on her breast (for instance, he imagines his father 'biting' on it). As Kikuji comes to recognize, however, in rejecting his father he is rejecting himself, since there is so much of his father in him. Thus he is drawn irresistibly to his father's old world – to Kurimoto's tea ceremonies and to Mrs. Ōta and her daughter – in an effort, one might say, to 'lay' his father's ghost.

Especially by making love to Mrs. Ōta, who seems hardly able to distinguish between him and his father, Kikuji is able to achieve an identification with his father which frees him from his emasculating father/self-hatred: 'He felt as if he had for the first time known woman, and as if for the first time he had known himself as a man. It was an extraordinary awakening'.[12] And, after even further lovemaking: 'he felt that the recesses of his mind had been washed clean'.[13] This is a fascinating twist on the usual procedure of the narcissistic Kawabata male, who seeks to 'purify' himself through the love of a virginal girl.

The story does not end there, however. There are complications – including the question of how much guilt arises from a relationship which is, after all – at least on a psychological level – close to incestuous. Mrs. Ōta's suicide, though, seems to free

145

Kikuji to live happily ever after with a perfect substitute, her daughter. But Fumiko has problems of her own: she has the same kind of guilt-tinged, resentful feelings towards her mother as Kikuji had towards his father. Nor does she relish the idea of serving as a substitute for her mother. This seems to be the message behind her breaking the Shino cup that is so imbued with her mother's presence – she wants Kikuji to 'love her for herself alone' (and not as her mother's heir). With the ghosts of his father and her mother thus duly exorcised, it seems that the novel might well have ended propitiously with a wedding. And indeed, Kawabata did later write a sequel along those lines.[14]

But, as it stands, the novel ends on a much more ambiguous (and so more interesting?) note. Perhaps Kawabata could not quite bring himself to believe in salvation through a woman who was not young, beautiful and virginal. At any rate, the fact that Kikuji is left alone and miserable at the end seems to lead us back to a suspicion that has been hinted at throughout the novel: namely, that it was Mrs. Ōta, not Kurimoto, who represented the real danger to Kikuji by drawing him away, as Kurimoto claimed, from Yukiko, where his real salvation lay. It is the lost Yukiko, after all, who is the lady of the 'thousand cranes'. This, perhaps, is the novel's ultimate ambiguity.

2. The Artist as Go-Player

Throughout *The Master of Go*, Kawabata maintains a steady level of dramatic tension. The 'match of the century' between Shūsai, the old master, and Ōtake, his young challenger, is presented as a 'life-and-death' affair from the very first chapter – we are told, in fact, that: 'One may say that in the end the match took the Master's life. He never quite recovered, and in upwards of a year he was dead'.[15] Kawabata continually heightens the tension by his vivid depiction of the almost incredible intensity of concentration required of the two master *go* players – the toll of which on Ōtake's nerves, for instance, is revealed by his frequent trips to the toilet – and by his equally vivid depiction of the cloistered, claustrophobic atmosphere of a *go* tournament which lasts almost half a year, and in which the players are 'sealed' in the close quarters of a Japanese inn.

The Master himself, however, seems to remain calm and detached in this pressure-cooker atmosphere – in keeping, of course, with the highest spiritual ideals of the tradition he represents. He is thus a figure of tremendous dignity, to whom our hearts very easily and naturally go out. And yet . . . .

There is, it seems, a false note here. Towards the end of the novel a rather surprising scene occurs in which the Master appears to succumb finally to all the pressure; not only does he lose his temper but he does so, according to the narrator, for no ultimately justifiable reason: 'He was angry at the time because the move [Ōtake's move No.121] was so unexpected. In his anger he unjustly questioned Ōtake's motives'.[16]

Should we then view the Master's sudden outburst as jarringly out-of-character – and as inconsistent with Kawabata's idealization of him as a 'culture hero'? Or is it that we do not perceive the Master's true character until this moment, so that the scene serves as a kind of 'denouement' or 'anticlimax' to all the previous 'buildup' of the Master as a heroic figure, the novel then turning out to be a sort of ironic satire on traditional cultural ideals?

The true answer, I think, is rather more complex than either of these two extremes, but to find it we must look more closely at the way Kawabata develops the character of the Master through the course of the novel. What we discover when we do so is that, almost from the beginning, the character we are presented with is split into two distinct and in some ways contradictory figures: namely, the Master as he is when he sits before the *go* board and as he is when he is away from the board.

Quite early in the novel, the narrator tells us that the Master 'seemed to grow larger when he seated himself before the *go* board'.[17] There is an elaboration of this theme somewhat later when the narrator describes his feeling that he is witnessing some kind of profound spiritual transformation as the Master readies himself to play:

> I wondered if I was witness to the workings of the Master's soul as, all unconsciously, it received its inspiration, was host to the afflatus. Or was I watching a passage to enlightenment as the soul threw off all sense of identity and the fires of combat were quenched? Was it what had made 'the invincible Master'?[18]

We are told in the same chapter that a certain clairvoyant had once told Ōtake that 'the proper method' for winning at *go* was to 'lose all awareness of self while awaiting an adversary's play'.[19] The fact that the Master does attain to something of this state while playing is shown later by his amazing endurance of the pain caused by his heart condition: 'Lost in the game, the Master seemed to give over custody of his physical self ....

Even during the great debate over the effects of his illness upon the game, the Master himself had sat absently apart, as if it did not concern him'.[20] By a startling contrast typical of Kawabata's technique, shortly after this statement we are presented with a picture of the two distraught wives, who are busily ministering to their hard-playing husbands: 'They looked ... like women who no longer sought to hide their egoism'.[21]

The Master's temporary 'egolessness' is further emphasized by contrast with Ōtake's restlessness: 'the Master and Ōtake presented a complete contrast, quiet against constant motion, nervelessness against nervous tension'.[22] It is also revealed, of course, in his style of play, which seems to flow naturally and spontaneously, as if directed by a force greater than his own individual self. The fact that Ōtake takes so much longer than the Master to make his moves seems to suggest that his whole approach to the game is, by contrast, deliberate and calculating – in other words, overly cerebral.

Away from the *go* board, however, the Master cuts quite a different figure, an almost pathetic one. As his doctor remarks:

> 'He has a body like an undernourished child ....
> There's no flesh at all on his calves. You wonder how
> he manages to carry himself. I can't prescribe
> medicine in ordinary doses. I have to give him what
> a thirteen- or fourteen-year-old might take'.[23]

This lack of physical substance on the part of the Master gives him an air of ethereal, almost ghost-like unreality which enables Kawabata to identify him all the more with a bygone culture and to present him as a living embodiment of such traditional Japanese sentiments and aesthetic values as *mono no aware* and *yūgen* (that mixture of 'beauty and sadness', to use Kawabata's words, or, in the more specific definition of Makoto Ueda, that beauty which results 'when refinement is combined with pathos'.[24]) The narrator's response to the sight of the diminutive figure of the Master walking unsteadily through the garden of the inn is an excellent example of this:

> His body, bent forward from the hips, was perfectly
> straight, making his legs seem all the more unreli-
> able. From below the thicket of dwarf bamboo,
> along the main road, came a sound of water down a
> narrow ditch. Nothing more – and yet the retreating
> figure of the Master somehow brought tears to my
> eyes. I was profoundly moved, for reasons I do not
> myself understand. In that figure walking absently

from the game there was the still sadness of another world. The Master seemed like a relic left behind by Meiji.[25]

Nevertheless, such dignified pathos is not the only sentiment evoked by the figure of the Master as he is away from the *go* board – because his body is not his only child-like feature. One would, of course, expect there to be something child-like about a man who has devoted his entire life to playing games; but in the Master's case this is taken to the extreme by his total addiction to games – by the way, for instance, in which he tries to cajole everyone into playing other games with him in between the sessions of *go*.

In one scene the narrator is touched by the way in which the Master reacts when he is told there are not enough people left to play mahjongg with him:

'Now we'll have a game of mahjongg', he said, as if scarcely able to await the outcome. Since I did not know mahjongg, however, they were one man short.
'Mr. Kumé?' said the Master.
'Mr. Kumé is seeing the doctor back to Tokyo'.
'Mr. Iwamoto?'
'He's gone back too'.
'Gone back', echoed the Master weakly. I found his disappointment most touching.[26]

The Master is here for all the world like a forlorn child left alone with no-one to play with. And the narrator states the point more explicitly later: 'The Master was like a starved urchin in his appetite for games'.[27]

There is something of the 'spoiled child' too in the Master's lack of manners and in his sometimes arbitrary and irascible behaviour. We are told that he rarely thanks anyone or excuses himself – these functions are performed by his wife on his behalf. Then again, problems are caused several times by the Master's attempts to violate the rules which had been devised to 'keep his old-fashioned willfulness under control, to deny him a special status'.[28] But he misbehaves like this only when he is away from the *go* board. When the 'Master lost himself in a game ... his waywardness left him'.[29]

In the other words, Kawabata's 'idealization' of the Master extends only to the dignified figure transformed momentarily by his art who sits before the *go* board – and not to the rather pathetic, vulnerable, infantile and narcissistic figure the Master becomes away from it. Thus the important point about the Master's outburst towards the end of the novel is that it occurs when he is a away from the board, and so is not out of character. Kawabata emphasizes this point twice in the novel: when he first refers to the incident in Chapter 20, he stresses that, although the Master expressed indignation at Ōtake's 'very curious play' during the recess: 'Seated before the board, however, he had not let his face reveal a trace of his feelings'.[30] And when the incident is more fully treated in Chapter 38, Kawabata again stresses: 'I had not been aware, at the moment of play, that the Master was so angry and so disappointed as to consider forfeiting the match. There was no sign of emotion on his face or in his manner *as he sat at the board*'.(my emphasis)[31] Only if the Master would have betrayed his anger while at the board would he have betrayed Kawabata's ideal of him.

What is the significance, then, of this dichotomy in the Master's character? I would suggest that a good part of the thematic structure of the novel is built upon the answer to this question.

In speaking of the photographs he took of the dead Master's face, Kawabata remarks: 'There was something unreal about the pictures, which may have come from the face, the ultimate in tragedy, of a man so disciplined in an art that he had lost the better part of reality. Perhaps I had photographed the face of a man meant from the outset for martyrdom to art'.[32]

We are given here a clear sense of the high price the Master has paid to achieve his mastery. Chess Master Bobby Fisher has been quoted as saying that he feels real only when he is playing chess. Obviously much the same is true of the Master of *go*. This is the real reason why he is such an addict of games, and why he seems to dwindle in size when he is away from the board. Away from the board, in fact, he seems hardly a real person. He has about him always an air of 'vagueness', as if he is not quite present; he is like 'some rarefied spirit floating over a void'.[33] His obsessive devotion to his art makes him 'forever true and clean', like the self-sacrificing virgins in Kawabata's other works – but this is a double-edged sword.[34] The art seems literally to suck the life-blood out of him. Comparing him to the writer, Naoki Sanjūgō, who 'wrote himself to death', the narrator remarks that both men were 'ghostlike' in their last days.[35] And this theme of art as a kind of blood-sucking vampire is reiterated two pages later when the narrator says of the Master's non-stop playing: 'It was less as if he were playing to dispel gloom or beguile tedium than as if he were giving himself up to the fangs of gaming devils'.[36] Thus the force that the Master gives himself up to is as much destructive as creative. Ultimately, in fact, it leads to his martyrdom. It is to emphasize this very point that Kawabata begins the novel with the Master's death. This reversal of the normal narrative sequence may lessen the drama but it adds to the pathos. Our knowledge, from the beginning, that the match being described is going to 'take the Master's life' makes his obsessive devotion to his art seem all the more tragic.

By equating the Master with the writer Naoki Sanjūgō, the narrator also makes it clear that this *go*-player is to be regarded as an artist in the full sense of the word. Indeed, one of the real achievements of the novel is that it succeeds in convincing us that *go* is a true art-form, capable of as much expressive range as any other complex art. At one point, for instance, Ōtake style of playing is characterized by another *go* Master, Iwamoto, as 'dark':

> 'There are bright and dark in Go?' [the narrator asks him.]
> 'There are indeed. A game takes on its own shading. There's something very cheerless about Ōtaké's. Something dark. Bright and dark have nothing to do with winning and losing. I'm not saying that Ōtaké game is any the worse for it'.[37]

Elucidating this purely aesthetic side of *go* further, the narrator himself remarks:

> I had not thought the Black game against the Master especially cheerful. There was something oppressive about it, something that seemed to push up from deep within, like a strangled cry. Concentrated power was on a collision course, one looked in vain for a free and natural flow. The opening moves had been heavy and a sort of inexorable gnawing had followed.[38]

By way of contrast, the Master's style of play does seem to maintain a 'free and natural flow'. In fact, the Master himself, during his 'outburst', draws attention to the great gulf that separates his own aesthetic of *go* from Ōtake's. His objections to Ōtake's move 121 seem to be primarily aesthetic: '"The match is over!"' he says, '"Mr. Ōtake ruined it with that sealed play. It was like smearing ink over the picture we had painted"'.[39] And the narrator goes on to explain in greater detail:

The Master had put the match together as a work of art. It was as if the work, likened to a painting, were smeared black at the moment of highest tension. That play of black upon white, white upon black, has the intent and takes the forms of creative art. It has a flow of the spirit and a harmony as of music. Everything is lost when suddenly a false note is struck, or one party in a duet suddenly launches forth on an eccentric flight of his own. A masterpiece of a game can be ruined by insensitivity to the feelings of an adversary. That Black 121 having been a source of wonder and surprise and doubt and suspicion for us all, its effect in cutting the flow and harmony of the game cannot be denied.[40]

But the narrator goes further than this: he claims more for *go* than even the status of an 'art'. After his encounter with the foreigner on the train (in Chapter 28), he is moved to identify *go* with the very soul of Japanese culture, on a level with the tea ceremony and the *nō* drama. The fact that the foreigner loses to him 'so effortlessly' causes him to reflect that:

> ... perhaps the conclusion might be valid ... that Western *go* is wanting in spirit. The Oriental game has gone beyond game and test of strength and become a way of art. It has about it a certain Oriental mystery and nobility. The 'Honnimbō' of Honnimbō Shūsai is the name of a cell at the Jakkōji Temple in Kyoto, and Shūsai the Master had himself taken holy orders.[41]

On the always thorny question of how 'Japanese' any art can be that was originally imported from China, the narrator (who, we may assume, voices Kawabata's own cultural nationalism fairly directly[42]) is in this case quite unequivocal:

> Go came to Japan from China. Real Go, however, developed in Japan. The art of Go in China, now and three hundred years ago, does not bear comparison with that in Japan. Go was elevated and deepened by the Japanese .... It is clear that in Go the Japanese spirit has transcended the merely imported and derivative ....
> Had Go, like the Nō drama and the tea ceremony, sunk deeper and deeper into the recesses of a strange Japanese tradition?[43]

Now we can begin to see the true dimensions of the Master as a symbolic figure, and the tragic meaning of the dichotomy in his nature, and of his final defeat and death. The contest between the Master and Ōtake is not merely a clash between two men but between two cultures – the deeply 'spiritual', highly aesthetic, nature-based culture of old Japan, represented by the Master, and the over-intellectualized, scientific, artificial culture that has now become world-wide, and is personified in the high-strung, aggressive, rule-obsessed Ōtake. The death of the Master is the death of the old culture, so that the novel certainly may be seen on one level as Kawabata's elegy for traditional Japan.

Nevertheless, there is another, and perhaps even more important, level to the novel, and this has to do with the dichotomy I have described in the Master's character. Because the Master is a symbolic figure, a symbol of the artist in particular as of traditional culture in general, the tragic dichotomy of his character – or, in other words, his martyrdom to his art – does not belong to him alone but suggests the fate of all artists. To become, like the Master of *go*, 'some rarefied spirit floating over a void' is the inevitable price anyone must pay who is 'so disciplined in an art he has lost the better part of reality'. And this, as the narrator of *The Master of Go* tells us, is the 'ultimate in tragedy'.[44]

CHAPTER SIX

TIME AND ANTI-TIME

1. Soundings in Time

It may be said that, in one way or another, all novels must come to terms with the problem of time, since the novel genre has evolved traditionally as the art of time *par excellence* – or, at least, the art of temporal mimesis. This is not merely a matter of length, although obviously by virtue of its length a novel may represent the passage of time more convincingly than, say, a sonnet or a *haiku*. But the epic poem is also a lengthy form, yet it cannot be said to be concerned with time in the same sense as is the traditional novel. Dealing as it does with mythic figures and events, the epic has a timeless quality which is beyond the scope of the novel as we usually know it. Even a novel such as James Joyce's *Ulysses* (1922), which borrows an epic framework, is still far more grounded than any epic in a particular time and place: quite specifically, the Dublin of 16 June 1904. *Ulysses*, in fact, also suggests another point: the span of time represented even by a lengthy novel need not be long – in this case it is barely sixteen hours. But what a sense we are given of the passing of those hours – a moment-by-moment experience of the physical presence, the sights, sounds and smells of that Dublin day. It is exactly in this that the novel has excelled as the quintessentially 'realistic' genre; it has given us as no other form has a sense of time as we all experience it in our everyday lives, not the immemorial time of gods and heroes but the ordinary quotidian time of men for whom 'time is money', the eighteenth-century merchants (and their wives) who were the first readers of modern 'realistic' novels.

A certain 'realistic' time-consciousness, then, may be regarded as inherent in the novel-form itself as it has existed since the eighteenth century. Nevertheless, it is equally obvious that in the twentieth century the novel has become conscious of its own time-bound nature to an unprecedented degree and has even shown signs of rebellion against this supposedly *sui generis* aspect of its nature. Certainly there can be few serious novels today which take as their narrative principle the progressive unfolding of a straightforward chronological time-span, without the intervention of at least a few unexpected 'flash-backs'. And, from early in the century, novels have appeared which consciously confront the problem of time as one of their central themes and do so with an originality which is manifest not only on a thematic but also on a formal, technical level, in a way that promised to revolutionize the very form of the novel itself. I have already mentioned Joyce: his *Ulysses* and especially his *Finnegans Wake (1939)* sought to raise the novel out of its bondage to quotidian time and up to the timeless level of myth – to achieve what Erich Auerbach calls the 'symbolic omnitemporality of an event'.[1] In a very different way, Marcel Proust's *In Search of Lost Time (A la Recherche du temps perdu,* 1913–27), achieves a sense of timelessness, as we shall see, by introducing the narrator's semi-mystical experiences of time-transcendence through what he calls 'involuntary memory'. With its own masterly and highly original treatment of the theme of time, Kawabata's *The Sound of the Mountain (Yama no oto,* 1954), generally regarded as the greatest of his works, seems by no means out of place among these great Western modernist novels.

In his *Time and the Novel*, A.A. Mendilow sees this preoccupation of modern novelists with time as part of the general 'time-obsession of the twentieth century', brought on in particular by the rapid pace of change of modern life, which tends to induce a strong sense of transiency.[2] He also quotes Oswald Spengler to the effect that this 'sense of the logic of time', this view of life 'not as things-become, but as things-becoming', is a distinctive product of Western civilization, since the civilizations of the East, according to Spengler, change at such an imperceptible pace that they are unable to develop much sense of historical time.[3] Spengler was aware that, even by his day, Japan had gone through more changes in less time than probably any other modern nation, but he tried to evade the challenge this posed to his Eurocentrism by claiming that Japan must now be regarded not as an Asian country but as merely an adjunct to Western civilization.[4]

Although some Japanese nationalists might gladly accept this dissociation of their country from the Asian mainland, the fact is that there has been a strong sense of time in Japanese culture from the beginning, and it derives largely from a pan-Asian influence: Buddhism. The sense of transiency which suffuses *The Tale of Genji, The Tale of the Heike,* medieval Japanese poetry, the Nō plays and much other Japanese literature comes from a sensitivity to passing time of an intensity rarely seen in Western literature, and certainly this has the sanction if not the inspiration of Buddhism behind it. If, as Lionel Trilling has claimed, our sense of time has changed dramatically since the nineteenth century, so that we no longer seem to have the leisure, for instance, to write lengthy journals and letters, then this is a phenomenon by no means confined to the West alone.[5] A common complaint heard among elderly Japanese, for example, is that the younger generation no longer seems to have the time for all the polite expressions that were current in the pre-war language. At any rate, the idea that Asians have no sense of time seems about as respectable now as another notion popular in Spengler's Germany: that Jews could not see the sun. Whether there are, however, cultural differences in the sense of time seems to me quite a legitimate question, and one which obviously has relevance to any comparison of a Japanese and a Western novelist's treatment of time.

Besides being regarded as a symptom of the *Zeitgeist*, in a purely literary context the obsession of modern novelists with time may also be seen as part of the increasing subjectification or inward-turning of the novel since the late nineteenth century (say, from Henry James on), a movement that has been well charted by Leon Edel, for one, in his *Modern Psychological Novel*.[6] The time-structure of the traditional novel was to some extent a 'given': since its intention was to project an 'objective' image of man in society, the established social rituals provided it with a ready-made 'time-table'. A novel such as *David Copperfield*, for instance, could achieve a very neat structure, with a clearly defined beginning, middle and end, simply by following its hero in strict chronological order from his birth and christening on to his school days and marriage and up to his successful career as a writer in middle-age. Similarly, in *Nicholas Nickleby*, as in so many Victorian novels, the hero's conflicts – and the novel – are all brought to a satisfying conclusion with his marriage. For the hero of a modern novel, needless to say, marriage is likely to be just the beginning of his problems! At any rate, once the novel's focus shifted from the central character's social life to his or her interior life, there could be no simple conformity to chronological time. The so-called stream of consciousness is not an orderly canal running in a straight line from past to present to future; it is rather a meandering river wandering at random through the total landscape of time.

In their struggle with temporal problems, then, both *The Sound of the Mountain* and *In Search of Lost Time* may be placed in the same general historical and literary context, despite the fact that they were written more than a quarter of a century apart. But this alone seems hardly enough to promise a fruitful comparison. Are there any affinities of more depth or detail? At first glance, one might not think so. The discrepancies between them are all too obvious – to begin with, in terms of sheer bulk. Proust's *magnum opus* is actually seven novels in one, a total of more than three thousand pages in the standard edition in English. Kawabata's is a work of more modest proportions – an average-sized novel, one might say, less than one-tenth the length of Proust's.

Such considerations of mere size may seem irrelevant but, in this case, they do have some bearing on a matter of more importance: the very different styles of the two authors, and the different aesthetic values embodied in their styles. Kawabata may be described as an intuitive and elliptical writer; he leaves much unstated, and even his statements are often only hints or half-questions, so that his style is pervaded by an air of mystery and ambiguity. In this, of course, he is very much a writer in the Japanese tradition, in which a certain subtle suggestiveness or indirection is usually valued over explicit statement or rational argument.

Proust, on his part, is as quintessentially French in style as Kawabata is Japanese. If Kawabata's style achieves its ultimate crystallization when it approaches, as it often does, the imagistic purity of *haiku*, then Proust's style seems to attain its ideal form when it achieves the witty lucidity of an aphorism. As the many quotations from his work in the *Oxford Book of Aphorisms* proves, Proust is one of the greatest aphorists of our century, a worthy successor of Montaigne, Pascal and La Rochefoucauld. It seems ironic now that certain Western interpreters of Japanese literature in the nineteenth century dismissed *haiku* on the grounds that they were mere aphorisms. These interpreters were English, of course, rather than French (otherwise they would not have taken the aphorism so lightly), but the point is that today the two forms seem to us in some sense opposites: the play of images versus the play of ideas. Certainly when we compare the two modern novels based on these stylistic ideals, the contrast seems great. And nowhere does it seem greater, as we shall see, than in the way in which each author deals with the time-related epiphanies of his central character.

In a work of art, of course, considerations of style are no small matter, and it is not my intention to downplay the difference in aesthetic effect between a Japanese '*haiku* novel',

The Sound of the Mountain, and a French 'aphoristic novel', *In Search of Lost Time*. One feels that it is rather like comparing Ginkakuji, the Temple of the Silver Pavilion in Kyoto, with Chartres Cathedral – or *sushi* and pickled ginger with, say, Chateaubriand steak in *sauce béarnaise*. The aesthetic pleasure afforded by the one experience seems almost of a different order than that afforded by the other. Nevertheless, despite the best efforts of Flaubert and his followers, no novel yet written is pure style; making use, as it does, of the most 'vulgar' of artistic media, language, which is so much less reducible to pure abstraction than sound, line or colour, it must have reference, willy-nilly, to some recognizable dimension of meaning. And it is in this dimension, that of plot and theme, that the two novels have some interesting affinities, made all the more striking by their stylistic discrepancies.

The plot-structure of both works, once unraveled from its reams of complications, is essentially a simple one. In fact, it may be regarded as one of the archetypal plots of literature: a hero is presented who suffers from a certain problem, and the story is of how that problem is resolved. Comparing the two novels, one finds that there are strong affinities between them on this fundamental level – both in the nature of their basic problem and in the way it is resolved. Both Kawabata's Shingo and Proust's Marcel are aging men confronted in very real terms by the problem of time: when they look to the past, they see a happiness which seems irretrievably lost; when they look to the present, they see the disappointment of all their hopes; when they look to the future, they see nothing but their own imminent death. What both characters fear is not so much death itself as the fact that they must die as frustrated men. Thus, if only they can overcome this sense of frustration, perhaps they will be able to confront death with relative equanimity. Herein lies the basic dynamic of both novels, what might be called the 'anti-time' tension which impels the central character towards his 'search for lost time' and, ultimately, towards a form of time-transcendence. But, before advancing any further with this general argument, I would like to look at the two works more closely, with the above-mentioned plot-structure in mind.

One significant difference is immediately apparent in the way the two authors order this basic plot-structure in the temporal context of the novel itself: unlike his earlier practice in novels such as *Snow Country*, Kawabata here arranges the plot in a simple chronological way; Proust, on the other hand, submits it to some complex reversals. That is to say, at the very beginning of Kawabata's novel we are introduced to the problem of Shingo's *present* situation: by the end of the first chapter we have learnt that he is an aging man suffering from loss of memory, dissatisfied with his wife and son, filled with longings for his dead sister-in-law and frightened by his own approaching death. The rest of the novel will show us how he confronts and ultimately resolves these problems; although there are a number of excursions into the past via Shingo's memories and dreams, the novel unfolds basically in a forward-moving, chronological progression. Proust's novel, on the other hand, from its very first sentence, plunges us immediately into the reminiscences of the central character: 'For a long time I used to go to bed early'.[7] We do not discover until almost the end of this vast enterprise what is Marcel's *present* situation and why it impels him to undertake his long journey into the past.

There are several literary motives behind Proust's strategy here. Firstly, by being immersed immediately in Marcel's memories we are given a strong sense of the 'subjectivity' of the narrative point-of-view. Unlike *The Sound of the Mountain, In Search of Lost Time* is written in the first person and derives much of its power from seeming to involve the reader in a very intimate way in the labyrinthine meanderings of Marcel's consciousness. Secondly, Proust learned from John Ruskin, whose works he translated into French, the dramatic effectiveness of 'delayed revelations', of keeping the reader in suspense as to one's main point until the end. But, thirdly and most importantly, the delayed revelation intensifies the sense of 'search' which is the central motif of the entire work – as we shall see, neither the reader nor Marcel knows until the penultimate phase of the novel what is about to become of him in this 'present' time. For there is one further complication in the time-structure of Proust's novel: once we have, so to speak, caught up to Marcel's present, we follow him then into his future, a future in which he makes his great discovery regarding time and self by the light of which his view of everything that has gone before is radically transformed.

At any rate, when finally we do discover Marcel's 'present situation', he is an aging and not very healthy man who is sorely disillusioned with his life and filled with despair at the thought of his approaching death. Marcel differs from Shingo in that he has attained most of what he desired in his youth: in particular, he has had love affairs with glamorous women and has satisfied his own profound snobbery by climbing high in Parisian society. But his success has left him with only a bitter taste in middle age; he has become convinced of the hollowness of

159

aristocracy and even of love. In this sense, Marcel may be described as an embittered cynic, forming a stark contrast with Shingo, who is something of a romantic in his continued longing for his lost love, the ideal of his youth.

Nevertheless, Marcel also has harboured one desire since his youth which is as yet still unrealized – his desire to be a writer – and this is the most important one of all because, unless it is achieved, he feels that his life will have been meaningless. Thus, like Shingo, he is confronted by the prospect of dying a frustrated man – like Shingo, he has not yet 'climbed Mount Fuji'. To both characters time therefore appears as the enemy, a ruthless force rushing them headlong away from the happiness they knew in youth and towards the frightening abyss of death.

It is in the ways the two protagonists deal with their similar predicaments that we have, I think, the most interesting and fruitful grounds for comparison of the two works. People who are told by their doctors that they have only a short time to live are said to go through several fairly predictable stages of reaction: from shocked disbelief to fear to anger and, finally, to resignation and even acceptance. This basic pattern, from resistance to resignation, may also be seen in the reactions of Shingo and Marcel to the 'time-problem' which confronts them: both attempt the seemingly impossible task of going against the natural flow of time, and even achieve some degree of success in this, a success which, in turn, seems to enable them both finally to accept the inevitable.

Despite their different time-schemes, both novels have important scenes early on which serve to announce the 'time-problem' in a suspenseful way – that is, they surround the problem with an air of mystery. Since both works are rather lacking in dramatic events by the standards of the traditional novel, this suspense obviously works to their advantage. In this sense, they may be regarded as 'mystery novels', the mystery to be solved being the problem of time. Something may be learned by a comparison of the two scenes in which the 'mystery' is first presented.

The scenes occur, respectively, in the first chapter of *The Sound of the Mountain*, when Shingo rises from bed and hears the sound of the mountain from which the novel derives its name, and in the 'Overture' to *In Search of Lost Time*, when Marcel experiences rapture on tasting a morsel of cake soaked in tea. Although the two scenes seem diametrically opposite in emotional tone – Shingo's fear versus Marcel's rapture – they do have some significant points in common. Firstly, in both cases the protagonist's state of mind immediately prior to the

experience is characterized by a certain world-weariness:
Shingo, we are told, is 'not in good spirits' tonight; he feels
something close to disgust for his aged wife asleep beside him:
'only when she snored did he reach out to touch her'.[8] He gets
up and opens the shutter to the garden outside, as if trying to
escape the oppressiveness of so much mundane reality – the
reality of time made manifest in his wife's body.

Marcel's preliminary mood is quite similar: he has been out
walking on a cold winter's day and he is 'dispirited after a
dreary day with the prospect of a depressing morrow'.[9] More
importantly, he tells us that: 'Many years had elapsed during
which nothing of Combray ... had any existence for me'.[10] In
other words, the whole paradisal world of his childhood is now
dead to him, and with it all the childhood ideals which seemed
to make life worth living. Thus, like Shingo, he is shown to be
suffering the consequences of the passage of time, though as
manifested in himself rather than in his wife. In this way both
authors skillfully prepare us for the experiences soon to come.

The second thing these two scenes have in common is the
aforementioned sense of mystery which surrounds the experiences. In both cases, in fact, we must distinguish between the
experience itself, which is essentially inexplicable, and the
protagonist's interpretation of it. Both experiences, in their
irreducible mystery, are apt symbols of the ineffable mystery of
time itself. And both protagonists do interpret them in terms
relevant to the problem of time: Shingo senses intuitively that
the mountain has sounded out to warn him of his approaching
death; Marcel, in his more rigorously analytical way, con-
centrates all his considerable mental energies on trying to
determine what it is about the taste of that particular cake,
madeleine, dipped in tea that awakens such rapturous feelings
in him:

> Ten times over I must essay the task, must lean down
> over the abyss. And each time the cowardice that
> deters us from every difficult task, every important
> enterprise, has urged me to leave the thing alone, to
> drink my tea and to think merely of the worries of
> today, and my hopes for tomorrow, which can be
> brooded over painlessly.[11]

But the dauntless Marcel presses on, and finally is rewarded
with a flash of insight: 'The taste was that of the little piece of
madeleine which on Sunday mornings at Combray ... when I
went to say good morning to her in her bedroom, my aunt
Leonie used to give me, dipping it first in her own cup of tea or

tisane'.[12] The whole of his childhood seems instantaneously resurrected by this simple taste. But even though he has succeeded in connecting the taste to a childhood memory, Marcel confesses that: 'I did not yet know and must long postpone the discovery of why this memory made me so happy'.[13] Thus his experience, like Shingo's, still retains its essential mystery.

But it is important to note that one thing Marcel *is* sure of is that his experience as a whole is no simple act of memory. Such a vivid 'resurrection' of the past cannot be attained by a conscious act of will:

> It is a labour in vain to attempt to recapture it [the past]: all the efforts of our intellect must prove futile. The past is hidden somewhere outside the realm, beyond the reach of intellect, in some material object (in the sensation which that material object will give us) of which we have no inkling. And it depends on chance whether or not we come upon this material object before we ourselves must die.[14]

This is why, incidentally, Scott Moncrieff's translation of Proust's title, *A la Recherche du temps perdu*, as *Remembrance of Things Past*, is inadequate; the word 'remembrance' is too weak. What Proust suggests by his title is that Marcel is in search of a way to resurrect the past in a far more real sense than by a mere act of remembrance – he desires no less than to actually make the past become present again, a seemingly impossible task of time-transcendence. We might also note from the passage quoted above that Marcel, like Shingo, is aware of the urgency of accomplishing this task, as he says, 'before we ourselves must die'. Thus, although the emotional tone of the two protagonists' initial experiences of the time-problem is so different, both come away from the experience with a pressing desire for some form of time-transcendence.

Judging from these initial experiences, the compulsion which Shingo feels to escape from time may seem to derive from a more negative source than Marcel's – a stark fear of death – but as the novel progresses we learn that he also has a compelling reason to attempt to recapture the past: his continuing love for his wife's elder sister whom he had lost in his youth. And, when Shingo does manage finally to transcend time and achieve some form of union with her, his experience is as blissful as Marcel's. The scene, however, is presented with such economy of means (especially in comparison with Proust's) that an unsuspecting reader might easily miss its significance. Shingo is spending a

restless night at an inn in the resort town of Atami, kept awake
by the sounds of a storm and of passing trains:

> For a time he was unable to sleep.
> 'Shingo-o-oh! Shingo-o-oh!' Half asleep and half
> awake, he heard someone calling him.
> The only person who called with that particular lilt
> was Yasuko's sister.
> For Shingo it was a piercingly sweet awakening.[15]

The name of the chapter of which this scene forms the quiet
but significant climax is *Fuyu no sakura* (*Cherry Trees in Winter*)
and there is a description of these trees, in full bloom in the
garden of the inn – although it is January – immediately prior to
the scene quoted above. With a delicately suggestive use of
symbolism typical of his style, Kawabata here foreshadows the
experience of time-transcendence that Shingo is about to
undergo. The cherry trees blossoming in mid-winter are only
one of a number of natural images of things blooming 'out of
season', and thus seeming to transcend the normal chronological sequence of time, scattered throughout the novel: perhaps
the most conspicuous one is of the lotus seed, discovered after
two thousand years of hibernation, which blooms into a flower
when planted.

Another feature which Shingo's experience shares with
Marcel's, besides its blissful tenor, is that it is an example of
what Proust calls 'involuntary memory'. The experience occurs
while Shingo is 'half asleep' and thus, like Marcel's, it is not the
result of a conscious act of memory. The two authors seem to
concur that the conscious mind alone is not powerful enough to
bring about a true resurrection of the past. The power of the
unconscious was, of course, a central theme of European
thought in Proust's day – Freudian psychoanalysis was just
becoming established. According to the psychoanalyst, Milton
Miller, however, Proust anticipated the discoveries of Freud by
several years, and Dr. Miller has written a book to prove it.[16]
The same claim, of course, has been made for other writers
who lived long before Proust, but suffice to say that in his
preoccupation with the unconscious also Proust was in tune
with the *Zeitgeist* of turn-of-the-century Europe. As for
Kawabata, I have mentioned his debt to Freud and to
European modernism in general in earlier chapters, but we
should also recognize that in this respect too he is also writing
in the mainstream of the Japanese tradition: one finds, for
instance, an awareness of the power of unconscious associations in a Japanese poetic form as old as the medieval *renga*.

Neither Shingo nor Marcel, however, relinquish any of the conscious means at their disposal in their struggle to transcend time. Perhaps the most conspicuous of these in both cases is art. Both Proust and Kawabata were known as quintessential aesthetes, so it is hardly surprising that their protagonists too should value art almost more, it sometimes seems, than life itself. Of all man's earthly creations, art alone seems to have the power to resist the flow of time. This is the old theme of *ars longa vita brevis* but, more than that, in both novels art is also shown to be able to bestow some of its eternal aspect on creatures of the present moment. When Shingo sees a puppy assume a certain pose, he is reminded of a puppy painted by Sōtatsu, and the puppy before his eyes, by association with the painting, seems to manifest a quality of eternal 'puppiness'. The most important instance of this in *The Sound of the Mountain* is no doubt the scene in which Kikuko, Shingo's daughter-in-law, puts on the *Jidō* Nō mask which, as Shingo tells her, is a 'symbol of eternal youth'. By this point we know that the beautiful young Kikuko has become for Shingo a kind of substitute for the ideal love of his own youth, his wife's sister. By putting on the mask of youth she thus seems to attain a form of eternity not only for herself but also for the dead sister, thus consoling Shingo with the knowledge that his sister is still somehow present for him. This is a dangerous moment for Shingo, though, because, by seeing Kikuko so closely identified with the eternal feminine, he is tempted to forget that she is also his daughter-in-law. But he does resist the temptation: 'Shingo could not look at Kikuko as she moved the glowing young mask this way and that'.[17] And the spell is abruptly broken by noises made by his granddaughter and the dog: 'Shingo felt something ominous in it all'.[18]

In a similar way, Marcel has the habit of identifying people of the present with figures in the art of the past: the baron de Charlus with a grand inquisitor in an El Greco painting, the duc de Guermantes with a *bourgemestre* painted by Rembrandt, Odette Swann with a girl painted by Botticelli and so on. Such allusions again give us a sense of the 'eternal recurrence' of certain types – and a sense that, beneath the ever-changing forms of life, there are certain eternal essences. If things remain always the same in essence, then time, which cannot exist without change, is merely an illusion created by the surface level of reality. Much of the function of art, in both Proust and Kawabata, seems to be to communicate some sense of these 'eternal essences', and thus to provide an experience of time-transcendence.

For the artist himself, moreover, art seems to offer something additional: a kind of personal immortality. This is
emphasized by Proust in particular. What we might call the
three primary types of artist: the writer, the painter and the
musician, all make an appearance as major characters in his
novel – Bergotte, Elstir and Vinteuil – and each is shown to
distill the essence of his life into his work in such a way that,
even after his death, his life may be quite literally relived by
another. Even the writer Bergotte, who is something of a
disappointment to Marcel when seen in the flesh, seems to
transcend his own vulgarity in his art. As Monsieur de Norpois
quite baldly states: 'the work is infinitely superior to the
author'.[19] Thus, when Bergotte dies, Marcel feels that the best
part of him will live on in his books: 'They buried him, but all
through that night of mourning in the lighted shop windows,
his books arranged three by three, kept vigil like angels with
outspread wings and seemed, for him who was no more, the
symbol of his resurrection'.[20]

We may note in this passage, by the way, a good example of
the quality of Proust's style I mentioned earlier: a lucidity that
sometimes seems to verge on the overly explicit. In contrast,
Kawabata usually just presents an image without telling us what
it symbolizes. Proust's drive for clear definition seems at times
relentless, almost obsessive. As André Gide once remarked, he
'is not satisfied unless he shows us together with the flower the
stem and the delicate net of roots'.[21] How much of this the
reader will accept probably depends as much on his patience as
on his aesthetic tastes. Certainly it is true that Proust plays this
game superbly well. One might easily agree with Joseph Conrad
that: 'Proust is a writer who has carried analysis to a point where
it becomes creative'.[22] And another quality of his style which
must be taken into account, because it does much to
compensate for any excessive explicitness, is its all-pervading
sense of irony. Kawabata also assumes at times an ironic tone, as
in the sentence quoted earlier: 'Only when she snored did he
reach out to touch her'. But in Proust the ironic tone is at the
core of his style, because he is preeminently what Kawabata
rarely if ever is: a satirist. *In Search of Lost Time* contains some of
the most delicious satire ever written on such human foibles as
snobbery, hypochondria, the self-delusions of 'love' and so on.
Looking again at the passage above, we may detect here too a
faintly mocking tone which warns us that the narrator should not
be taken too seriously. Just the association of 'angels' with the
lascivious Bergotte – he who boasted of spending more on
whores than a millionaire – should make us suspicious.

And, sure enough, when Marcel himself later begins his career as a writer, we find him aware that there is a certain naïveté in this view of the immortality of the work of art. 'No doubt my books too', he writes, 'like my fleshly being, would in the end one day die . . . . Eternal duration is promised no more to men's works than to men'.[23] Yet he still remains convinced that there is a sense in which works of art are eternal; otherwise, he would not be prepared to struggle to complete his one great novel before the death which he feels to be imminent. This confidence is based on a new vision he has had of what he calls the 'form of Time':[24]

> The happiness which I was feeling was the product . . .
> of an enlargement of my mind, within which the past
> was reforming and actualizing itself, giving me – but
> alas! only momentarily – something whose value was
> eternal. This I should have liked to bequeath to those
> who might have been enriched by my treasure.[25]

The emphasis now, then, is not on an 'eternity' in terms of chronological time, but on an eternity felt within the lived moment itself, an eternal 'value' experienced momentarily. It is such 'eternal moments' that Marcel wishes to communicate to the reader of his work, and he believes that by doing so he will confer upon his work an eternal value of its own, whether or not it actually survives in chronological time. But, to understand this point fully, we must look more closely at Marcel's experiences of 'time-transcendence', the significance of which is at the very core of the novel's thematic structure.

Marcel himself makes very clear the importance he attaches to these privileged moments of his life, these 'moments bien hereux'. He describes them as 'moments of perception which had made me think that life was worth living'.[26] As I have already mentioned, the first description of such a moment – provoked by the taste of madeleine dipped in tea – occurs as the climax of the 'Overture', in which, as in an operatic overture, all the major themes of the work to come are announced. But the most detailed depiction and discussion of these incidents comes as the climax to the novel as a whole. Again Marcel's preliminary mood is dark: he feels himself old and ailing, and is convinced of his 'incurable lack of literary talent'. Unable to work in this mood, he accepts an invitation to an afternoon party at the Princesse de Guermantes. Just as he is approaching the Guermantes' house, he is startled by a car coming towards him; he must step out of the way quickly, and in doing so he trips against some uneven paving-stones.

> And at the moment when, recovering my balance, I
> put my foot on a stone which was slightly lower than
> its neighbour, all my discouragement vanished and
> in its place was the same happiness which at various
> epochs of my life had been given to me by ... the
> flavour of a madeleine dipped in tea, and by all those
> other sensations of which I have spoken ....[27]

He soon realizes that the sensation of the two uneven paving
stones has evoked a memory of another two such stones he had
experienced years before in Venice:

> In the same way the taste of the little madeleine had
> recalled Combray to me. But why had the images of
> Combray and of Venice, at these two different
> moments, given me a joy which was like a certainty
> and which sufficed, without any other proof, to make
> death a matter of indifference to me?[28]

Marcel is determined to find the answer to this question that
very day. Entering the Guermantes' house, he experiences
more such 'lightning-flashes': when a servant knocks a spoon
against a plate, when he wipes his mouth with a napkin, etc.,
each of which revives a moment from his past in the same vivid
way. Bringing all his considerable powers of analysis to bear
now on these experiences, in which 'the past was made to
encroach upon the present and I was made to doubt whether I
was in the one or the other', Marcel finally discovers what he
believes to be the cause of his happiness.[29]

> The truth surely was that the being within me which
> had enjoyed these impressions had enjoyed them
> because they had in them something that was
> common to a day long past and to the present,
> because in some way they were extra-temporal, and
> this being made its appearance only when, through
> one of these identifications of the present with the
> past, it was likely to find itself in the one and only
> medium in which it could exist and enjoy the essence
> of things, that is to say: outside time. This explained
> why it was that my anxiety on the subject of my
> death had ceased at the moment when I had
> unconsciously recognized the taste of the little
> madeleine, since the being which at that moment I
> had been was an extratemporal being and therefore
> unalarmed by the vicissitudes of the future. This
> being had only come to me, only manifested itself
> outside of activity and immediate enjoyment, on
> those rare occasions when the miracle of an analogy

had made me escape from the present. And only this
being had the power to perform that task which had
always defeated the efforts of my memory and my
intellect, the power to make me rediscover days that
were long past, the Time that was Lost.[30]

In these experiences, then, Marcel seems to discover within
himself some essence which transcends time, a deeper being to
whom the past is ever present. One immediate temptation, of
course, is to interpret this in traditional religious terms: has
Marcel discovered, as if by chance, that he possesses the
immortal soul of the Christians, or the *atman* of the Hindus?

A more interesting interpretation, at least from a Japano-
logist's point of view, is provided by R.C. Zaehner, an
authority on mysticism in world religions. In his *Mysticism,
Sacred and Profane*, Zaehner devotes a good part of a chapter
to proving his thesis that Marcel's experiences are a form of
'natural mysticism' comparable to the *satori* experiences of
Zen Buddhism. As evidence Zaehner points to the suddenness
of the experience – Marcel himself calls them 'lightning
flashes' – and to the fact that they are occasioned by physical
stimuli: tastes, smells, touches and sounds. The sense of
egolessness also seems quite Buddhistic: what is realized is
''the real self set free form the order of time' which, for Proust,
seemed to have very little to do with his transient ego .... '[31]
Thus the immortality of the self, as with the immortality of the
work of art, does not necessarily mean continuous survival in
chronological time; it is a quality sensed in a realm beyond
time, the 'eternal moment' of the mystics. But Zaehner also
points out an important difference between Marcel's experience and that of the Zen adept: in Marcel's experience 'there is
no merging into Nature, there is only a complete realization of
the self. It is not what Jung calls a case of inflation, but a
genuine case of "integration"' – though of a self beyond the
transient ego.[32]

What Zaehner calls 'natural mysticism' is, of course, a
deeply-ingrained part of Kawabata's own cultural tradition,
fostered by Shintō as much as by Buddhism, so it is hardly
surprising that the ultimate form of Shingo's time-transcendence should differ from Marcel's in this respect. Throughout
The Sound of the Mountain, in fact, the presence of nature is
much more strongly felt than in Proust's novel. From the
moment early in the novel when Shingo hears the ominous
sound of the mountain, we feel nature as an overwhelming,
mysterious power always in the background and completely

independent of man. Through a skillful use of natural imagery we are made continuously aware of the passing seasons.

In Proust's novel, on the contrary, when nature appears it is almost always in an anthropomorphic guise, filtered through an individual human consciousness – a tamed nature made to serve human ends. In the famous 'moonlight scene' of the 'Overture', for example, we may note, first, that the landscape outside Marcel's window is offered as merely a reflection of his state of mind: the boy Marcel is sitting in rapt attention, listening to the adults below him, and outside 'things too seemed frozen, rapt in a mute intentness not to disturb the moonlight'.[33] Secondly, we may note that the analogies used in his descriptions of nature are drawn from the human world: the whole landscape is compared to a map, and distant sounds are said to resemble 'pianissimo' movements on muted strings performed by the orchestra of the Conservatoire. If we compare this to Kawabata's own 'moonlight scene' quoted earlier, in which Shingo first hears the sound of the mountain, we see that what might be called the flow of psychic power is in an opposite direction: whereas Shingo opens his mind to the natural world and receives a message from it, Marcel imprints his own mental state on the landscape outside. 'Kawabata's achievement', according to Masao Miyoshi, 'lies in just this, his keen awareness of the objects around men that exist in themselves as solidly as people do'.[34] Proust's world, on the other hand, is an entirely human one. It is rather like the difference between a *sumi-e* landscape in which the human figures are tiny against the vast mountains and a Renaissance portrait in which the human figure occupies almost the entire canvas.

Indeed, Proust may be regarded as one of the last great artists in the Western humanist tradition that began with Renaissance portraits and biographies. With this in mind we can understand further why he adopts the first-person as his narrative point-of-view. *In Search of Lost Time* is, of course, largely autobiographical but, more than that, it is a highly introspective novel which traces the growth of the narrator's consciousness from boyhood ideals to middle-age disillusion and beyond that to final enlightenment. Even though a large cast of other characters does appear, their ultimate interest lies in the effect they have on the growth of Marcel's consciousness. In Kawabata's novel, on the other hand, the natural world in particular appears very much as a force independent of the protagonist's consciousness, continually exerting its own subtle pressure, and to maintain the greater sense of objectivity this requires the author naturally adopts the third-person point-of-view.

It is nature which first calls out to Shingo, warning him of the approach of death, and it is to nature that he must finally return to resolve his problem with time. As with Marcel, art alone is not enough. Art may afford a momentary glimpse of a realm beyond time, the realm of eternal ideals or essences represented, for instance, by the *Jidō* mask for Shingo and Vermeer's *View of Delft* for Marcel, but what is needed is a radical change of consciousness in regard to self and time. Marcel achieved this by delving deep within himself and finding there an 'extratemporal being'; Shingo achieves it by surrendering himself to the larger world of nature, in which linear, chronological, human time is superseded by the cyclical time of nature's eternal seasons. Before he can attain this cathartic release, however, Shingo must purge himself of his sense of personal frustration and lay to rest the ghosts of the past. In this painful process Kikuko, his daughter-in-law, is like a heaven-sent helper to him: by serving as a substitute for the beautiful girl he had loved and lost in his youth, she enables him to achieve at last a soul-satisfying sense of union with this feminine ideal. Thus purified of his frustrated longings, Shingo attains a state of egolessness similar to Marcel's; he is now an empty vessel open to receive the healing powers of nature.

But, again, Kawabata conveys this fact to us in a subtle and indirect way – in this respect quite opposite the almost over-insistent Proust. Whereas Proust surrounds Marcel's 'blissful moments' with long disquisitions on the nature of time and so on, Kawabata barely hints at what is going on, so that an inattentive reader might easily miss the significance. The title of the final chapter of *The Sound of the Mountain*, 'Fish in Autumn', is our first hint. Then, in the very last scene of this chapter and of the novel, Shingo sits down to a fish dinner with his entire family, and is reminded of some *haiku* about trout:

> '"A trout in the autumn, abandoning itself to the water". "Trout swimming down the shallows, not knowing they must die". That sort of old poem. I imagine they would apply to me'.[35]

This is the most direct indication we have of the revolution that has occurred in Shingo's state of mind, but for anyone familiar with Kawabata's style of indirection it is enough: Shingo here affirms that, like the trout in autumn, he has at last surrendered himself to the river of time and is at peace. Again we may note a contrast in the final pose of the two protagonists which bespeaks perhaps a fundamental difference in the spiritual values of their respective cultures. In his serenity, absorption in nature and resignation, Shingo reminds us of the Daoist sage who is reputed to have said: 'My every act is an act of surrender'. Marcel, despite the Buddhistic tenor of his 'enlightenment', still seems basically the Faustian man of the West, struggling to master nature and even time itself. To return to a question that was raised at the beginning of this chapter: if there is a true cultural difference between the Japanese and the Western sense of time, then these two works show us how closely related this must be to the difference between the Japanese and Western sense of self. Indeed, they reveal to us how intimately related the time-sense is to the whole range of cultural values, from the aesthetic to the philosophic. In both cases, it would be hard to find any other twentieth-century novel which better expressed in modern form these fundamental values of the native tradition.

2. Questions of Form

> 'In so far as "creation" is defined by "order", disorder is essential to it'.
>
> Paul Valéry[36]

In the West, at least since Plato, the contemplation of formal beauty, whether in the aptness of a metaphor or the grandeur of a Gothic cathedral, has been considered the very heart of aesthetic pleasure. In the neo-Platonic poetics which has flourished since the Renaissance, this is the level at which the beautiful becomes the good, the true, and art is reconciled with philosophy – although Plato himself, the banisher of poets, might have objected to any such reconciliation. Modern theoretical critics, of course, have assigned this pleasure a psychological rather than a metaphysical locus: formal structures are thought to satisfy not because they reflect some absolute universal order but simply because they satiate the human mind's desire for order – or, in other words, because they reflect the mind itself. At any rate, this stress upon formal beauty has remained, for millennia, at the core of Western literary aesthetics, and continues to remain so, despite attacks on such 'formalism' by Marxists and others of their ilk. (Structuralism, for instance, may be regarded as one of its more recent manifestations, and poststructuralism or 'deconstruction' as merely a more than usually pronounced swing of the pendulum in the direction of that 'disorder' which, as the great French poet Valéry noted, is its indispensable concomitant.)

Given this Western emphasis on form, it is hardly surprising that perhaps the most common complaint of Western readers on first contact with Japanese literature is of its formlessness. It is as if someone who had spent his whole life in Louis Quatorze gardens, with their geometrically perfect patterns, were suddenly confronted by the stone garden of Ryōanji: a few rocks scattered seemingly at random over raked sand, it might appear not only poor in materials (not even a single flower!) but totally without order. Similarly, someone used to reading the epic poetry of Homer, Virgil and Milton, in which there is a clear syllogistic progression from one event to another, might find himself puzzled if not exasperated by the lengthy poetic sequences of Sōgi, Shōhaku and Sōchō, in which syllogistic progression is purposely frustrated. But order, like beauty, is in the eye of the beholder. And the eye must be educated. The Zen monk who scatters a few leaves along the garden path so that it will not seem unnaturally neat, and the *renga* poet who avoids carrying an association beyond two verses in a chain so as to eschew any clear narrative progression, are both following a principle of asymmetrical order that is culturally imbued and, ultimately, a matter of taste. But asymmetry is not chaos; it is, at most, a studied disorder, the formless element serving only to 'balance off' the underlying form. First one cleans the path, and only then scatters about a few leaves. A path smothered in leaves would have no aesthetic value whatever. Nor would a poem consisting of nothing but random associations. And, as a matter of fact, there is probably no poetic genre anywhere governed by such an intricate body of rules as *renga*.

To explain the aesthetic appeal of any modern novel, too, it is not enough simply to analyse its themes; one must also take its formal structure into account. Of course, any discriminations one makes between 'form' and 'theme' are a matter of relative critical perspective and are not to be taken as rigid or absolute distinctions. The relation between theme and form in literature is not like the relation between, say, beer and bottle; it is more like that between dance and dancer – and, as W.B. Yeats asked, 'How can we know the dancer from the dance?' Nonetheless, unless one is to forego the critical enterprise altogether (a prospect not without its temptations), one must try, however tentatively, to separate the inseparable. Since this is such a delicate and difficult task, one needs a rather sophisticated critical apparatus in order to carry it out. It seems to me that, for this purpose, no finer set of tools has been designed than Kenneth Burke's *Lexicon Rhetoricae*. Burke's analysis of the 'five aspects of form' is not to be taken, of course, as the last word on the subject but, as shown by the extensive use made of it by later critics such as Wayne Booth and Ralph Freedman, it provides some highly useful guidelines – or, as Burke himself promised, it provides us with a 'machine for criticism'.[37] And I have found it a useful point of reference in my analysis of the formal structures of *The Sound of the Mountain* and *In Search of Lost Time*.

Both works are episodic in character, divide easily into independent parts and were left unfinished – all of which seems to bespeak the casual, almost off-hand attitude of both authors towards formal structure. The impression of 'casualness' is, of course, in good part intended: neither writer had much taste for the artificialities of the nineteenth century well-made plot, with its clear-cut beginning, middle and end. On the other hand, it would be wrong to say that their works are 'formless'. Though they may appear so on first reading, this is only because their formal principles are subtle and original and thus difficult, at first, to discern. And this subtlety and originality derives, it seems to me, from one central fact about both works: what I have called the 'resistance to time' or 'anti-time' tension expressed on the thematic level of the two works is also fully embodied in their formal structures. As with all major works of art, this consonance of form and theme constitutes the basis of their aesthetic integrity – and, indeed, is their main claim to greatness.

Of the two kinds of progressive form, what Burke calls 'syllogistic progression' has been, of course, the predominant formal principle of the traditional Western novel. As the term implies, it is a principle which, in essence, is the same as that which underlies formal logic.

> We call it syllogistic because, given certain things, certain things must follow, the premises forcing the conclusion. Insofar as the audience, from its acquaintance with the premises, feels the rightness of the conclusion, the work is formal. The arrows of our desires are turned in a certain direction, and the plot follows the direction of the arrows.[38]

Any narrative work naturally must have this syllogistic aspect, and, since it is so intimately involved with the work's major themes, I have already sketched its outlines for the two novels under comparison in the first part of this chapter. This is also the aspect of form which most adequately conveys a sense of linear time: past cause leading to present consequence which carries within it the possibility of further consequence in the future. Thus it follows that any novel which seeks to set up a time/anti-time tension in formal terms must downplay this syllogistic element, in which the traditional novel is so naturally strong, and balance it off with some of the other aspects of form. This is exactly what both *The Sound of the Mountain* and *In Search of Lost Time* do. And this is also why any mere plot summary does even less justice to these works than to more conventional novels.

Early readers of Proust were shocked by the apparent formlessness of his *magnum opus*. To the French *literati*, even to one so perceptive as André Gide, he seemed finally to have achieved Flaubert's infamous ambition to write a novel about nothing. Instead of an orderly series of narrative events, they were confronted by the seemingly random flow of associations in the mind of a half-sleeping narrator. One publisher, it is said, sent an indignant note back to the unfortunate Proust rejecting his manuscript on the grounds that no gentleman should spend the first fifty pages of his novel describing how he gets to sleep!

France, of course, is the land where classical symmetry has been carried to its most artificial extremes – in literature as much as in gardening. Kawabata, in writing his novel, did not have to contend with the same cultural prejudices against 'formlessness'. Indeed, the whole tradition of Japanese literary aesthetics was on his side. Even the word *suji*, for instance, though usually translated as 'plot', connotes something like a thin line running through a loosely related series of episodes rather than a solid 'plot' which ramifies through all dimensions of theme, character, setting and story. Certainly one could find countless examples of such 'loosely structured' novels in modern Japanese literature, the *suji* of which is not quite a 'plot'. (And a good many of our problems in crosscultural studies derive precisely from the misconceptions which arise because our respective terms of reference do not always exactly coincide.) But to understand the deepest reason for Kawabata's 'underdevelopment' of syllogistic progression, it may help to look beyond the modern period to that most 'anti-syllogistic' of all literary genres, the medieval *renga*.

Several commentators have already pointed out, in a general way, the affinities between Kawabata's narrative art and the *renga*. Judging by the way some of them have phrased this, however, they seem to think that Kawabata's novels assume a *renga*-like form not so much by aesthetic choice as 'by default'. Edward Seidensticker, for instance, claims that: 'It is quite obvious that Kawabata cannot have known where he was going when he started to write, any more than a group of poets know where they are going when they sit down to compose a *renga* sequence'.[39] And Yamamoto Kenkichi, in his postscript to a 1957 edition of *The Sound of the Mountain*, remarks that Kawabata's habit of writing a novel as it was being serialized, chapter by chapter, in various literary magazines, so that each chapter was semi-independent, may be responsible for the *renga*-like structure of the work as a whole – since *renga* poets also write verse by verse, *ichiku ichiku*.[40] Nakamura Mitsuo seems to have something similar in mind when he proposes a rather startling analogy for the typical Kawabata novel: it is like an earthworm, claims Nakamura, because you may cut it up into any number of parts and each part will be able to survive on its own.[41] Kawabata's writing habits may indeed have been rather desultory, and the exigencies of serial publication may also have taken their toll, but it seems to me that there are also some more positive reasons for the *renga*-like structure of his works, reasons which may emerge if we look more closely at the *renga*-form itself.

Renga has been described as a 'plotless narrative' by Earl Miner, the leading Western authority on the subject.[42] I must confess that I do not find this definition completely satisfactory. One understands why a random series of images should be called 'plotless', but in what sense does it form a narrative? Admittedly, there are some narrative-like elements in the overall structure of *renga:* for example, a basic *jo-ha-kyū* structure as in Nō, and a rhythmic pacing of highpoints and lowpoints, but this is a highly artificial, impersonal structure, externally imposed and governed by a large number of inflexible rules; it is not, like the narrative structure of a modern novel, the personal creation of an individual artist which grows organically out of the work's thematic core. It is a purely formal rather than a narrative or thematic structure in the true sense. Besides, how can there be true narrative without some form of sustained progression – and it is exactly this which is explicitly prohibited in *renga*.

Are we to say, then, that there is absolutely no relation between narrative and *renga*? This does not seem quite right either. Why is there such a strict prohibition in the rules of *renga* against any direct continuity of meaning beyond two verses of the series (usually a hundred verses)? Is it not for the very reason that *renga* aims to frustrate the natural narrative tendency of the human mind, the tendency to develop images or ideas in a logical, linear series – that very 'syllogistic progression' of which Burke speaks – or, in the specific *renga* context, the natural tendency of one poet to continue developing the nascent story, image or thought of the previous poet? Thus *renga* does have a definite relation with narrative but it is an adversary one. To call it 'plotless narrative' is not only misleading but understates the importance of this unique verse-genre; for *renga* is by far the earliest example in world literature of a sustained structure that is deliberately anti-narrative – that is, anti-narrative by aesthetic choice. It is not until the twentieth century that we find such a phenomenon in Western literature – as, for instance, in the temporal distortions of Robbe-Grillet's *nouveau roman* or the satirically repetitive narrative games of Raymond Queneau.

If one were to search for a philosophical basis for this apparently unique and 'modernistic' stance of medieval *renga,* one need look no further than the Zen Buddhism which was a dominant influence in the age which gave rise to this art, as well as to the Nō drama, the tea ceremony, rock gardens and other Zen-related arts. By cutting off rational, linear thinking, and its concomitant sense of the continuity of an individual ego through a continuum of time, *renga,* like Zen, seeks to release the moment-to-moment enjoyment of the unbound consciousness. As we would expect, being anti-narrative means that it is also anti-time: it seeks to cut off all sense of past and future in order to concentrate the mind on an eternal present. This is why Nijō Yoshimoto (1320-88), the 'poet who helped most in elevating linked verse to the level of a serious art form',[43] and who first lay down its theoretical basis, could make the rather startling claim that *renga* might help one achieve a Buddhistic enlightenment.[44]

To put this in more strictly literary terms, by turning the reader's attention away from narrative development, *renga* is able to focus it on the random flow of poetic imagery which, as Konishi Jin'ichi asserts, constitutes its principal beauty. Konishi describes *renga* as a 'symphony of images' and goes on to say:

> Each verse taken either singly, or as linked with either the preceding or succeeding verse, has its specific semantic value, and these values are part of the pleasure of *renga.* But the essence of *renga* is the essentially *meaningless* pattern of images.[45]

And, needless to say, without a sustained meaning there can be no narrative in the true sense.

But this anti-narrative, anti-time impetus is not confined to *renga* alone in traditional Japanese culture. The *haiku* poet, for instance, avoids all temptation towards syllogistic progression simply by not developing his inspiration beyond a single seventeen-syllable verse, and by trying to capture imagistically a timeless instant of union: as of frog and water, crow and evening. The same impetus may be found even in the theatrical arts, in which, perhaps, one would expect the structural support of a strong narrative to be indispensable. Most conspicuously, in both the Nō *kata* and the Kabuki *mie* there is a sudden stoppage of the narrative flow as the actor assumes a motionless pose. Such conventions may seem to resemble Brechtian techniques of audience 'alienation', but the resultant detachment is, of course, for quite different purposes. As with Kawabata's moments of narrative stasis, such theatrical moments give a sense of timelessness and also a strong intuition of a kind of Zen-style 'emptiness': the sudden arrest of the action reveals the illusory nature of all that is happening on the stage.

By studying such examples, in fact, we begin to realize that the mainstream of Japanese aesthetics seems to include a whole dimension that is lacking in its Western counterpart; or, to put it another way, its 'aesthetics of form' is counterbalanced by an 'aesthetics of emptiness'. As Kawabata himself once pointed out, however, this Eastern sense of emptiness does not connote the mere nullity of Western nihilism – rather it suggests the creative, spiritual reality that is the obverse side of all phenomena.[46] In the words of the great Zen scholar, Suzuki Daisetsu: 'Sunyata is formless, but it is the fountainhead of all possibilities'.[47] Obviously no artist can directly represent this formless source of all form, and so the aesthetic problem becomes how to hint at it or symbolize it. A well-known passage of the *Heart Sutra,* chanted every day in Zen monasteries, tells us that 'form is emptiness, emptiness is form', and, for the artist, this would seem to imply that any form he uses will manifest emptiness, and that, therefore, the distinction between an aesthetics of form and an aesthetics of emptiness is an artificial one. From an absolute point of view, this is no doubt correct. Indeed, Kawabata himself made much of a passage regarding the Buddhist poet Saigyō who said of himself that, when 'confronted with all the varied forms of nature, his eyes and his ears were filled with emptiness'.[48] But, because everyone is not a Saigyō, artists have developed certain techniques or conventions like those mentioned above to suggest to the unenlightened the mysterious truth that form is emptiness. Such devices, we might say, are meant to awaken an intuition of emptiness. Perhaps the clearest example of this may be found in Sino-Japanese ink painting or *sumi-e:* in contrast to the oil painter, who covers every last square inch of canvas with colour and form, the ink painter leaves much of his paper untouched so as to suggest by this 'white space' the emptiness from which the pictured forms arise.

The question then arises: is there any way that this 'aesthètics of emptiness', found so widely in traditional Japanese culture, expresses itself also in narrative form? One might answer immediately with another question: how else but in the various formal devices which might be called 'anti-narrative?' We may understand this more clearly by taking a closer look at the structure of *The Sound of the Mountain*.

Paradoxically, in view of its central anti-time theme, *The Sound of the Mountain* is probably the most 'novelistic' of all Kawabata's novels. Kobayashi Hideo once claimed that Kawabata:

> ... has not written a single work that is like a novel. Anyone who reads his work with the slightest attention will soon realize how little this writer is interested in the things which generally become the objects of a novelist's curiosity, things suggested by such questions as: what is the nature of our everyday life? how do we collide with and submit to social systems and conventions? what sort of complications arise between two people of different character or ideology? Consider the fact that he lacks the ability even to describe two men or women in such a way that we can distinguish between them .... Disqualification as a novelist (*shōsetsuka shikkaku*) occurs at the very centre of this writer's individuality; the sense of *dōwa* (fairy tale) ripens within his 'heart's sorrow'.[49]

Coming from the leading literary critic of Kawabata's own generation, this rather severe and dismissive judgement warrants serious consideration. One might argue that Kobayashi's concept of *shōsetsu* was unduly influenced here by Western models of the 'novel' – his love of the Dostoevskian novel, for instance, was often expressed. On the other hand, since the general idea of what constitutes or should constitute a *shōsetsu* itself only came into being as part of the Meiji response to the Western novel, it is not entirely unreasonable to have the Western model in mind in defining it – whether or not one believes that the *shōsetsu* ultimately stands on its own as a uniquely Japanese genre. At any rate, one must admit that the elements which Kobayashi lists as typically novelistic – the textures of mundane life, social problems, ideological conflicts, the peculiarities of individual characters – are indeed conspicuously lacking in most of Kawabata's novels, as are the formal structures which go along with these thematic elements. But Kobayashi made this statement in 1941, more than a decade before *The Sound of the Mountain*. In this creation of a more mature Kawabata we find not only a great deal more everyday 'mundanity' and a sharper delineation of character than is usual with him, but there are even some passing references to the social problems and moral conflicts current in postwar Japan. Although the work is not exactly a *Zeitsroman*, perhaps Kawabata, sensing that this was going to be his most purposely 'anti-narrative' novel, made the aesthetic decision, consciously or unconsciously, to create more of a dialectical balance by increasing his quota of traditionally novelistic elements. After all, how can there be any sense of an escape from a mundane, timebound world unless we are first given a strong impression of what that world is like? And so, for instance, in the first chapter, we are told some of the unpleasant details of Shingo's married life – such details as would have entirely preoccupied earlier 'naturalist' writers like Shimazaki Tōson and Tayama Katai. The consequence of this increased mundanity on a formal level is that *The Sound of the Mountain* has a more pronounced plot-structure than other works by Kawabata – and, of course, I tried to show what I consider to be its main outlines in my earlier discussion the novel's themes. Indeed, if one were to give a cursory summary of the novel's plot, any unsuspecting person who had not read the work might conclude that it was a typical kind of nineteenth-century domestic novel or, in a modern Japanese context, a *yoromeki dorama*. True, the theme of incest is usually taboo in popular fiction, and certainly was in the bourgeois novel a hundred years ago, but Kawabata presents it in such an understated way that it might easily be missed.

I have already remarked on the danger of plot summaries. The obvious fact is that Kawabata's works, more than the works of most writers, are grotesquely misrepresented by any mere plot summary, and this fact in itself clearly suggests that the conventional narrative side of these works, though it undoubtedly exists, is of relatively less importance here than elsewhere. To reconstruct the 'plot' of *The Sound of the Mountain* in any linear fashion one must extract it from a complexly interwoven fabric of both narrative and non-narrative elements, meanwhile ignoring all those vital elements considered 'non-novelistic', i.e., which do not contribute directly to the syllogistic progression. To do this is like trying to come to an aesthetic appreciation of an opulent Persian carpet by unravelling its complex design into reams of its component threads: one is left with yards of linear thread but no more design, and only when the threads are part of a design do they transcend linearity. What, then, are the non-linear, nonsyllogistic elements in the formal structure of *The Sound of the Mountain*? And in what way, if at all, do these function as part of a traditional 'aesthetics of emptiness'?

Regarding both *Thousand Cranes* and *The Sound of the Mountain*, Kawabata once wrote:

> Each should have been a short story that concluded in one episode. All I did was to keep sounding the overtones of what I had written. For that reason, I should have ended both works after the first chapter: such is the brutal truth. The rest was probably mere self-indulgence.[50]

The final sentence reads in the original: '*Ato wa amaete iru dake darō*' – a charming way to put it.

The first reaction of anyone who admires Kawabata's masterpiece for what it is will probably be to smile at the excessive modesty of his self-deprecation here. Perhaps, also, one might relish the Zen-like spirit of a man who thinks he is being too soft (*amae*) on himself when he allows himself to write more than the bare minimum number of words necessary to make his point. This is the spirit, after all, which produced that ultimate flower of Japanese culture, the *haiku*, a poem as close to silence as any verbal medium could possibly come. Perhaps here, too, one might discern another manifestation of Kawabata's taste for the 'joy of emptiness' – *kyomu no arigatasa* – silence being preferable to words.[51]

But, on second look, this statement also contains an important hint, though negatively phrased, regarding the evolution of a Kawabataesque narrative structure. Of course, there is nothing wrong with a writer who 'keeps sounding the overtones' – this is precisely, as we have seen, the method of *renga*. But what this means in structural terms is that the first chapter of a Kawabata novel, like the opening verse or *hokku* of a *renga* sequence, assumes a preponderant importance: one might say that it contains not only the beginning but also the end of the entire novel – or, at least, the end in embryo. As the author himself suggests, all that follows in the rest of the novel may be regarded as essentially variations on the themes sounded in the first chapter. 'Variations on themes' suggests, of course, a musical analogy and, indeed, one may trace to Wagner's influence the fact that Proust's novel also assumes a structure of repeated *leitmotifs*. (One doubts, in fact, whether any nineteenth-century model of the novel has had an impact on twentieth-century novelistic structure equal to that of Wagner's tetralogical *Gesamtkunstwerk*.) At any rate, in the overall structure of *The Sound of the Mountain*, there is a large element of what Burke calls 'repetitive form'. In analyzing the work, we may thus reverse the direction of the author's procedure of 'sounding the overtones' and find the seeds of the whole novel in its first chapter.

I have already dealt with the key 'mountain sound' scene of the first chapter on a thematic level, but I would like to reconsider it now from the viewpoint of structure. The scene occurs in the second section of the chapter, a section which may be divided into three parts, almost with a traditional *jo-ha-kyū* rhythm (introduction, development, climax). The *jo* part introduces us to the mundane side of Shingo's existence. The narrator assumes an objective, matter-of-fact tone and tells us of Shingo's unhappy marital situation and of his bad health. Of the three parts, this is the most conventionally novelistic, the narrator imparting some necessary information about the central character in a prosaic and efficient manner: '*Shingo no tsuma no Yasuko wa hitotsu toshi-ue no roku-jū-san de aru*',[52] etc. (Shingo's wife, Yasuko, was sixty-three, a year older than him.) Compare this to the first sentence of the second, *ha* part: '*Tsukiyo datta*'.[53] (It was a moonlit night.) A short, lyrical gasp, the poetic effect of which is heightened by its being written as a single paragraph – like a *sumi-e* painter, Kawabata makes evocative use of 'empty space', and, since *kanji* and *kana* are written vertically rather than horizontally, there is actually more of it to use per line in a Japanese than in a Western text!

One might detect a causal, syllogistic link between the first and second parts of this section: Shingo gets up to open the shutter because the room is 'sultry'. But this is hardly the main reason why they are juxtaposed. As Burke says, a true syllogistic progression must have a 'pronounced anticipatory nature': for example, Macbeth assassinates the king and so we expect him, in turn, to be assassinated.[54] The real reason why the account of Shingo's married life is juxtaposed with the account of his communing with nature in his back garden is because of the contrast of moods involved. This is what Burke calls a 'qualitative progression', and he says of this:

> We recognize its rightness after the event. We are put
> into a state of mind which another state of mind can
> appropriately follow.[55]

Note that Burke is concerned here with the reader's state of mind, not the character's. The character's mental or emotional state may, of course, influence that of the reader, but it is only one of many factors which do so, and in forming the total structure of his work, the writer must ultimately have the reader's responses in mind. In short, literary form is fundamentally based on reader psychology. For those purists who dream of some Platonic ideal of form independent of the vagaries of individual human reactions, this formal relativism may seem to compromise the aesthetic autonomy and universality of the literary work. But the plain fact is that literature is a product of and for the human mind, and can have no meaningful existence apart from that mind. Thus, for instance, when Kawabata introduces certain images of nature in the scene under consideration, it is with a carefully calculated aesthetic effect – in other words, with the aim to arouse a particular emotional response in his readers. One may be more specific about this: it is a Japanese readership in particular for whom Kawabata is writing, and it is their particular responses which he must judge and even 'manipulate' to achieve the desired structure of his work. Obviously it would not be in my interest, as a 'blue-eyed' interpreter, to argue that only Japanese readers can respond properly to – and thus perceive the true structure of – a Kawabata novel. Nor do I wish to offend the spirit of open-minded internationalism which is currently so fashionable – one product of which is the kind of comparative study I have attempted in this chapter. But, on the other hand, it seems obvious that any work of art is to some extent culture-bound, and that this simple fact clearly demonstrates the above-mentioned relativity of form.

This is exactly why some Western readers, unresponsive to the formal devices of certain Japanese writers, have found their works 'formless'. In the present instance, if the 'mountain sound' scene were read by, say, a North American who had spent his entire life on the prairies, one doubts that his response would in any way resemble that of, say, an educated Japanese of Kawabata's generation, who had not only spent his life among mountains but had absorbed the whole sense of the mysterious spiritual reality of mountains which has deep roots in Japanese culture. Thus, for our hypothetical North American, it is doubtful that the scene would have the appropriate aesthetic effect, and it may well appear meaningless and thus formless. Indeed, the same may have been true for any Western reader before the Romantics taught us to love nature – and mountains in particular. As Marjorie Nicholson points out in her interesting study of the subject, *Mountain Gloom and Mountain Glory*, before Romanticism Europeans usually regarded mountains as mere obstacles and eye-sores, disfiguring the natural roundness of the earth. Although in Japan both Shintō and Buddhism encouraged reverence for mountains as symbolic centres of spiritual power, in the West the 'idea that mountains are a blemish to the earth goes back to theological positions long argued by the Christian and Jewish Fathers'.[56]

At any rate, with a novel such as *The Sound of the Mountain*, it is particularly important, when analyzing its structure, to clearly distinguish between the subjective states of character and reader. Because the novel is centred on the consciousness of a single character, it is all too easy for the reader to identify with that character so closely that he or she fails to distinguish at all between his or her own responses and those of the character. Obviously, this can result in various distortions in one's perception of the work's 'true' structure. Although the novel centres on a single character, it is not a *shishōsetsu* or autobiographical novel; if it were, perhaps there would be little harm in this confusion of subjective states, since in such a novel, unless it is written ironically, the writer intends the reader to identify with the character so closely that the 'emotional chart' of the two is almost identical in structure. But this is far from being the case in *The Sound of the Mountain*. The narrator (with whom the reader identifies *prima facie)* establishes himself at some distance from Shingo in the very opening scene: he is shown to be an old man prone to mistaken perceptions, and perhaps moments of self-indulgent sentimentality based on these perceptions, and we see him this way partly through the eyes of his son: 'Used to these problems, Shuichi offered his father no sympathy'.[57]

Thus Kawabata, perhaps for the very reason that he is aware of the dangers inherent in writing a novel around a single character, takes pains to warn us, in the very first scene of the novel, against any too close identification with this character's point of view – in other words, against taking any of Shingo's thoughts or feelings too quickly at face value. And there is a further difficulty here: because Kawabata frequently works through imagery rather than explicit statement, there is often considerable ambiguity about what a character is really feeling. In the 'mountain sound' scene, there seems to be a notable exception to this: we are told that Shingo, convinced that the sound has notified him of his approaching death, feels afraid. But Shingo's 'fear', though it is the only emotion that is explicitly mentioned, is surely not the only one that will be communicated to the reader by this scene. If such were the case, there would be little element of qualitative progression in the second section of the first chapter: from Shingo's disgust with his married life to his fear of death is hardly much of a progression, qualitative, syllogistic or otherwise. To discover the 'deep structure' of this scene, then, we must look to our own responses more than to Shingo's.

At the moment of transition I have already mentioned, for instance, there appears the image of a 'moonlit night' (*tsukiyo*). We are not told directly whether this relieves Shingo's gloomy state of mind, but I would venture to say that for any reader, Japanese or Western, the image is a poetic, 'uplifting' one, in sharp contrast to the mundane and rather depressing imagery in the scene up to this point: Shingo spitting up blood, Yasuko's aging, sweat-soaked body, Shingo twisting her nose to stop her snoring, etc. Thus, for the reader at least, the vast depth of the moonlit night, the singing of autumn insects, the cherry tree, and even the mysterious mountain sound, bring with them a liberating sense of escape into the natural world from the oppressive atmosphere of Shingo's bedroom. (And, incidentally, one wonders if Kawabata's works would be bearable, whether their generally dark mood would not repel most readers, without frequent interjections of such 'mood-raising' natural or artistic imagery. After all, there is very little in the way of humour to provide 'light relief'. Thus such qualitative progressions may be seen to play a crucial role in the aesthetic appeal of his work as a whole.) It is also important to note that the form of this particular qualitative progression has great symbolic meaning in the context of the novel as a whole. For, as we have seen in discussing the novel's themes, although Shingo may be frightened by his initial experience of the natural world, ultimately he must return to nature in order to achieve some degree of transcendence of the time-bound human world. This qualitative progression which occurs so early in the novel, then, may be said to contain in microcosmic form the fundamental action, the mainspring, of the entire novel. In other words, *The Sound of the Mountain* as a whole consists essentially of a qualitative progression.

In view of the novel's anti-time theme, one should also take note that qualitative progressions are less bound to any sense of linear time than are their syllogistic counterparts. In this sense, Burke's term 'qualitative progression' is not quite satisfactory; perhaps 'qualitative leap' would be more appropriate in some cases. For, although in syllogistic narrative there is always a sense of a logical progression from causes to effects over a certain period of time, there is often a suddenness and fortuitousness about qualitative narratives which precludes all sense of a progression through time. The transition often comes with a startling spontaneity, as if out of nowhere – or nothingness – like a Zen *satori: Tsukiyo datta.* (And we may recall, in this particular scene, that the moon is the age-old symbol of enlightenment.) Between the two terms of this 'leap' there is a 'space' or *ma,* a pregnant pause like that of the *mie* or the *kata,* and, as in these theatrical cases, there comes with this sudden break in the narrative a sense of timelessness and emptiness.

Another kind of narrative form of which Kawabata makes frequent use is what might be called 'associative progression', in which a transition is effected by a *renga*-like associative leap in the mind of the central character. The way the 'mountain sound' scene comes to an end is a conspicuous example of this: just as he closes the shutter on his garden, Shingo recalls the story told him by a *geisha* of how she had recently planned to commit love suicide with a carpenter, but had called it off because she did not trust that the poison was in the correct dosage. Obviously it is Shingo's presentiment of his own death, evoked by the mountain sound, which has led him to recall this strange tale of an aborted death (which prefigures, by the way, the several other forms of abortion which occur later – an example of Kawabata' use of *leitmotifs).* Paradoxically, though, rather than deepen his gloom the memory seems to lighten his (and our) mood, for the *geisha*'s story is curious and even somewhat absurd. Thus the progression here is not only associative but also qualitative – for, as Burke himself points out, these formal categories are by no means exclusive, and, indeed, are often mixed to good effect.[58] At any rate, referring back again to the *jo-ha-kyū* model, the mood of this final part is more of an anti-climax than a climax.

If it is true that the form of this section, as of others in the novel, is reminiscent of the *jo-ha-kyū* structure, then Kawabata is here, consciously or unconsciously, making use of what Burke calls 'conventional form', which 'involves to some degree the appeal of form *as form*'.[59] Other examples might be those transitions in the novel which are *renga*-like, or those single sentences which are *haiku*-like. But these examples are cross-generic. Strictly speaking, *qua* novelist Kawabata is anything but conventional – indeed, he might be considered anti-conventional. Thus the 'studied informality' I spoke of earlier: for instance, his beginnings do not read like beginnings, nor his endings like endings. As *The Sound of the Mountain* opens we are plunged immediately into Shingo's memory problem – there are no lengthy introductions or scene-settings. The ending is equally abrupt; there are no elaborate summations or tyings up of loose ends, nor even a hint of drama: simply the flat statement that Kikuko could not hear Shingo above the sound of the dishes.

Nevertheless, such 'anti-conventional' forms have not only the aesthetic charm of a casual appearance but also their own implicit power. There is a kind of 'playing off' of the seeming inconsequentiality of the statement against the obvious formal importance of its position. If the statement had occurred, for instance, in the middle of the novel, we might not have paid it much heed; but, coming as it does at the end, it immediately assumes a symbolic importance and our minds rush on to puzzle it out: does it mean, for example, a final alienation of Kikuko from Shingo? This holds true whether or not Kawabata really intended it as his final sentence (and apparently he did not – at least not at one point in time): the work as it stands is an aesthetic *fait accompli,* regardless of the author's original intentions. Besides, one cannot really imagine Kawabata finishing this novel in any other way but 'low key'. An artist of his maturity is aware of the implicit 'power of context', and thus knows that it is unnecessary to make his endings read like endings. Here, as elsewhere, he prefers the implicit to the explicit. After all, the novel, being a 'time-bound' art, must come to an end somewhere, but why make a big to-do about it? Life itself goes on, with its own natural forms and rhythms, and it is of these timeless natural forms, more than of literary forms *per se,* that a novel such as *The Sound of the Mountain* gives a strong and lasting impression.

But this is not to say that Kawabata neglects literary style. He is no Stendhalian naturalist whose only ambition is to hold a mirror up to life, and who thus writes in a featureless, 'transparent' prose. No reader can help but notice the beauty of Kawabata's medium, his sentences that, as Nakamura Mitsuo pointed out, often assume the formal beauty of prose poetry.[60] Hence, we might say, the naturalistic 'looseness' of the overall structure of his novels is counterbalanced by the formal rigour of his prose style – and surely the aesthetic tension implicit here is one of the secret pleasures of his work. If Kawabata were a Western writer, we might describe him as a classicist in romantic clothing, as Apollo playing Dionysus. Or would it be the other way round? At any rate, we may see how Kawabata's development of what Burke calls the 'minor form' of eloquence also serves his larger purposes. As Burke points out, a novelist such as Stendhal, for whom syllogistic progression is all-important, purposely avoids any form of stylistic eloquence which would draw attention to individual sentences and thus slow down the ongoing rush of narrative events. 'Each sentence in Stendhal deliberately eschews any saliency as a minor or incidental form – it aims to be imperceptible – and if the reader forgets that he is reading, he is reading as Stendhal would have him read'.[61] Conversely, we may see how Kawabata's cultivation of a poetic intensity of language contributes to his overall antinarrative purpose. But more on this point shortly.

I have already mentioned that 'repetitive form' plays a predominant role in the overall structure of *The Sound of the Mountain*, and many of the major themes and images which recur throughout the work are initially sounded in its first chapter: themes such as Shingo's aging, his family problems and his fear of death, and images such as the cherry tree, the train commuting between Tokyo and Kamakura, and the all-important mountain itself. But, as Burke points out, repetitive form may also operate on a smaller scale, such as in a 'succession of images, each of them giving the same lyric mood'.[62] As a 'lyrical' novelist, Kawabata naturally makes frequent use of this device – as in the above-mentioned series of images in the 'mountain sound' scene: moonlit night, autumn insects, cherry tree, mountain and so on. In this respect, Kawabata's work also might be described, to use Konishi's words about *renga*, as a 'symphony of images'. And, just as with *renga*, as the reader is 'transfixed' by these individual images, his or her attention is diverted away from any ongoing narrative development; in other words, he or she is released from a time-bound into a timeless realm.

We may begin to see, then, how Kawabata's 'aesthetics of emptiness' functions on both a formal and a thematic level. To put this in *kōan* form: when the narrator announces, *Tsukiyo datta*, where is Shingo? We might say either that he has vanished entirely or that he has become the moonlit night. Either way, at that moment the ego-bound, time-bound Shingo is nowhere to be found. There is a sudden suspension of his personal presence as there is of the narrative flow; what we have instead is the all-pervasive, impersonal presence of nature. A sense of liberation may come with this, but also a certain bittersweet sadness. One critic, Katō Shū-ichi, has described the metaphysic implicit in Kawabata's style as *setsuna-shugi*, a term difficult to render into English (ephemeralism?) but implying a consciousness that human existence is only moment to moment and is lacking in any continuous identity.[63] Thus, although, as many critics have pointed out, Kawabata's works are redolent with the traditional aesthetic/Buddhistic sentiment of *mono no aware* (literally, a 'sensitivity to things', but with a suggestion of something like the old Roman *lacrimae rerum*), it arises not only from a sense of the transitoriness of perceived objects but also of the perceiving subject. Just as, in *renga*, there is no sustained continuity of narrative voice but rather what Donald Keene has called a 'multiple stream of consciousness', so in Kawabata the moments of narrative stasis have the effect of a sudden break in the ego-centred consciousness of the central character.[64] A dramatic and sustained example of this is the final, climactic scene of *Snow Country*, discussed in Chapter Four, in which Shimamura loses all sense of self and is described as being filled with and overwhelmed by the Milky Way.

There are some interesting parallels between Kawabata's aesthetic here (and its implicit metaphysic) and that of the French 'new novel' which came to prominence in the 1950s, the decade in which *The Sound of the Mountain* was also published. In his *For a New Novel*, Alain Robbe-Grillet, the leading novelist and theorist of this movement, attacks the 'obsolete notion' that a 'true novelist' must create 'characters'.[65] 'The novel of characters belongs entirely to the past, it describes a period: that which marked the apogee of the individual'.[66] In this age of mass man, in which psychologists also have demonstrated that there is no such thing as an absolute personal identity, major novelists such as Kafka, Sartre, Céline, Camus, Faulkner and Beckett have no interest in perpetuating the illusion of 'round' characters. The truth of Robbe-Grillet's contention is further confirmed, it seems to me, by the example of Japanese literature – and perhaps this is a good example of the kind of insight we may expect from East/West comparative studies. Since Japan never experienced such a golden age of individualism as occurred in nineteenth-century Europe, it is hardly surprising that the 'novel of character' never really took root there – despite the best efforts of even such a considerable practitioner of the form as Natsume Sōseki.

But, as Robbe-Grillet also points out, there is another, more positive side to all of this: what the novel has lost in humanistic value it has gained in a wider vision. 'The exclusive cult of the "human" has given way to a larger consciousness, one that is less anthropocentric'.[67] Here the French novelist, pursuing his own 'postmodern' course, seems to approach remarkably close to the 'aesthetics of emptiness' of medieval Japanese culture:

the personal gives way to the impersonal, and as the sense of the presence of man lessens, the sense of the presence of objects – especially natural and aesthetic objects – greatly increases. This is the 'new objectivity' of the *nouveaux romanciers.* And I might repeat here Masao Miyoshi's claim that: 'Kawabata's achievement lies in just this, his keen awareness of the objects around men that exist in themselves as solidly as people do'.[68] This is particularly true, I would say, with Kawabata's later works, beginning with *Thousand Cranes,* in which the tea implements seem to have more 'character' than the human beings, and *The Sound of the Mountain,* in which objects such as the ancient lotus seed and the *Jidō* nō mask play a role at least equal to that of the minor characters. By the time of *Sleeping Beauties* (*Nemureru bijo,* 1961), even human beings have become objects: the drugged girls whom Eguchi, the old man, spends the night with, exist only as physical presences for him; given the state they are in, they are not even allowed the possibility of individual identity. In the surrealistic fantasy, 'One Arm' (*Kataude,* 1964), which could be regarded as a kind of companion piece to *Sleeping Beauties,* woman's body is so objectified that her limbs may be detached at will, as if she were no more than a doll. I might add that Kawabata's interest in pornography as an extreme form of the objectification of human beings is shared by *nouveaux romanciers* such as Robbe-Grillet, whose *Maison de rendez-vous,* for instance, parallels *Sleeping Beauties* on this as on other points.

Reviewing, now, all of the non-syllogistic forms which Kawabata makes so much use of in *The Sound of the Mountain*: qualitative and associative progression, repetitive and minor forms, we may see that they all incline towards the creation of moments of stasis or 'gaps' in the narrative and so function as an integral part of an 'aesthetics of emptiness'. By disrupting the on-going progress of the narrative they disrupt all sense of the flow of linear time, and thus serve as a perfect 'objective correlative' in formal terms of the anti-time theme at the novel's core. This formal/thematic consonance is the hallmark of the novel's aesthetic integrity.

It would, perhaps, be somewhat monotonous to go over all this same ground with Proust's novel, but suffice it to say that here, too, we may find the same reliance on non-syllogistic forms to 'slow down' the narrative and afford some sense of time-transcendence in line with the novel's theme. To give but one conspicuous example, one could hardly imagine a less 'transparent' or Stendhalian style than Proust's: not only because of the frequently epigrammatic quality of his sentences but also because of their sheer density. No reader would go to Proust merely for a 'good story' – if anyone did, they would probably find him unreadable. With Proust one must readjust one's sense of narrative pace and relish each lengthy sentence, each extended analogy or metaphor, as it comes. What Burke has to say in this regard is interesting:

> A writer like Proust, any single page of whom is out-standing, becomes wearisome after extended reading. Proust's technical forms, one might say, are limited to the exploitation of parenthesis within parenthesis, a process which is carried down from whole chapters, through parts of chapters, into the paragraph and thence into the halting of the single sentence.[69]

But perhaps Burke is not being quite fair to Proust here; perhaps what he fails to see is that it is exactly this 'halting of the single sentence' which serves Proust's larger purpose: namely, the paradoxical one of representing within a linear narrative the transcendence of linear time.

Finally, are there any general lessons to be learned by Western theorists of the novel from a consideration of Kawabata's use of non-syllogistic forms? There is already a long tradition in modern Western criticism, beginning perhaps with Georg Lukacs' *Die Theorie des Romans* (1920), of conceiving of temporal mimesis as somehow central to the poetics of the novel. Lukacs pointed out that the extended forms of antiquity, tragedy and the epic, were time-transcendent, but that the novel was inescapably timebound.[70] In that case, what was Lukacs, and those critics who followed him, to make of all those modern novels such as Proust's which aimed, at least, to be time-transcendent? Having defined the novel as time-bound, they must necessarily characterize these heretical modern novels as 'anti-novelistic'. Eleanor Hutchens, for instance, pronounces quite strictly on the matter:

> When we consider the novels that seem to defy temporal control, it becomes evident that they make up the body of the anti-novelistic novel: that is, every test of the novel is a temporal test. From Sterne to Robbe-Grillet, the writers who strain the genre strain it by flouting a temporal norm. The more defiant they are, the more they call attention to the primary importance of time.[71]

One can almost imagine Ms. Hutchens pursuing these 'defiant' novelists with a schoolmarm's stick! But how many 'anti-novelistic' novels must we have before they themselves are accepted as a novelistic norm? And if they ever are, would we not begin to agree with Robbe-Grillet that the time-bound novel is a product of the bourgeois culture of nineteenth-century Europe – or, at least, of European humanist culture since the Renaissance? Certainly the Japanese example seems to confirm this sense of relativity.

Is it possible, then, to have anti-temporal or even anti-narrative elements as an integral part of a novel's structure? Looking at *The Sound of the Mountain*, we must answer emphatically in the affirmative. Furthermore, it may not be said that Kawabata, in writing this work, took an adversary stance to any tradition of the novel as temporal mimesis. Quite the contrary: not only does his novel fall well within the tradition of the modern *shōsetsu*, but also, as we have seen, it harks back in many ways to such older traditions as the *renga*. It would be Eurocentric, to say the least, to characterize the *shōsetsu* as anti-novelistic. The non-syllogistic novel, then, begins to seem like a natural, *bona fide* form of the genre. From a wider perspective, across cultures and centuries, it may even seem more natural or normative than the syllogistic, time-bound novel. Be that as it may, I think we may conclude, at least, that if such masterworks as *The Sound of the Mountain* and *In Search of Lost Time* are 'disqualified as novels' by our critical doctrines, it is time those critical doctrines were revised.

CHAPTER SEVEN

NARCISSUS IN WINTER

Each man kills the thing he loves . . . .

Oscar Wilde

Why should not old men be mad?

W.B.Yeats

The Buddha realm is easy to enter, but it is difficult to enter the realm of devils.

Ikkyū

1. Narcissus and the Virgin Whore

Seen in the perspective of Kawabata's entire career, his two late stories, *Sleeping Beauties* (*Nemureru bijo*, 1961) and 'One Arm' (*Kataude*, 1964) are, first of all, of great interest technically or aesthetically, as bold and startling new experiments on the part of a rather elderly writer. He seems here to be returning with a vengeance to the modernist experiments of his youth. On a thematic level also, in the context of Kawabata's lifelong preoccupations and obsessions – especially in regard to sexual relations beteen men and women, these stories form a powerful and enlightening climax, providing the most radical solution yet to the eternal conundrum of the Kawabata male: how can he relate with the kind of woman he desires without destroying that very quality in her which he finds desirable? This 'outer' contradiction is paralleled by an 'inner' contradiction: his narcissism impels him to preserve his isolation, while his self-hatred impels him to seek self-affirmation and 'purification' through relations with a virginal girl. But this same self-hatred convinces him that any virginal girl touched by him will immediately be defiled, thus losing the capacity for purification – except perhaps for one all-too-brief ecstatic moment. Furthermore, although both his narcissism and his self-hatred demand a virginal girl, they also demand that she will offer herself to him without any threatening

192

counter-demands for reciprocity. In other words, she must be a virgin who is willing to be used like a whore. On the face of it, it is an impossible and contradictory demand, and yet in these two stories Kawabata seems to find a way, at least in fantasy, to resolve this contradiction and realize his desires at last.

The title 'Sleeping Beauties' has, of course, a fairy-tale resonance which may seem ironic, given the rather seedy nature of the business being transacted at the 'brothel for impotent old men'.[1] But there is something more to it than that: the fairy-tale aspect of Kawabata's work, here as elsewhere, has its deepest roots in what we might call his mystical/romantic idealism, his longing, or the longing of his protagonists, for an innocent, paradisal, transcendental realm, an ideal monistic realm such as that dreamt of by the scientist's wife in *Crystal Fantasies*, a 'fairytale world in which baby peacocks were born to dogs'.[2] Only by entering such a realm will Kawabata's troubled protagonists find themselves purified of the 'dirt of the world' and of their own egotism. In other words, although *Sleeping Beauties* certainly has its erotic or even pornographic aspect – naked girls drugged so that impotent old men may enjoy them freely as 'sex objects' – what raises the work above the level of commonplace erotica is that ultimately it is a story more of unsatisfied spiritual than of sexual longings. In short, innocence is never presented in a merely ironic way in Kawabata – it is too much the object of longing for his protagonists. In the case of *Sleeping Beauties*, despite the protagonist's 'immoral' actions – indeed, because of them – he is, in fact, trying to gain admittance into exactly that fairy-tale realm of innocence. The story's title is thus a brilliantly appropriate one (which is why one regrets Edward Seidensticker's 'dilution' of it in his otherwise excellent translation, *House of the Sleeping Beauties*).

To say that the male hero longs for innocence is not to say, of course, that his behaviour is innocent. Indeed, *Sleeping Beauties* is obviously Kawabata's ultimate and most extreme expression of a theme he had explored – unconsciously at first perhaps, but with increasing consciousness and conscience – since his earliest works: male narcissism and the kind of objectification and exploitation of women which results from it. In this sense *Sleeping Beauties* is his most ruthless formulation of the familiar paradox and conundrum of the Kawabata male mentioned above, but explored now in a new context: that of old age. Indeed, it is old age which introduces a new and ironic twist on an old Kawabata problem: in this story the males are sexually inhibited not because of their narcissism but because of their impotence – or so it is supposed, and yet, even more ironically, this is one of the few Kawabata stories in which the male protagonist, despite his advanced age, actually threatens to become sexually active.

Like *The Sound of the Mountain*, *Sleeping Beauties* may be regarded as a study in old age, and of sex and death in old age – although in a very different mood to the earlier work. The protagonist is repeatedly referred to as '*Eguchi rōjin*' ('old man Eguchi'), so that his age becomes his main defining characteristic. He asks himself whether he has not come to the house of sleeping beauties seeking, paradoxically, the 'ultimate in the ugliness of old age'.[3] In other words, is he driven by a perverse impulse to experience the bitterness of his old age to the depths through the obscene contrast between himself and the beautiful young girls? But to what purpose? No doubt he is searching in this way for some form of transcendence. According to Buddhist teaching, first one must experience life as suffering – especially the basic realities of sickness, old age and death – and only then will one be motivated to attain spiritual liberation. But does Eguchi's 'liberation' consist in anything more than oblivion and death? Certainly the shadow of death already casts a chill over his old age. Just as Shingo's hearing of the sound of the mountain warns him of the approach of death, so also, in the first scene of this story, with Eguchi's hearing the violent sound of wind and waves just outside the house where he is seeking momentary refuge. The wind, it is said, carries 'the sound of approaching winter'.[4] This 'winter', of course, is meant symbolically as well as literally. Time in this story progresses from autumn to mid-winter, symbolizing Eguchi's own movement towards old age and death. Seasonal correspondences are often meaningful in this way in Kawabata, as in traditional Japanese literature. Whereas the mood of *The Sound of the Mountain* is gently autumnal, the mood of *Sleeping Beauties* becomes increasingly that of bleak midwinter.

The literal meaning of 'Eguchi', the protagonists family name, is 'river mouth', signifying that he is near the end of the river of life. The Chinese characters of his personal name, 'Yoshio', can be read to mean 'as if a man' or 'like a man', implying that, like Shingo too, he is filled with regrets about his life and feels that he has not realized his full potential as a human being. He senses that life is leaving him before he has really lived, and this creates a sense of enormous pent-up frustration which causes him to have violent impulses. Despite all his boasts of potency and that, unlike the other old men, he is 'not yet a guest to be trusted', his efforts to set himself apart from all the other pitiful old men – and, at one point, his vow even to get revenge for them by violating the house rule against sexual intercourse – all this comes increasingly to seem empty posturing based on illusion.[5] His threats are never carried out and by the story's end he seems to belong with the other old men in this respect as well. His violent and even murderous impulses towards the girls, which culminate in his 'inadvertent' killing of the 'black girl', his fury towards life itself, derive from this increasing sense of his own impotency, and from his desire to 'leave his mark on the girl' – that is, to take possession of her by an act of violence rather than sex, since he seems incapable of the latter.[6]

Like Shingo too, Eguchi is troubled by incestuous impulses, as revealed in his dreams about his mother and his daughters. And like Shingo again he seeks escape from the flow of time – but not merely through dreams or the quiet contemplation of art or nature. More desperate than Shingo, Eguchi is a 'mad old man' who seeks to rejuvenate himself by taking the desperate and dangerous measure of visiting the 'house of the sleeping beauties'.

Like the fairy tale 'sleeping beauty' who does not age in her long sleep, who is as young when she is kissed awake as when she was put to sleep, Kawabata's drugged girls too in their death-like sleep seem suspended outside of time, statue-like humans who approach the condition of works of art in their pure physicality, void of any ego, eternal virgins who promise to 'purify' and rejuvenate old men. Eguchi describes them as offering 'ageless freedom for old men'.[7] His friend Kiga introduced him to this 'secret' house with the promise that the experience it offered was 'like sleeping with a secret Buddha', and he had also assured him that 'only when he was beside a girl who had been put to sleep could he himself feel alive'.[8]

The promise, then, is of a kind of salvation as well as of rejuvenation. And Eguchi himself seems motivated by something much more than just the lustful fantasies of a 'dirty old man'. When he goes back, despite his guilt feelings, it is because he feels he has never 'spent another night so clean'.[9] And this had enabled him to sleep deeper and longer than usual, a sleep of young innocence rather than of aged guilt, and when he had woken up in the morning it had been 'a sweet, childlike awakening, in her young warmth and soft scent'.[10] Again, the virginity of the girls is also emphasized, adding to their aura of 'youthful innocence'. Thus Eguchi seems motivated, like other Kawabata males in their pursuit of women, more by psychological or spiritual needs than by erotic or lustful desires (although the latter, of course, are not entirely absent).

But is this too all an illusion? Are the pleasures and satisfactions the house offers really so 'innocent', 'purifying' and life-affirming? Is there not an obvious contradiction, first of all, in the promise upon which this secret establishment is built: that old men will feel more 'alive' by sleeping with young woman who seem 'dead'. What then does the house really offer?

There are hints from the beginning of something far from innocent – a suggestion, for instance, of necrophilia. When he first visits the house, Eguchi is afraid the drugged girl might look like 'a corpse from a drowning'.[11] And when finally he approaches the girl, he finds that her sleep is indeed death-like – she is unresponsive even when he touches her. Close to death themselves, it seems that the old men can feel comfortable only with girls drugged into a death-like sleep. For them the girls are 'life to be touched with confidence'.[12] In other words, because the girls are fast asleep, the old men need not feel ashamed of their own ugliness and impotence. They can indulge freely in 'dreams and memories of women', the sleeping girls serving as a kind of catalyst for these.[13]

But Eguchi, supposedly not yet as 'impotent' or as 'senile' as the other old men, sometimes feels a contradictory impulse to awaken the girls, even by resorting to violence, and to force them to relate with him in a more human way. When he confides to the madam his desire to know the girls as people and to have them know him, she replies paradoxically that this would be a 'crime' and admonishes him: '"Just take sleeping girls as sleeping girls."'[14] But Eguchi finds this hard to do: sometimes he can no longer bear the fact that they are completely oblivious of his presence – or of his existence. The girls confront him like blank walls; the experience which seemed pleasant on a physical level begins to torment him on a psychological level. The 'blank surface' of the girls soon becomes another of those dangerous 'mirrors of the heart' which we have so often encountered in Kawabata's works, reflecting back to old Eguchi all that troubles him now and in the past. In particular, the girl lying asleep beside him, being an 'absent presence' herself, and so incapable of engaging him in a present relationship, has the effect of 'reawakening' his past relationships with other women. Since old Eguchi was obviously quite a 'womanizer' in his day, there are quite a few of these – *geisha* and mistresses as well as casual affairs. He is also reminded of how much he misses his three daughters, now married and lost to him, since they seldom visit. And this provokes disturbing dreams in him: for instance, of one of his daughters hacking to death her deformed baby. The theme of incestuous desire implicit here becomes more explicit when he broods over his favourite, youngest daughter's loss of virginity before she was married, and feels shame and degradation over this. Oppressed in this way by his present loneliness and his bitter memories, he feels that it would be 'just as well' if he too, like the girl beside him, 'would fall into a sleep of death'.[15] And so he takes two sleeping pills.

Indeed, by his third visit Eguchi has begun to realize what the real attraction of the house is for him:

> It was a house frequented by old men who could no longer use women as women; but Eguchi, on his third visit, knew that to sleep with such a girl was a fleeting consolation, the pursuit of a vanished happiness in being alive. And were there among them old men who secretly asked to sleep forever beside a girl who had been put to sleep? There seemed to be a sadness in a young girl's body that called up in an old man a longing for death.[16]

Immediately after these ruminations supposedly about the most secret desire of other old men, Eguchi decides to ask for the stronger sleeping pill which the girls have been given – even though he knows it is dangerous for a man of his age and might induce, perhaps all too literally, a 'sleep as of the dead'.[17] And lying beside the girls also, on two occasions he has a vision of white butterflies – a symbol of death.

By his fourth visit, with the season now in midwinter, Eguchi has begun to entertain more friendly thoughts towards death, such as: 'the aged have death, and the young have love'.[18] And he registers his 'dissatisfaction at not being able to die'.[19] The sinister madam, who presumably is already thoroughly experienced in these matters, shows that she knows full well what he is really asking for when he asks for the same strong 'medicine' the girls have been given: '"You're asking a lot for someone who has only been here three times"', she says, and then stares at him with 'a faint smile on her lips'.[20] One notes that this is not a categorical refusal, but implies rather that with longer patronage he will be granted his wish. And, in fact, it does not take very long: on his next visit the madam herself suggests that '"it would be paradise"' for an old man to die there, and when Eguchi hints that he might want to commit suicide with one of the girls, she replies coldly: '"Please do, if you feel lonely about doing it by yourself"'.[21]

On his fifth and final visit, when the madam expresses surprise that he has come out on such a cold night, Eguchi answers immediately: '"That's why I've come .... To die on a night like this, with a young woman's skin to warm him – that would be paradise for an old man"'.[22] And when he assures her that he has come 'with open eyes' even though he knows that another old man has died there recently, the madam laughs 'diabolically'.[23] Eguchi remembers too that his cynical friend Kiga had described this man's death as 'a kind of euthanasia'.[24]

Finally, the choice Eguchi makes between life and death is symbolized by his behaviour towards the two girls with whom he is provided on his fifth visit. The 'dark girl' (literally 'black girl', *kuroi musume*) is described by Eguchi as 'life itself'; she is black because full of life-force, or life-blood – quite literally, since Eguchi sees 'the colour of blood' beneath her finger-nails.[25] Being so overpoweringly alive, she makes him feel more keenly than the other girls the ebbing of his own life-force, the fact that he is not far from the impotence and sterility of the other old men. Thus it is not surprising that she is the one he chooses, however 'inadvertently', to kill – by turning off her electric blanket after the madam has admonished him explicitly not to do so (since it is getting cold and, being naked, the girl might freeze). And by killing her he seems to be taking his revenge on 'life itself'. The 'fair girl' ('white girl', *shiroi musume*), on the other hand, is 'slender and graceful' and has skin so white that 'it might have been bleached', and she gives Eguchi a 'voluptuous' welcome – unlike the black girl, who had pushed him away.[26] White, of course, is the colour of bloodlessness and therefore death. Thus, quite clearly, by killing the black girl and returning to sleep with the white girl, Eguchi chooses death over life. And when, finally, he threatens to make trouble over the dead 'black girl', the madam is only too willing to grant his wish for a dangerous extra dose of 'white' sleeping medicine and invites him, suggestively, to return to the white girl and 'sleep late tomorrow' (in the original her words are even more suggestive of a 'long sleep': '*Kore de ashita no asa wa, doozo goyukkuri oyasumi ni natte ite kudasaimase*'.)[27]

★ ★ ★

Despite his age, Eguchi's psychology and behaviour are still recognizably those of the narcissistic male familiar to us from earlier Kawabata works. After all, the 'relation' between impotent old men and drugged virgins is an 'ideal' form of sexual relation from a narcissistic point of view: an intense union of eros and thanatos, but with more of the latter than the former. In other words, the story is the most extreme expression to date – though shortly afterwards it would be outdone in this respect by 'One Arm' – of the narcissistic Kawabata male's reluctance to become involved in a mutual relationship with women: finally now he can relate safely with beautiful virgins, taking an aesthetic and erotic pleasure in them but not having to give anything of himself in return – except, of course, his money. As the madam assures him, the girls will not even know who has been with them – they are live objects, inhabiting the twilight zone between life and death.[28]

But there is also an exploitative aspect of his relationship with the girls which is a far more sinister manifestation of his narcissism. He receives the 'current of life' from them, but this seems to awaken something like a vampirish impulse in him, as if, feeling his own life-force draining away, he wants to suck new life out of the girls – quite literally.[29] In an eerie foreshadowing of 'One Arm', at one point he even feels tempted to take a girl's finger in his mouth and suck blood from it.[30]

As with other Kawabata protagonists – Shimamura with Komako, for instance – what draws Eguchi back to his strange 'relationship' with the sleeping girls, unsatisfactory as it is in other respects, is the attraction of self-knowledge – always an irresistable attraction for the narcissist! One might say that he visits the house in order to discover why he wants to visit the house. The novella's main 'plot-line', if such it may be called, consists of Eguchi's journey towards a frightening self-discovery, the discovery of his 'secret' desire for death. The house of the sleeping beauties stands revealed, in the end, as a house of death. And not only a house of death. At one point Eguchi speculates that, although it may be 'evil' for an old man to lie beside a drugged girl, the 'evil would become clearer were he to kill her'.[31] Since that is exactly what Eguchi finally does, perhaps we might say that ultimately, in his bitterness towards life, he embraces evil as well as death, thus entering that nihilistic, anti-life 'realm of devils' which, according to Ikkyū in an epigram Kawabata was very fond of, was the most difficult realm to enter. The house of the sleeping beauties turns out to be a house of evil as well as a house of death: we realize this clearly with the madam's final casual but devastating remark: 'There is the other girl', showing how cruelly expendable the girls are.[32]

The discovery of his own growing impotency and the violent impulses aroused by this is another unexpected and unpleasant insight Eguchi gains from his encounter with the sleeping beauties. By his fourth visit he himself has realized the connection between these two 'evils', as indicated by a typically Kawabataesque juxtaposition:

> The impotence of the other old men was probably not very far off for Eguchi himself. Thoughts of atrocities rose in him .... [33]

After which he has another vision of white butterflies, which he imagines to have been evoked in him by the sleeping girl 'to quiet the bad impulses in an old man'.[34]

By bringing out these murderous impulses which cause even Eguchi himself to 'shiver', the girls are true 'mirrors of the heart' which reveal his 'shadow side' to him – a fascinating if unpleasant form of self-knowledge.[35]

For the aging narcissist too, being able to spend the night with these sleeping virgins, immersing himself in their aura of innocent femininity, offers him a chance to indulge in fantasies of infantile regression: embracing them, he experiences a 'mindless rapture' – that is, something akin to the egoless 'oceanic consciousness' of infants as described by Freud.[36] As we have seen, after spending his first night at the house, he feels that he has never 'spent another night so clean' and he enjoys a 'sweet, childlike awakening'.[37] Paradoxically but predictably, he also manages to find something 'motherly' in the girls: as when he smells baby milk on one of them, or when he has a 'childlike feeling that he was loved by the girl' and, like a suckling infant, he immediately reaches for her breast – indeed, he even has the illusion that it is his own mother's breast.[38] Thus the girls conform to the male narcissist's ideal of the 'virgin mother' and allow him to indulge his incestuous fantasies.

Regressing back to his infancy, Eguchi ultimately encounters his mother and, sleeping with the motherly virgins, he is able to imagine that he can 'possess' her before she was 'violated' by his father. When the thought occurs to him that his mother had been his 'first woman', he asks himself: '"But can I say that Mother was my woman?"'[39] He can, in fact, with the help of the 'sleeping beauties'. But now that he finally 'takes possession' of his mother, where does this lead him?

Coming at the strategic point that it does, just before the story's end and climax, Eguchi's confrontation with the greatest trauma of his life – the loss of his mother – obviously plays a crucial role in determining his ultimate choice between life and death. He remembers how, when he was only seventeen, he had watched his mother die painfully from tuberculosis, coughing up blood and calling out his name as she died. As the narrator tells us: 'It was natural that when old Eguchi thought of his mother as the first woman in his life, he thought too of her death'.[40] When he looks around the room now, the curtains that had once seemed a sensual scarlet seem 'the colour of blood'.[41] For the first time in this novella, there are tears in his eyes. Holding the girls' breasts, he remembers his mother's breasts, 'groping for them and going to sleep, one day when he was still an infant'.[42] Now too he falls asleep, but not to enjoy the innocent sleep of an infant: he has a succession of nightmares which are 'disturbingly erotic'.[43] In the last of these, the only one that is described, Eguchi comes home from his honeymoon to find his house surrounded by blood-coloured flowers and his mother there to welcome him but asking pointedly: '"Is your wife afraid of us?"'[44] When Eguchi then goes out into the garden with his new bride to admire the flowers, he finds that one of them is oozing blood – and he awakes with a groan. Clearly this nightmare expresses the guilt he had felt on 'betraying' his dead mother with another woman, his wife. But now, finally, near the end of his life, he has a chance to be 'reconciled' and 'reunited' with his mother by joining her in death.

After this powerful dream, it is almost anti-climactic when Eguchi awakens to find that the 'black girl' is dead and when, as a result of this, the madam offers him a potentially fatal extra dose of sleeping medicine. The real climax, after all, is Eguchi's confrontation with the ghost which has haunted him all his life. Is *Sleeping Beauties*, then, a story of salvation or of damnation? And does Kawabata indicate anything about the answer to this question by the obvious intertextual relations he establishes between his novella and the medieval Nō play, *Eguchi*?

Eguchi's name is doubly significant: besides indicating, as already mentioned, that he is near the end of life, it also conjures up Zeami's Nō play, *Eguchi* (1424), and the legends upon which this play was based. Now part of Osaka, Eguchi is an area around the mouth of the Yodo River which was once famous for its brothels. Various legends arose regarding a courtesan known as Eguchi no kimi or Princess Eguchi, who once plied her trade there, and her encounters with some famous Buddhist monks. In the Nō play, *Eguchi*, she is revealed to be a manifestation of the bodhisattva Fugen, and the story is told of how she was once visited by the famous twelfth-century poet-monk Saigyō. Saigyō had requested a night's lodging in her house, but she had first refused him this, warning: 'Set not your heart upon a moment's refuge'.[45] As the play further explains:

> ... she, a known woman of pleasure,
> harboured in her house forgotten troubles,
> secrets disowned by all. Upon that house,
> set not your heart, her poem warned,
> only because she cared for him
> who had renounced the world.[46]

Her warning certainly applies well to Eguchi too, who also seeks 'a moment's refuge' in a house which harbours 'forgotten troubles' and 'secrets disowned by all'.

Are then Kawabata's sleeping beauties, whom we already know to be 'virgin prostitutes', also '*bohisattva* whores' like Princess Eguchi? Do they guide the old man Eguchi to any kind of enlightenment or spiritual liberation? The legend of the '*bodhisattva* whore' traditionally symbolizes one of the most profound doctrines of the monistic philosophy of Mahayana Buddhism: since all phenomena are ultimately manifestations of the same universal mind, then *samsara* is *nirvana*, ignorance is enlightenment, the impure is pure, the low is high, and even whores have Buddha-nature and can be *bodhisattvas*. (*Sleeping Beauties* seems to be structured on a similar pattern of apparent contradictions and merging opposites: age becomes youth, beauty becomes ugliness, purity becomes pollution, pleasure becomes pain, good becomes evil, life becomes death, heaven becomes hell – it is probably Kawabata's most 'dialectically' structured story.) Furthermore, the whore, in offering her body to all men without distinction, is an excellent symbol of non-discriminative wisdom and compassion. Last but not least, who knows with more conviction than a whore – as Princess Eguchi so eloquently demonstrates – the 'noble truth' that desire leads to suffering, and that sensual pleasures are fleeting and illusory?

Of course, since Kawabata's girls are drugged into an unwakeable sleep, they cannot be as eloquent as Princess Eguchi. Any instructive 'role' they play must necessarily be passive, silent and unconscious. But, on the other hand, perhaps that is the only kind of 'instruction' which the old cynic Eguchi would tolerate. Certainly he is not in any mood to listen to a Buddhist sermon, such as the one preached in the Nō play by the whore of Eguchi! Indeed, in their very unconscious, egoless, timeless state, the girls may be said to represent the ideal state of 'nothingness' which Eguchi himself longs for. But whether this is a Buddhist nothingness or a merely nihilistic one is another question. In his Nobel Prize acceptance speech Kawabata made much of this distinction. At the very end of the speech, after having evoked at length the paradisiacal monistic vision of traditional Japanese poetry and Zen, he says: 'We have here the emptiness, the nothingness, of the Orient. My own works have often been described as works of emptiness, but it is not to be taken for the nihilism of the West. The spiritual foundation would seem to be quite different'.[47] And, earlier in the same speech, he defines this 'Oriental emptiness' in his favourite monistic terms: 'This is not the nothingness or the emptiness of the West. It is rather the reverse, a universe of the spirit in which everything communicates freely with everything, transcending bounds, limitless'.[48] It is difficult to believe, however, that the nothingness which looms like a dark shadow behind this late work is anything but nihilistic – and, indeed, is anything but the shadow of death.

The girls are described as 'secret Buddhas' by Eguchi's friend Kiga, but coming from such a cynic this can only seem ironic – at first glance, at least.[49] Nonetheless, Eguchi himself has similar thoughts about one of the girls because of the 'comfort' she has given to old men:

> He almost thought that, as in old legends, she was the incarnation of a Buddha. Were there not old stories in which prostitutes and courtesans were Buddhas incarnate?[50]

Indeed there were – one of which, by strange coincidence, was about a whore called Eguchi. Kawabata is not just being coy here; obviously he wants to make sure that even readers unfamiliar with Nō will not miss his point about the sleeping beauties as '*bodhisattva* whores'. But what exactly is his point?

From a Buddhist point of view the house itself, built on the very desires which lead to suffering, may be seen to symbolize *maya*, the realm of illusion – like the whorehouse in the Nō play upon which the monk is warned not to 'set your heart:' it promises the old men youth, beauty, pleasure, and a renewal of life, but ultimately gives them an intensified sense of old age, ugliness, suffering and death. What seemed to be heaven turns out to be hell, and the promised salvation is really damnation. As Eguchi discovers, once one is ensnared by the 'charms' of this house, the only possible exit is by death. But, then again, is not this death the very liberation he has been seeking, the closest he can come, as a troubled modern soul, to the medieval Buddhist goal of *nirvana*? Perhaps so, but this would be a sorry decline from the ideal of transcendence Kawabata had expressed only a decade earlier, in *The Sound of the Mountain*. Although it is true that Freud, with whom Kawabata seemed to agree on many points, equated his idea of a 'death-drive' with the Buddhist aspiration for *nirvana*, Kawabata was too deeply versed in the Buddhist scriptures – and, it must be said, too much in love with them – to make such a simplistic equivalence, except ironically.

The correspondences between *Sleeping Beauties* and the Nō play *Eguchi*, then, must be said to function in an essentially ironic way, just as the correspondences between Western classics and modernist works often do – for instance, between the heroic *Odyssey* and Joyce's anti-heroic *Ulysses*. These echoes from an age of faith only intensify the bitterness and the nostalgic sense of loss in an age of nihilistic despair.

As Royall Tyler has pointed out, *Eguchi* was one of those Nō plays which touched on an 'important religious issue for thinking people in medieval Japan', which was 'the relationship between art (especially dance, music, and poetry) and enlightenment, since art actually creates objects of sense'.[51] In other words, does art entangle one further in the snares of the sensory world, the realm of illusion and desire, or does it sometimes enable one to see through the illusion and thus liberate oneself from it? As we have seen, Kawabata was concerned with the spiritual function of art throughout his career – he had even begun with the optimistic Arnoldian view that literature was destined to replace religion in the new age of science. In this respect also, then, his choice of the play *Eguchi* as the 'corresponding' work of classic literature for his own late story, *Sleeping Beauties*, is obviously meaningful. But, again, what the story seems to tell us is that by this time he had lost all confidence in literature's 'salvational' power. If so, then this 'loss of faith' is yet another thing he had in common with his great *haiku* forbear, Bashō, of whom Makoto Ueda has written:

> Bashō, who once thought of becoming a monk, did not do so but clung to the thin line of poetry, no doubt because he thought poetry could solve problems that are usually the preserve of religion .... He thought he could attain supreme serenity of mind by means of poetry, but, ironically, it was poetry itself that forever disturbed his mind. Towards the end of his life he is said to have called poetry a 'sinful attachment'. His deathbed poem of dreams roaming on a withered moor also seems to suggest Bashō's ultimate failure to enter a realm of religious enlightenment.[52]

Sleeping Beauties is Kawabata's own 'withered moor', his *Waste Land*, a powerful vision of spiritual sterility. It is his most pessimistic, anti-life and despairing work, a work which seems favourably disposed towards both nihilism and suicide, despite his disavowal of these just a few years later in his Nobel Prize speech. Like the Nō play *Eguchi*, *Sleeping Beauties* is suffused with a medieval sense of life as suffering, and of old age as the surest token of this 'noble truth', but, unlike the Nō play, it offers no corresponding promise of 'liberation' from suffering – apart from death. In Mishima's memorable image, the atmosphere of this story is like that of a 'submarine in which people are trapped and the air is gradually disappearing'.[53] From a literary biographical point of view, we might say that the work was born out of Kawabata's own struggle in old age with insomnia and sleeping pills, so that finally, it seems, his longing for sleep became a longing for death. Like Eguchi, Kawabata himself often needed whisky and sleeping pills to put himself to sleep, and when Eguchi thinks of the nightmares engendered by sleepless nights, the "toads and black dogs and corpses of the drowned', he might well be thinking of *Sleeping Beauties* itself.[54] Sad to say, the work thus reflects Kawabata's own ultimate choice of death over life – despite, again, the disavowals of his Nobel speech.

2. The Blood of the Virgin Whore

Although *Sleeping Beauties* presents us with an unusual or, as Mishima described it, an 'esoteric' situation, it still remains, if just barely, within the rational bounds dictated by the mainstream 'realistic' tradition of fictional narrative. In 'One Arm', however, Kawabata takes his solution of the 'virgin whore' conundrum to a surreal extremity – as if he had finally reached the conclusion that only a suprarational solution to that *kōan*-like puzzle were possible.

This account of a man who 'borrows a girl's arm for the night' is perhaps Kawabata's most baffling short story, and yet it is also very evidently a *tour de force* in the style and technique of its narrative art. In this sense it is unmistakably a late product of the period of Kawabata's artistic maturity, a period when he had attained such a mastery of his craft that anything seemed possible to him. Indeed, it is easy to imagine how, in the hands of a lesser writer, the same story might have turned out unconvincing and even grotesque. Like earlier masters of fantasy such as Gogol and Kafka, Kawabata is able to draw his readers into the dream-like world of his story by the skillful use of palpable, graphic descriptions, the kind of precise physical details which make even the most fantastic occurences seem

real. Of course, this sort of vividly imagistic writing had long
been his particular *forte*, especially, as we have seen, his peculiar
power of making an inanimate object seem intensely alive –
often more alive, indeed, than some of his shadowy, ethereal
human characters. But in 'One Arm' he was able to put this
imagistic talent to a daring new use.

Expressing his admiration for the vivifying power of
Kawabata's descriptions in *Sleeping Beauties*, Mishima Yukio
once remarked that: 'It must be very rare for literature to give
so vividly a sense of individual life through descriptions of
sleeping figures'.[55] In 'One Arm', however, we can say that
Kawabata goes even one step further, for the object which
assumes 'individual life' so vividly is not the whole body of a girl
who has been placed in a death-like sleep, but merely a single
arm which has been detached from the girl's body.

A detached arm, after all, even if it once belonged to a
beautiful girl, is usually regarded as a rather repulsive object.
Kawabata quickly overcomes our sensitivities on this point and
persuades us to respond to the arm as we would to a lovely girl
in toto by the sheer force of his style and by the use of a
technique akin to the traditional rhetorical device of synecdoche. One can trace various stages in the arm's progressive
'vivication', a process by which it soon becomes more than just
an arm, gradually taking on a quite charming feminine
presence of its own.

As the story opens, the arm is merely a part of the girl which
she takes off to lend to the narrator 'for the night'. She puts her
ring on one of its fingers, '"to remind you that it's mine"'.[56]
Before the narrator leaves with the arm, however, the girl kisses
its elbow and fingers in order to 'make them bend for you'.
This is the proverbial 'kiss of life', for the arm is already
beginning to assume a life of its own. She also touches it with
her other hand 'as if to infuse it with a spirit of its own'.[57] Once
alone with the arm, the narrator begins to see it in such a way
that it soon takes on the qualities and presence of the whole
woman. Indeed, one is even made to feel its delicately erotic
attractiveness, as in the synecdochic passage in which its
'roundness' – often symbolic in Kawabata of the very essence of
femininity – becomes the 'roundness' of the whole girl:

> She had taken off the arm at the point I liked. It was
> plump and round – was it at the top of the arm or the
> beginning of the shoulder? The roundness was that
> of a beautiful Occidental girl, rare in a Japanese. It
> was in the girl herself, a clean, elegant roundness,
> like a sphere glowing with a faint, fresh light. When

the girl was no longer clean that gentle roundness
would fade, grow flabby. Something that lasted for a
brief moment in the life of a beautiful girl, the
roundness of the arm made me feel the roundness of
her body. Her breasts would not be large. Shy, only
large enough to cup in the hands, they would have a
clinging softness and strength. And in the roundness
of the arm I could feel her legs as she walked along.
She would carry them lightly, like a small bird, or a
butterfly moving from flower to flower. There would
be the same subtle melody in the tip of her tongue
when she kissed.[58]

Then comes a startling incident which is an impressive
example of Kawabata's imaginative power: crossing a street on
his way home, with the arm held under his raincoat, the
narrator is narrowly missed by a car, which honks its horn at
him. Then he notices: 'Perhaps the arm had been frightened by
the horn. The fingers were clenched'.[59] This is the arm's first
'autonomous' action.

The next stage and a further synecdochic leap occurs when
the arm begins to actively relate with the narrator, to converse
with him like a complete woman. This happens, significantly,
when he reaches his room and is about to be overwhelmed by
its loneliness: 'perhaps my own solitude waited there to
intimidate me'.[60] At first the arm only seems to speak: '"Are
you afraid of something?" the arm seemed to say'.[61] But the
final step is soon taken, and Kawabata's narrative skill
convinces us that there is nothing unnatural in this. Further
on still he manages even to convince us that the arm smiles:

A smile did come over the arm, crossing it like light.
It was exactly the fresh smile on the girl's cheek . . . .
The light of her smile flowed across the skin of her
arm.[62]

Finally the arm is referred to simply as 'a woman': 'Never before
had a woman watched me undress in my room'.[63] And, like a
woman, it embraces him of its own accord. Thus, in the space of
a few pages, the arm has been subtly transformed from an
inanimate object into a 'full-blooded' character in its own right.

But to what purpose? Is the story merely a virtuoso
performance, Kawabata 'showing off' his technical skill by
demonstrating how he can 'breathe life' into inanimate objects
and outlandish fantasies? If such were the case, then this 'adult
fairy tale' would hardly be as powerfully compelling as it is.
What makes the story ultimately so convincing is not the

verisimilitude of its surface detail but its truth on a deeper, psychological level. For in this final completed work of his career Kawabata found a unique and powerful way of addressing and attempting to resolve issues which had preoccupied him from the beginning.

If we take a closer look at the story's central character, the narrator himself, it soon becomes apparent that he is the archetypal Kawabata protagonist, such as may be found, in one form or another, in his works of fiction from the *Dancing Girl of Izu* to *Sleeping Beauties*: a lonely man suffering from the classic modern disease of alienation, and frustrated particularly in his relations with women. Our first strong sense of this comes in the strange scene in which the narrator, on his way home with the arm, sees a young woman driving alone in a car. At first he is frightened, thinking that it is the girl coming to retrieve her arm. But 'then I suddenly remembered that she would hardly be able to drive with only one'.[64] Surrounded by a strange purple light, the woman, all alone in an empty car, seems to him like an apparition that reflects his own psychic condition: 'Was it because I went around carrying girls' arms that I felt so unnerved by emptiness?'[65] And, as we have already seen, this theme of the narrator's loneliness and alienation is sounded again when he arrives at his room.

More specifically, in one of the key moments of the story, the narrator is reminded by the arm of an incident from his past demonstrating his inability to relate fully with women: when the arm asks him to 'please' exchange it for his own arm, he is reminded of a 'strange' woman who had once offered herself to him in the same way. It was, indeed, an unusual sort of love scene:

> I pushed her down with my arm.
> 'You're hurting me!' She put her hand to the back of her head.
> There was a small spot of blood on the white pillow.
> Parting her hair, I put my lips to the drop of blood swelling on her head.[66]

This last detail is vintage Kawabata, making the man seem more like a 'vampire' than a conventional lover. And the narrator tells us of his surprise over the fact that women present themselves as such willing victims.[67]

The plot or 'action' of this story, then, revolves around the problem of how the protagonist is to be made whole and 'redeemed' from his psychic distress. And the solution – that he be purified somehow by contact with a 'clean', virginal girl – is also vintage Kawabata, but with a twist. It is not the girl herself he seeks to relate with, like the young hero of the *Dancing Girl of Izu*, nor even the drugged body of the girl, like the old protagonist of *Sleeping Beauties*, but merely with one of her arms. In other words, this seems to represent the ultimate level of abstraction in man-woman relations in Kawabata's writings. An 'innocent reader' might well pose a simple but significant question here: why indeed does the narrator take only the girl's arm – why not the whole girl? Surely the girl *in toto* would be a far more appetizing 'thing' to take home with him? Or, to phrase the question from a different point of view: why does Kawabata take the aesthetic risk of substituting a detached arm – not, after all, a very pleasing object – for the whole girl? Is he merely after 'shock value', like so many modernist artists before him, or does he 'legitimize' his seemingly bizarre choice on a deeper level than this?

One may answer this question both in a general way, within the wider context of Kawabata's works, and more specifically, within the particular context of 'One Arm'. Within the context of Kawabata's works as a whole, his protagonists, as we have seen, often shun direct relations with 'full-bodied', autonomous women, and the present male's 'relationship' with a detached female arm may be seen as a logical if surreal culmination of this tendency. In, for instance, a more 'realistic' novel Kawabata wrote a few years before 'One Arm', *The Lake* (*Mizuumi*, 1954), the hero, Gimpei, is again a man severely frustrated in his relations with women – in fact, he is a kind of highly aesthetic voyeur who follows his 'ideal' women always at a distance. And that is the point. When, at the novel's end, the tables are turned and a woman actually pursues him, his aesthetic/psychological sensibilities find the close physical presence of a woman too much to bear: 'To have seen Machie by the moat was a beautiful dream, but this ugly woman in a cheap restaurant was real'.[68] And again: 'She seemed ready to give herself to him. Gimpei felt overwhelmed with sadness, as though the world were at an end ...'.[69] And finally he pushes the woman away and returns home alone.

Thus we can understand why, in 'One Arm', Kawabata has his hero relate to only one part of a woman – the whole woman would have been altogether too much of a good thing. In this story, it seems, the narcissistic male has finally found a way of having intimate intercourse with a woman while still preserving his and her virginity – a kind of 'virgin intercourse' which brings to mind the 'virgin birth' dreamt of by the embryologist's wife in *Crystal Fantasies*.

Nevertheless, it is still paradoxically the case, as we shall see, that the protagonist of *'One Arm'* achieves a far profounder communion with woman and thus perhaps a deeper healing of his spirit than any previous Kawabata hero. He is able to do this, however, not because of any particular virtue of his own but because of the girl's supreme self-sacrifice.

Within the particular context of 'One Arm' itself, there is a more specific reason why the narrator needs only the girl's arm. At first the arm seems merely to provide him with erotic pleasure, as in the passage quoted above in which he rhapsodizes on its delectable 'roundness'. Then, when the arm begins to speak, its function seems to be to keep him company, to ward off his loneliness. But still deeper needs are hinted at from the start. The girl herself is aware of these, as revealed by her apprehensive question: "'I don't suppose you'll try to change it for your own arm?'"[70] Being so perfectly kind and self-sacrificing, however, she quickly acquiesces: "'But it will be all right. Go ahead, do.'"[71] Later, when the arm itself consents to be exchanged for his own, another hint is given in the incident remembered from the narrator's past and already quoted above. We remember that, when a certain woman had offered herself to him, he had 'pushed her down' and then, at a small prick on her head caused by her hairpin, he had sucked some blood from her. It is important to note that this girl had been a virgin:

> Her anguish was not common to all women in the act of surrender. And it was with her only the one time. The silver thread was cut, the golden bowl destroyed.[72]

Likewise the girl who has now given him her arm. Who, after all, is this strange girl who is willing to lend her arm to a man 'for the night'? On one level, of course, she is Kawabata's eternal virgin, in a direct line from the Izu dancer down through Yōko of *Snow Country* and Kikuko of the *Sound of the Mountain*. When the narrator is first admiring her arm, praising its 'roundness', he remarks: 'It was in the girl herself, a *clean*, elegant roundness, like a sphere glowing with a faint, fresh light'.[73] [my emphasis] She possesses the kind of cleanness and ethereal purity which serves as a form of balm to the psychic wounds of the Kawabata male. And speaking further of the pleasant sensation he receives from touching her arm, the narrator says: 'the slight coolness in my hand passed on to me the pleasure of the arm. It was like her breasts, not yet touched by a man'.[74] To put it bluntly, what the narrator is after is the blood of a virgin.

More than this, though, the girl is a symbolic and, it is hardly too much to say, a 'religious' figure. Other Kawabata virgins are self-sacrificing, but none to this extent. Lafadio Hearn, in his famous paean to the traditional Japanese woman, compares her to a 'boddhisattva' in her capacity for compassion and self-sacrifice. Certainly the girl in 'One Arm' displays these qualities to a saintly degree in the opening scene – when she kisses the elbow and fingers to 'make them bend for you', when she gives permission for the man to exchange her arm for his own, and so on. One is reminded, indeed, of a certain Jataka story of the Buddha in which he gives his body to feed a hungry tiger.

But, interestingly enough, it is Christian rather than Buddhist allusions which Kawabata uses to suggest this 'parable-like' level of the work. There are two points in the story at which there are direct quotations from the *New Testament*. Both of them, significantly, are uttered by a virgin just before the narrator takes blood from her and both of them, just as significantly, deal with incidents of resurrection. The first is from the story of Christ resurrecting Lazarus (*John* 11:35-36) and the second from the story of Christ's own resurrection (*John* 20:15). The first is actually a slight misquotation: the virgin of the narrator's past substitutes 'her' for 'him' in the quote: '"Jesus wept. Then said the Jews, Behold how he loved *her*!"' The narrator remarks: 'perhaps she had made the substitution intentionally'.[75] By doing so, indeed, the girl has put herself in the position of Lazarus – the dead one – and obviously hopes to put her lover in the position of Christ, the life-giver. Rather than 'raising her up', however, the narrator had 'pushed her down' and had proceeded to suck the life-blood out of her – more like a Dracula than a Christ-figure! The whole scene, then, is the ironic reverse of a resurrection.

The second quotation is uttered by the arm just after the narrator has attached it to his body and has asked it the highly pertinent question: '"Is the blood flowing?"' The arm asks him in reply:

> '"Woman, whom seekest thou". You know the passage?'[76]

These are the words addressed by the resurrected Christ to his mother who has come to visit his tomb. Thus their significance here: the narrator is literally cleansed by the virgin's blood just as, in Christian terms, Christ's blood is said to have 'washed away the sins of the world'. And thus, perhaps, he is 'resurrected' to a new life, to a new sense of wholeness. With the girl's arm attached to his shoulder, he begins to feel her 'purifying' blood flow through his body: 'The clean blood of the girl was now, this very moment, flowing through me; but would there not be unpleasantness when the arm was returned to the girl, this dirty male blood flowing through it?'[77] Despite this last scruple, however, immediately after being 'purified' the narrator falls into a blissful sleep:

> Our sleep was probably light, but I had never before known sleep so warm, so sweet. A restless sleeper, I had never before been blessed with the sleep of a child.[78]

Another Christian reference may be detected here, of course: 'Unless you become like a little child, you shall not enter the kingdom of heaven'.

The final scene of the story – a kind of anti-climax – depicts yet another attempted 'resurrection', but one which is more ambiguous than the first two. The narrator awakes from his blissful, nirvanic sleep and has a moment of panic when he sees his own arm lying detached from his body. He tears the girl's arm from his shoulder and quickly reattaches his own: 'The act was like murder on a sudden, diabolic impulse'.[79] This 'impulse' may be equated with the aversion already mentioned of the Kawabata hero towards an overly intimate contact with women. Also, by now, presumably, the girl's arm has performed its 'purifying' function, so that the narrator, no longer needing it, is able to cast it ruthlessly aside. At this point he may remind us of previous Kawabata heroes who behave in a similarly ruthless fashion towards women they have 'used' – Shimamura of *Snow Country*, for instance.

But here there is a difference. Once the moment of 'panic' has passed, the narrator seems to feel some remorse for what he has done – an act that, as he himself remarks, has about it the feel of 'murder'. And indeed, when he looks at the arm which he has cast aside, it seems quite 'dead': 'The outstretched fingers did not move. The arm was faintly white in the dim light'.[80]

The story ends with one final Biblical image, again symbolic of life-giving force. The narrator picks up the arm and tries to restore it to life: 'If the dew of woman would but come from between the long nails and the fingertips!'[81] As Takeda Katsuhiko has pointed out: 'Kawabata was familiar with the imagery of dewdrops as a symbol of a life-creating substance in *Song of Solomon* and, surely, intended his image to convey this symbolic Biblical meaning'.[82] In his last act of the story, then, the narrator seems ready to take on the life-giving role of a Christ-figure which he had previously rejected: he picks up the girl's arm and tries to restore it to life. 'I embraced it as one would a small child from whom life was going. I brought the fingers to my lips'.[83] He thus seems about to repeat the life-giving gesture of the girl at the beginning of the story, when she kissed the fingers so that they would move.[84]

Read in this way, the story's climax is a striking symbolic statement of a theme which, as we have seen, had been persistent in Kawabata's work since his early novella, *The Dancing Girl of Izu* (1926): the alienated, self-loathing male hero somehow 'purified' or even spiritually 'enlightened' by contact with a beautiful and virginal girl. And indeed, there is a suggestion of something like *nirvana* in his blissful sleep, in which 'I disappeared'.[85] The major source of the story's symbolism, though, as already noted, is Christianity, and quite naturally so, since it is the religious tradition in which the 'blood of the redeemer' is a central image.

Indeed, there are some strange intertextural echoes in 'One Arm' of that most Christian of modern European novelists, Dostoyevsky. Given Kawabata's familiarity with and admiration for the great Russian writer, it is quite possible that he was inspired to restate his familiar theme of a man's 'redemption' by a woman in Christian terms by a reading of Dostoyevsky's most popular novel, *Crime and Punishment*. At any rate, it seems to me that 'One Arm' may profitably be read as a kind of surrealistic 'haiku version' of that novel.

Whether or not this is a case of 'direct influence', there are a number of illuminating parallels between the Japanese short story and the Russian novel, not least of which is Dostoyevsky's use of the same Biblical story of Lazarus for a similar symbolic purpose. Lest it seem incongruous to compare a short story with such a massive novel – more even than my earlier comparison of *The Sound of the Mountain* with Proust's *magnum opus* – let me repeat that 'One Arm' may be regarded as a kind of 'summing up' of Kawabata's entire lifework – in a sense, it is only the tip of a very large iceberg. Then again, Kawabata's economical style and his highly charged symbolic technique enable him to express much within a narrow compass – he is the modern fictional equivalent of a writer of *haiku*, and in this respect certainly contrasts markedly with the rather long-winded Dostoyevsky. Of course, this particular contrast may simply be attributed to literary-historical factors: any post-Kafka writer of 'symbolic' fiction does not feel it necessary to present his characters, plots, and settings with such a plethora of detail as was customary with the nineteenth-century 'psychological' novelist. From this perspective, Kawabata's economy of means not only makes him seem quintessentially Japanese but also places him squarely within the worldwide modernist tradition.

What interests me more than the obvious contrasts, however, are the perhaps less obvious affinities between these two works. To begin with, Kawabata's narrator has more in common with Raskolnikov than may first appear. Since both stories climax in a symbolic 'resurrection' of their respective protagonists, it follows that both men are in a sense 'dead' – that is, spiritually dead, alienated from themselves and from the world. (Raskolnikov's name derives from the Russian word *raskolnik,* meaning 'schismatic', thus signifying that he has split himself off from man and God.) In Raskolnikov's case, of course, this psychic malaise is given a more explicit objective correlative: he commits murder. Kawabata is working on a more symbolic level but, when we look closely at the narrator of 'One Arm', we find that, although literally he may not be a murderer, he has, so to speak, the soul of one.

The story begins, after all, with the narrator taking the arm from the girl, an act of dismemberment that suggests rape if not murder. This impression is strengthened all the more later when we discover that he has taken the girl's arm because he thirsts for her blood. The scene which immediately follows the story's opening, in which the narrator is depicted walking through the streets guiltily hiding the girl's arm under his raincoat, is strangely reminiscent of the scene in which Raskolnikov is on his way through the streets of St. Petersberg to murder the old pawnbroker woman, guiltily hiding an ax under *his* coat. When Kawabata's narrator arrives at his room, his hand trembles with nervous guilt when he tries to unlock his door: 'The harder I tried the more my hand trembled – *as if in terror after a crime*'.[86] (my emphasis) And, as we have already seen, in the incident remembered from his past he pushes the girl down, wounding her in the process, and then proceeds to suck her blood. Finally, towards the end of the story, when he tears the girl's arm from his shoulder after having ingested enough of her blood, he himself confesses that: 'The act was like murder upon a sudden, diabolic impulse'.[87]

One other important similarity in the way the spiritual malaise of both men is made manifest may be remarked upon: both are such monsters of pride and egotism that they resist being saved by the self-sacrifice of a woman, although they know instinctively that this is what they are in desperate need of. At one point Raskolnikov tells his sister bluntly: "'I don't want your sacrifice'".[88] And at first he associates Sonia, his ultimate 'savior', with one of his murder victims, Lizaveta, as one of the 'poor creatures' with 'meek eyes' who 'give everything away' – in other words, as one of the sheep-like masses from whom Raskolnikov, the pseudo-Napoleon, desperately wishes to dissociate himself by his act of murder. Kawabata's narrator also feels himself alien to woman's Christ-like act of giving: 'I could never really accept the surrender, even knowing that the body of every woman was made for it'.[89] At the same time, though, he recognizes that his very inability to accept may be a symptom of 'some spiritual debility I suffer from'.[90]

In the case of both men, in fact, being confronted like this with a woman's self-sacrifice is not only deeply disturbing to their own sense of self but is potentially the seed of their spiritual growth towards an ultimate 'resurrection'. We have already seen that Kawabata's narrator feels at least a moment of remorse at his ruthless treatment of the girl's arm; Raskolnikov too asks himself why he has to 'poison' Sonia's life by confessing his crime and thus unburdening himself of his guilt to her.[91] This resembles the Kawabata narrator's worry that when he returns the arm to the girl she will be troubled by the 'dirty male blood' now flowing through it.[92] And Raskolnikov is even more reminiscent of the Kawabata narrator when he compares himself to a spider 'catching everybody in my web and sucking the living juices out of them'.[93]

Both writers make the guilt of their protagonists seem all the greater by emphasizing the absolute purity of the girls who are 'dirtied'. Both girls, then, come to seem as much the victims as the saviors of the two men. It may seem incongruous to compare Kawabata's virgin with Dostoyevsky's whore, but in Dostoyevsky *spiritual* purity is all that matters, and even the cynical Raskolnikov recognizes that the life of prostitution which has been forced on Sonia has not really touched her spirit:

> There was not a drop of real depravity in her. He could see that. She stood transparent before him.[94]

Indeed, in a typically Dostoyevskian fashion, Sonia, whose name signifies 'holy wisdom' or *sophia* in the Russian Orthodox tradition, is made to seem all the more 'holy' because of the suffering and degradation she has undergone – in this respect she reminds one of the traditional '*boddhisattva* whore' alluded to in the companion piece to 'One Arm', *Sleeping Beauties*. Just

215

as Christ washed the feet of the prostitute, Mary Magdilene, Raskolnikov kneels down before Sonia and kisses her feet because she seems to him to represent 'all suffering humanity'.[95] It is the purity of both women, in fact, combined with their infinite capacity for self-sacrifice, which enables them to play the resurrecting Christ-role to the two Lazarus-like protagonists.

Although the 'Lazarus theme' is a symbolic keystone in the thematic structure of both works, in Dostoyevsky's novel it is, of course, developed at much greater length. It is first introduced ironically by Raskolnikov himself when he is on his way to his first meeting with the police investigator, Porfiry Petrovich, and he thinks to himself that: 'I'll have to play the part of Lazarus for him too'.[96] By a strange coincidence, shortly afterwards the investigator asks him: '". . . do you believe in the resurrection of Lazarus? . . . . Do you believe literally?"', and Raskolnikov answers that he does. With the theme thus prefigured, it emerges several times again with ever greater significance as the novel moves towards its climax in Raskolnikov's own hard-earned 'resurrection'. On his first visit to Sonia he asks her to read the Lazarus story, Christ's 'greatest miracle', to him from a Bible given to her by one of his murder victims; Sonia reads the passage at length, including the part quoted in 'One Arm'. And in almost the last paragraph of the novel, after the moving scene in which Raskolnikov is spiritually 'reborn' in his Siberian prison camp, we are told that: 'Under his pillow lay the New Testament . . . . it belonged to her, the one from which she had read him the resurrection of Lazarus'.[97]

Raskolnikov's own 'resurrection' forms the last important scene of the novel, in which he finally surrenders himself to Sonia in a sudden explosion of love, throwing himself at her feet, weeping and embracing her knees (much as Kawabata's narrator embraces the girl's arm). In a passage that somehow has a peculiarly Japanese ring to it, we are told that from now on for Raskolnikov: 'Life replaced logic, and in his consciousness something quite different now had to elaborate and articulate itself'.[98] Although this is undeniably a moving scene, for many critics Raskolnikov's 'resurrection' is altogether too facile and abrupt to be as powerfully convincing as was his previous egotism and alienation. As one of the most perceptive commentators, Prince Mirsky, says: 'the truth is (and here lies the exceptional significance of Dostoyevsky as a spiritual case) that the tragedies of Dostoyevsky are irreducible tragedies that cannot be solved or pacified. His harmonies and his solutions are all on a lower or shallower level than his conflicts and his tragedies'.[99] The final 'resurrection' or 'salvation' of Kawabata's narrator is also of uncertain success, but the ambiguity here is intended and must be regarded as an enrichment rather than as an aesthetic flaw.

The 'positive', Dostoyevskian reading of 'One Arm' as a story of redemption is consistent with its Christian imagery of self-sacrifice, death and rebirth, and seems to work up to a point. But the story's ambiguous final scene leaves us with a rather tantalizing question: does Kawabata mean us to take this 'redemption' seriously as a genuine moral and spiritual 'reformation' in the Christian or Buddhist tradition, or does he use all of these religious allusions and symbols merely for ironic or even satiric effect, perhaps to emphasize all the more the hypocrisy of his narcissistic male, who exploits women ruthlessly for his own purposes, however 'spiritual'?

At the very least, we might question whether the Kawabata male is ever really cured of his narcissism, even by such a radical means as the direct transfusion into him of a self-sacrificing virgin's blood. Certainly there is an exploitative, 'vampirish' side to this whole process. Thus the male's actions in the final scene may be interpreted in two quite contrary ways. When he 'cries out in alarm' at the arm's death and embraces it 'as one would a small child from whom life was going', is this out of genuine concern for the girl and guilt over what he has done to her, or merely because he wishes to feast again on the 'dew of woman'? In other words, does he regret having destroyed her because of a newly developed moral sensitivity or merely because this means that he can no longer exploit her? And when, as he says, he brings the 'fingers to my lips', will he give them a Christ-like kiss of life or a vampirish kiss of death? It seems to me that Kawabata purposely leaves these questions unanswered, for the very good reason that they are related to that irresolvable, *kōan*-like conundrum from which, as we have seen, his male protagonists have long suffered.

Thus I would not say that Kawabata's purpose in this story is mainly ironic or satiric. He places the male's longing for purity and innocence in a traditional religious context because he does intend to point to a genuinely spiritual quality in this – certainly his males are not driven merely by simple lust – but where the crucial difference with traditional religion emerges is in the quality of the 'redemption'. The Kawabata male's redemption does not conform to any religious ideal; on the contrary, it is problematical in the extreme, tragic in its effect on the female partner and pathetic in its short-lived efficacy for the male himself. The tragic irony and irresolvable conundrum of the male's situation is that, although his spiritual aspirations are genuine and, indeed, inescapable, when he acts on them he cannot help but destroy his female partner – rather like the mating tarantula. In other words, he destroys the very thing he needs for his salvation the moment he reaches out to embrace it. And this fact alone certainly compromises any brief, nirvanic sense of ego-transcendence which the experience affords him. Although there is evidence that he feels some guilt about this, the force of his longings ensure that, like John Fowles' 'collector', he will always be driven to seek another partner – and another victim.

Thus in these two remarkable and courageous late works, *Sleeping Beauties* and 'One Arm', Kawabata calls into question in a new and disturbing way perhaps *the* major theme of his lifework: the ceaseless attempts of his male heroes to free themselves from their alienation and egotism and to achieve a kind of monistic state of grace by a purifying contact with a beautiful, virginal girl. One might also say that in these works he finally tears away his male hero's mask of aestheticism and offers us a glimpse of the rather ugly reality which lurks behind it. Thus Kawabata maintained his restless, questing genius even into old age, and with the haunting note of ambiguity which ends 'One Arm' he also ended his entire career.[100]

NOTES

Introduction

1 The review was later published in Japanese with the 'gushing headline' quite literally translated as 'Parafureezu sareta haiku ni kakusareta yutakasa' in *Yama no oto bunseki kenkyū*, edited by Hasegawa Izumi and Tsuruta Kinya (Tokyo: Nansōsha, 1980).

2 Kenzaburō Ōe, *Japan, the Ambiguous, and Myself: The Nobel Prize Speech and Other Lectures* (Tokyo: Kodansha, 1995), p.116.

Chapter One: An Orphan Psychology

1 As Katō Shūichi claims in his 'Saraba Kawabata Yasunari', in *Genzai no naka no rekishi* (Tokyo: Shinchōsha, 1976), p.191.

2 The title of a well-known collection of essays on the early Kawabata in Japanese, which I refer to below, is *A Wounded Youth* (*Shōkon no seishun*).

3 The most extreme presentation of this 'literary fraud' theory is made by Kawashima Itaru in his *Kawabata Yasunari no sekai* (Tokyo: Kōdansha, 1969), especially on p.56.

4 Hasegawa Izumi, *Kawabata Yasunari ronkō* (Tokyo: Meiji Shoin, 1969), p.90.

5 See Isogai Hideo, '*Jū-roku-sai no nikki* to sofu', in *Shōkon no seishun*, ed. Kawabata Bungaku Kenkyūkai (Tokyo: Kyōiku Shuppan Sentā, 1976), p.47, and Tsuruta Kinya, 'Kawabata bungaku ni okeru jiden-teki yōso', in *Jiden bungaku no sekai*, ed. Saeki Shōichi (Asahi Shuppansha, 1983), p.447.

6 Arthur Waley, *The Nō Plays of Japan* (London: George Allen and Unwin, 1921), p.17.

7 Quoted in Hasegawa, *Ronkō*, p.97.

8 See, for instance, Hadori Tetsuya, *Sakka Kawabata no kitei* (Tokyo: Kyōiku shuppan sentā, 1979), p.48, and Isogai Hideo, *Shōwa shotō no sakka to sakuhin* (Meiji Shoin, 1980), pp.172–73.

9 For instance, Isogai in *Shōwa shotō*, p.165, and Tsuruta, *Jiden bungaku*, pp.450–51.

10 *Kawabata Yasunari zenshū*, vol.2 (Tokyo: Shinchōsha, 1980), p.9. (My translation.)

11 Ibid., p.10.

12 Donald Keene, *Dawn to the West: Japanese Literature in the Modern Era (Fiction)*, (New York: Holt, Rinehart and Winston, 1984), p.788.

13 Hasegawa, *Ronkō*, pp.118–19.
14 See Hayashi Takeshi's review of critical studies of the *Diary* in *Shōkon no seishun*, p.221.
15 Ibid.
16 Sasabuchi Tomoichi, 'Kawabata bungaku to shūrurearizumu', in *Kawabata Yasunari*, ed. Nihon Bungaku Kenkyū Shiryō Kankō-kai, (Tokyo: Yūseidō, 1973), p.265.
17 Tsuruta, *Jiden bungaku*, p.442.
18 Ibid.
19 Nakamura Hajime, *Ways of Thinking of Eastern Peoples*, (Honolulu: East-West Center Press, 1964), especially pp.361–7.
20 *Mumonkan*, edited by Hirata Takashi (Tokyo: Chikuma Shobō, 1969).
21 *Zenshū* 2, p.10.
22 Sasabuchi, *Kawabata*, p.265.
23 R.H. Blyth, *Zen in English Literature and Oriental Classics*, (Tokyo: Hokuseido, 1942), especially pp.212–43.
24 Dante, *The Divine Comedy*, translated by C.H. Sisson (London: Pan Books, 1980), p.498.
25 Quoted in ibid., p.684.
26 Hadori Tetsuya, 'Kawabata Yasunari to banbutsu ichinyo, rinne tensei shisō', in *Sakka*, pp.275–93.
27 ibid., pp.276–77.
28 Quoted in Hadori, *Sakka*, p.271.
29 See *A Guide to the New Criticism*, by William Elton (Chicago: Modern Poetry Association, 1948), p.29.
30 Kawabata, *Sora ni ugoku hi* ('Lights Moving Through the Sky', 1924), in *Zenshū* 2, p.112.
31 *Zenshū* 2, pp.10–11.
32 Kobayashi Hideo, *Sakka no kao* (Tokyo: Shinchōsha, 1961), p.167.
33 Hadori, *Sakka*, p.149.
34 Isogai, *Shōwa shotō*, p.175.
35 ibid.
36 *Zenshū* 2, p.14.
37 ibid., p.18.
38 ibid., p.26.
39 ibid., p.22.
40 ibid., p.27.
41 For an interesting account of this method, see Masao Miyoshi, *Accomplices of Silence* (Berkeley: Univ. of Calif. Press, 1974), pp.96–100.
42 *Zenshū* 2, p.33.
43 For definitions of *ma* in various cultural and artistic contexts, see *Nihonjin to ma*, ed. Kenmochi Takehiko et al. (Tokyo: Kōdansha, 1981).
44 *Zenshū* 2, p.20.
45 ibid., p.22.
46 ibid., p.27.
47 ibid., pp.33–34.

48 ibid., p.34.
49 ibid., p.37.
50 ibid., p.36.
51 ibid., pp.36–37.
52 ibid., p.42.
53 ibid., p.21.
54 See Hadori, 'Kawabata Yasunari to shinreigaku', in *Sakka*, pp.294–335.
55 *Zenshū* 2, p.17.
56 ibid., p.42.
57 ibid., p.43.
58 ibid., p.35.
59 ibid., pp.35–36.
60 ibid., p.42
61 See *Zenshū* 33, p.388.
62 Samuel Beckett, *Proust* (New York: Grove Press, 1957), p.17.
63 Leon Edel, *Stuff of Sleep and Dreams: Experiments in Literary Psychology* (New York: Avon Books, 1982), p.X.
64 *Zenshū* 2, p.43.
65 See, for instance, his story, *Koji no kanjō* in *Zenshū* 2, pp.153–72. An almost identical phrase, *koji konjō* ('orphan nature') figures importantly in *The Dancing Girl of Izu (Izu no odoriko)*, *Zenshū* 2, p.318.
66 Hayashi, *Shōkon no seishun*, p.218.
67 ibid., pp.227–28.
68 On the role of *amae* in Japanese psychology and social conditioning see Takeo Doi, *The Anatomy of Dependence* (Tokyo: Kodansha, 1973).
69 Kawashima, *Sekai*, p.36.
70 Isogai, *Shōwa shotō*, p.176.
71 Hadori, *Sakka*, p.62.
72 Shakespeare, *Julius Caesar* I, ii, 134.
73 Hadori, *Sakka*, p.69.
74 ibid.
75 ibid.
76 Kobayashi, *Sakka no kao*, p.168
77 Ralph Freedman, *The Lyrical Novel* (Princeton: Princeton University Press, 1963).
78 Quoted in Hayashi, *Shōkon no seishun*, p.227.
79 Kawabata himself confesses this solipsism in his *Literary Autobiography (Bungakuteki jijoden*, 1934), *Zenshū* 33.
80 Hayashi, *Shōkon no seishun*, p.228.
81 See Hadori, *Sakka*, p.294.
82 Quoted in Hadori, *Sakka*, p.279.
83 ibid., p.287.
84 ibid.
85 As so well recounted in Ralph Freedman's *The Lyrical Novel* and Leon Edel's *The Modern Psychological Novel* (Gloucester, Mass.: Peter Smith, 1972).
86 A term made good use of by Colin Wilson in his seminal study of modern literature and philosophy, *The Outsider* (Boston: Houghton Mifflin, 1956).

87 A term applied to Kawabata by Mishima Yukio among others. See his 'Eien no tabibito', in *Kawabata Yasunari nyūmon*, ed. Mie Yasutaka (Yūshindō, 1975).

88 Kawabata's own term, quoted in Hayashi, *Shōkon no seishun*, p.228.

89 Kawashima Itaru, for instance, in *Sekai*, p.41.

90 Sasabuchi Tomoichi makes this point in his *Kawabata*, p.263.

91 ibid.

92 Jean Jacques Rousseau, *Emile*, trans. Barbara Foxley (London: J.M. Dent & Sons, 1911).

93 Sasabuchi, *Kawabata*, p.292.

94 ibid., pp.262–63.

95 Katō Shūichi, 'Saraba Kawabata Yasunari', in *Genzai no naka no rekishi* (Shinchōsha, 1976), p.191.

96 On dreams in *The Sound of the Mountain*, see, for instance, Tsuruta, *Kawabata Yasunari no geijutsu* (Meiji shoin, 1981), pp.169–93.

97 Keene, *Dawn*, p.802. Keene is referring here in particular to the *tanagokoro shōsetsu* ('palm-sized story'), *Shinjū*.

98 Kawashima, *Sekai*, p.36.

99 ibid., p.37.

100 Besides Kawashima, Isogai Hideo argues the former position in *Shōwa shotō*, p.174, and Hasegawa Izumi, Kawabata's most devoted apologist, argues the latter position in *Ronkō*, p.107.

101 See Edward Seidensticker's expliqué of these Japanese critical canons in his 'The "Pure" and the "In-Between" in Modern Japanese Theories of the Novel', in *This Country, Japan* (Tokyo: Kodansha, 1979), pp.98–111.

102 See my *An Artless Art: The Zen Aesthetic of Shiga Naoya* (Folkestone: Japan Library/Curzon Press, 1998).

103 Hasegawa, *Ronkō*, p.95.

104 ibid., p.97.

105 Kawashima, *Sekai*, p.56.

106 Isogai, *Shōwa shotō*, p.165.

107 Hozumi Ikan, 'Chikamatsu on the Art of the Puppet Stage', translated by Donald Keene in his *Anthology of Japanese Literature* (New York: Grove Press, 1955), p.388.

108 ibid., p.389.

109 Quoted by Kawabata Kaori in *Kawabata Yasunari no seishun*, in *Bungakkai*, August 1979, p.145.

110 *Zenshū* 10, p.163.

111 For a detailed and fascinating account of the elite level of the prewar Japanese educational system, see Donald Roden, *Schooldays in Imperial Japan: A Study in the Culture of a Student Elite* (Berkeley: University of California Press, 1980).

112 See Seidensticker, *This Country, Japan*, p.169

Chapter Two: An Ambiguous Redemption

1 See Hayashi, '*Jū-roku-sai* (*Jū-yon-sai*) *no nikki*, *Izu no odoriko kenkyū no tenbō to mondai-ten*', in *Shōkon no seishun*, p.230.
2 *Zenshū* 2, p.318.
3 Ernest Hemingway, 'Big Two-Hearted River', in *In Our Time* (New York: Charles Scribner's Sons, 1925).
4 See Julian Smith's article, 'Hemingway and the Thing Left Out', in Jackson Benson, *The Short Stories of Ernest Hemingway: Critical Essays* (Durham: Duke University Press, 1975).
5 Hayashi, *Shōkon no seishun*, p.241.
6 ibid., p.234.
7 Hasegawa, '*Izu no odoriko no sōsaku dōki*', in *Shōkon no seishun*, p.89.
8 ibid., pp.95–6.
9 Quoted in ibid., p.96.
10 ibid., p.97.
11 ibid., p.95.
12 Kawashima, *Sekai*, p.106.
13 ibid., pp.95–109.
14 ibid., p.105.
15 ibid., p.106.
16 ibid., p.107.
17 Fujimori Shigenori, '*Izu no odoriko no kōzō*', in *Shōkon no seishun*, p.140.
18 ibid., p.148.
19 ibid., pp.150–52.
20 James Joyce, *Ulysses*, (New York: Random House, 1934), pp. 186-7 and 205-6.
21 W.H. Auden, 'Introduction' to William Shakespeare, *The Sonnets*, (New York: New American Library, 1965), p.xvii.
22 ibid., pp.xviii-xix.
23 Fujimori, *Shōkon no seishun*, p.153.
24 ibid., p.155.
25 ibid., p.156.
26 ibid., p.142.
27 *Zenshū* 2, pp.304–5.
28 Mishima Yukio, '*Izu no odoriko ni tsuite*', in *Izu no odoriko*, (Tokyo: Shinchōsha, 1950), p.166.
29 *Zenshū* 2, p.304.
30 For example, Senuma, Nakamura, Hayashi, Takada, Takeda and Tsuruta, as we shall see shortly.
31 *Zenshū* 2, p.307.
32 ibid., pp.309–13.
33 ibid., p.312.
34 ibid., pp.315–6.
35 See *Yukiguni* (*Snow Country*) in *Zenshū* 10, p.18.
36 *Zenshū* 2, p.316.
37 ibid.
38 ibid., p.308.

39 ibid., p.318.
40 ibid.
41 ibid., p.313.
42 ibid., p.318.
43 See Hayashi, *Shōkon no seishun*, pp.245-6.
44 *Zenshū* 2, p.321.
45 For example, Tsuruta Kinya and Kobayashi Ichirō, as we shall see.
46 Fujimori, *Shōkon no seishun*, p.153.
47 See Hayashi, *Shōkon no seishun*, p.232.
48 Kobayashi Ichirō, '*Izu no odoriko* ron', in *Shōkon no seishun*, p.119.
49 ibid., p.121.
50 Tsuruta Kinya, *Kawabata Yasunari no geijutsu*, (Tokyo: Meiji Shoin, 1981), pp.8-9.
51 ibid., p.23.
52 ibid., p.11. It should be noted, for those who have read only Edward Seidensticker's English translation of the story, that he omits both of these scenes.
53 ibid., pp.25–6.
54 Takeda Katsuhiko, 'Kawabata bungaku ni okeru *Izu no odoriko* no ichi', in *Shōkon no seishun*, p.168.
55 ibid., p.167.
56 Takada Kōda, '*Izu no odoriko* no bungakushi-teki igi', in *Shōkon no seishun*, p.187.
57 Nakamura Mitsuo, *Ronkō: Kawabata Yasunari* (Chikuma Shobō, 1978), p.147 and pp.160–1.
58 ibid., p.163.
59 ibid., p.166.
60 ibid., p.170.
61 See Gabriele Rico, *Writing the Natural Way* (Los Angeles: J.P. Toucher, 1983) for an account of the applicability of recent brain research to writing.
62 *Zenshū* 2, p.324.
63 ibid., p.323.
64 ibid., p.321.
65 Tsuruta, *Geijutsu*, p.15.
66 *Zenshū* 2, p.323.
67 ibid.
68 ibid., p.324.
69 Fujimori, *Shōkon no seishun*, p.155.
70 Tsuruta, *Geijutsu*, p.11.
71 Takeda Katsuhiko, 'Walt Whitman's Impact on Modern Japanese Writers', (Paper delivered at the East-West Symposium at the University of Indiana, 1979), p.9.
72 Paul Zweig, *The Heresy of Self-Love* (Princeton: Princeton University Press, 1980).
73 See Shiga Naoya, *A Dark Night's Passing*, trans. Edwin McClellan (Tokyo: Kodansha, 1976), especially the final chapter. And my own study of Shiga: *An Artless Art: The Zen Aesthetic of Shiga Naoya*.

Chapter Three: Experiment and Expansion

1 Quoted in Donald Keene, *Dawn to the West* (New York: Holt, Rinehart and Winston, 1984), p.825.
2 Quoted in Masao Miyoshi, *Accomplices of Silence* (Berkeley: University of California Press, 1974), p.95.
3 Keene, *Dawn*, p.631.
4 Gwenn Boardman Petersen, *The Moon in the Water* (Honolulu: The University Press of Hawaii, 1979), p.126.
5 Keene, *Dawn*, p.802.
6 As Edward Fowler has pointed out, there are, of course, significant culturally-based differences between the *shishōsetsu* and Western autobiographical fiction, but they do share, at least, a general subjective orientation and a 'confessional' impulse. See Edward Fowler, *The Rhetoric of Confession: Shishōsetsu in Early Twentieth-Century Japanese Fiction*, p.xi.
7 For a gripping account of the great earthquake and its aftereffects, see Edward Seidensticker, *Low City, High City: Tokyo from Edo to the Earthquake* (New York: Alfred A. Knopf, 1983), especially pp.3–9.
8 *Kawabata Yasunari Zenshū* 30 (Tokyo: Shinchōsha, 1980), pp.172–83.
9 ibid., pp.198–203.
10 Quoted in Paul Zweig, *The Heresy of Self-Love* (Princeton University Press, 1980), p.157.
11 *Zenshū* 4, p.417.
12 See Percy Lubbock, *The Craft of Fiction* (London: Jonathan Cape, 1939).
13 *Zenshū* 4, p.417.
14 ibid.
15 ibid., p.421.
16 ibid.
17 ibid.
18 ibid., p.422.
19 In, for instance, *Introductory Lectures on Psychoanalysis* 1. (London: Penguin, 1991), p.477, Freud contends: 'A strong libidinal fixation to the narcissistic type of object-choice is to be included in the predisposition to manifest homosexuality'.
20 *Zenshū* 4, p.422.
21 ibid., p.423.
22 ibid., p.425.
23 ibid., p.424.
24 ibid., p.426.
25 ibid.
26 ibid.
27 ibid.
28 ibid.
29 As Borges has shown so convincingly, we often 'reread' classics by the light of modern authors, and quite legitimately so, since there are no real anachronisms in the 'eternal present' of literature. See Jorge Luis Borges, 'Pierre Menard, Author of the *Quixote*', in *Labyrinths* (New York: New Directions, 1964), pp.36–44.

30 *Zenshū* 4, p.420.

31 ibid.

32 See below, pp.108–112.

33 Sir James Fraser, *The Golden Bough* (London: Macmillan, 1957), p.253.

34 ibid., p.254.

35 *The Upanishads*, translated by Juan Mascaró (London: Penguin, 1965), p.49.

36 Perhaps the best scientific account of the general characteristics of mystical experience is still to be found in William James, *The Varieties of Religious Experience* (New York: Macmillan, 1961), especially pp.299–336.

37 Paul Zweig, *The Heresy of Self-Love: A Study of Subversive Individualism* (Princeton: Princeton University Press, 1980), p.viii.

38 ibid.

39 ibid., p.143.

40 ibid., p.xii.

41 ibid., p.ix.

42 For a fascinating account of Motoori's literary theories, see Makoto Ueda, *Literary and Art Theories of Japan.*

43 Zweig, p.24.

44 Quoted in ibid., p.23.

45 Yasunari Kawabata, *Japan the Beautiful and Myself*, translated by Edward G. Seidensticker (Tokyo: Kodansha, 1969), p.56.

46 At this very moment, in January 1995, the media report that Sri Lankan Buddhist monks have boycotted a planned meeting with Pope John Paul II, who is visiting their country, as a protest against his contention that 'the objective of Buddhist meditation is to reach "indifference" to the world, not to draw nearer to God'. (*Japan Times*, 23 January 1995, p.3.) It seems that Zweig's 'cultural dialectic', far from being confined only to the West, has now begun to shape even East/West relations.

47 Quoted in George Steiner, *Language and Silence* (London: Faber and Faber, 1967), p.31.

48 Quoted in Zweig, pp.202–3.

49 Quoted in Richard Boothby, *Death and Desire: Psychoanalytic Theory in Lacan's Return to Freud* (New York: Routledge, 1991), p.228.

50 ibid., pp.31–7.

51 ibid., pp.37–41.

52 See Takeo Doi, *Anatomy of Dependency.*

53 See above, p.83

54 See Zweig, p.155.

55 ibid., p.163.

56 ibid., p.153.

57 See my *An Artless Art: The Zen Aesthetic of Shiga Naoya* (Folkestone, England: Japan Library, 1998).

58 Malcolm Cowley, *The Flower and the Leaf* (New York: Viking, 1985), p.227. Cowley gives as examples of such supreme fictional creations: Moll Flanders, Valerie Marneffe, Emma Bovary, Anna Karenina and Molly Bloom. Present standards of strict sexual egalitarianism would

seem to call for a caveat here: that the contrary is true for women novelists, who must prove their imaginative powers by creating 'passionately living' men. But perhaps not. Perhaps we may be permitted to acknowledge that women are innately superior as subjects, at least in the realm of fiction.

59 Kawabata Yasunari, *Zenshū 3* (Tokyo: Shinchōsha, 1980), p.372.
60 ibid., p.345.
61 ibid., pp.345–6.
62 ibid., p.346.
63 ibid.
64 ibid.
65 ibid.
66 ibid.
67 ibid., p.347.
68 ibid.
69 ibid.
70 ibid., p.348.
71 ibid., pp.348–9.
72 ibid., p.349.
73 ibid.
74 ibid.
75 ibid.
76 ibid., pp.349–50.
77 ibid., pp.350–3.
78 ibid., p.364.
79 ibid., p.362.
80 One need not belabour the autobiographical import of this Kawabata heroine's obsession with her childlessness and need to justify it, but the fact is that Kawabata's own childlessness is yet another thing he had in common with her – as well as, one assumes, a concomitant need for art and religion.
81 Kawabata Yasunari, *Zenshū 3*, p.367.
82 ibid., pp.367–8.
83 ibid., p.370.
84 ibid.
85 ibid., p.371.
86 ibid., p.373.
87 ibid.
88 ibid., p.374.
89 ibid., pp.374–5.
90 ibid., p.376.
91 ibid., p.377.
92 ibid., p.376.
93 Kawabata Yasunari, 'Lyric Poem', translated by Francis Mathy. *Monumenta Nipponica*, XXVI, 3–4 (1971), p.288.
94 ibid., p.292.
95 ibid., p.287.
96 ibid., p.295.
97 Quoted in Keene, *Dawn to the West*, p.811.

98 Kawabata, *House of the Sleeping Beauties and Other Stories*, trans. Edward Seidensticker, p.134.

99 ibid., p.131.

100 ibid., p.147.

101 See p.91.

102 I have discussed this issue at much greater length in regard to the experience of nothingness in Mishima's novels, which in my view is 'genuinely' nihilistic. See my *Deadly Dialectics: Sex, Violence and Nihilism in the World of Yukio Mishima* (Honolulu: University of Hawaii Press, and London: Curzon Press, 1994).

103 *House of the Sleeping Beauties*, p.147.

104 This theme of 'the price an artist must pay' – in psychological terms, of course – is developed at much greater length in Kawabata's later novel, *The Master of Go*. See my discussion of this below, pp.146–153

105 *House of the Sleeping Beauties*, p.146.

106 ibid., p.147.

107 ibid., p.148.

108 ibid.

Chapter Four: Between Tradition and Modernity

1 Yasunari Kawabata, *Snow Country*, translated by Edward G. Seidensticker (New York: Berkley, 1960), p.115.

2 ibid., p.16.

3 ibid., p.45.

4 ibid., p.52.

5 ibid., pp.38–41.

6 Masayuki Akiyama, for instance, claims that Kawabata relies exclusively on Shimamura's 'limited point of view' to make the setting and characters come vividly alive. See his 'Point of View in Kawabata Yasunari and Henry James', in *Comparative Literature Studies*, Vol.26, No.3, 1989 (University Park: Pennsylvania State University Press), p.197.

7 *Snow Country*, p.74.

8 ibid., p.73.

9 ibid., p.74.

10 ibid., p.75.

11 Quoted by Malcolm Bradbury, *The Modern British Novel* (London: Penguin Books, 1994), p.347.

12 Quoted in Earl Miner, *The Japanese Tradition in British and American Literature* (Princeton: Princeton University Press, 1966), pp.113–4.

13 ibid., p.114.

14 ibid., p.115.

15 Joseph Frank, 'Spatial Form in the Modern Novel', in John W. Aldridge, *Critiques and Essays on Modern Fiction 1920–51* (New York: Ronald Press, 1952), p.43.

16 ibid., p.54.

17 See Tadao Satō, *Currents in Japanese Cinema* (Tokyo: Kodansha, 1982), pp.8 and 57.
18 See Paul Zweig, *The Heresy of Self-Love*, p.vi.
19 Tajima Yoko, 'A Rereading of *Snow Country* from Komako's Point of View', translated by Donna George Storey, in *U.S.-Japan Women's Journal*, No.4, January 1993, p.26.
20 *Snow Country*, p.17.
21 ibid., pp.13–4.
22 ibid., p.20.
23 ibid., p.33.
24 ibid., p.34.
25 ibid., p.29.
26 ibid., p.35.
27 This is not necessarily to say that any of us ever completely outgrow the narcissistic stage, or that narcissism is a problem only of narcissists. Long into our maturity, most of us still have our narcissistic moments. The narcissist is simply one who seems incapable of having anything else. Perhaps a vertical, 'archaeological' model of the human psyche is preferable to a horizontal, 'historical' one: that is, one layer of 'maturity' or social conditioning is laid upon another, but the primal layers – including the narcissistic ego – still survive 'underground'.
28 *Snow Country*, p.121.
29 ibid., p.122.
30 ibid., pp.126–7.
31 ibid., p.142.
32 ibid., p.15.
33 Søren Kierkegaard, *Either/Or*, vol.1, translated by David F. Swenson and Lillian Marvin Swenson, with revisions by Howard A. Johnson (Princeton: Princeton University Press, 1971), pp.xi-xii.
34 Yasunari Kawabata, *The Existence and Discovery of Beauty*, translated by V.H. Viglielmo (Tokyo: Mainichi, 1969), pp.18–9.
35 *Snow Country*, p.52.
36 Quoted and translated in Makoto Ueda, *Matsuo Bashō* (New York: Twayne, 1970), p.48.
37 *Snow Country*, p.63.
38 ibid., p.142.
39 ibid., p.127.
40 Ueda, *Matsuo Bashō*, (New York: Twayne, 1970), p.178.
41 ibid., p.179.
42 Shiga Naoya, *A Night's Passing*, translated by Edwin McClellan (Tokyo: Kodansha, 1976), p.407. For a more in-depth discussion of this scene, see my: *An Artless Art: The Zen Aesthetic of Shiga Naoya*, Chapter Four.
43 ibid., pp.400–1.

Chapter Five: Elegies for a Dying Tradition

1 Kuwabara Takeo, *Japan and Western Civilization: Essays on Comparative Culture*, edited by Katō Hidetoshi, translated by Kano Tsutomu and Patricia Murray (Tokyo: University of Tokyo Press, 1983), p.187.

2 ibid.
3 Quoted in Donald Keene, *Dawn to the West: Japanese Literature in the Modern Era: Fiction* (New York: Holt, Rinehart and Winston, 1984), p.825.
4 The terms, of course, are borrowed from one of the most celebrated studies of Japanese culture ever written by a foreigner, Ruth Benedict's *The Chrysanthemum and the Sword*, which, published in 1946, had a considerable influence on the way both Japanese and Westerners viewed Japan in the immediate postwar period.
5 Yasunari Kawabata, *Thousand Cranes*, translated by Edward G. Seidensticker (New York, 1958), p.14.
6 ibid., p.128.
7 ibid., p.65.
8 ibid., p.134.
9 ibid., p.122.
10 ibid., p.120.
11 ibid., p.142.
12 ibid., p.33.
13 ibid., p.38.
14 This sequel remains yet another of Kawabata's unfinished works, but its first installment was published as *Nami chidori* (*Wave Plovers*) in 1953.
15 Yasunari Kawabata, *The Master of Go*, translated by Edward G. Seidensticker (New York: Alfred A. Knopf, Inc., 1973), p.5.
16 ibid., p.166.
17 ibid., p.20.
18 ibid., pp.39–40.
19 ibid., p.42.
20 ibid. p.106.
21 ibid., p.107.
22 ibid., p.42.
23 ibid., p.19.
24 Makoto Ueda, *Literary and Art Theories of Japan* (Western Reserve Univ., 1967), p.222.
25 *The Master of Go*, p.63.
26 ibid., pp.99–100.
27 ibid., p.109.
28 ibid., pp.46–7.
29 ibid., p.62.
30 ibid., p.85.
31 ibid., p.163–4.
32 ibid., p.32.
33 ibid., p.64.
34 ibid., p.109.
35 ibid., p.108.
36 ibid., p.109.
37 ibid., pp.135–6.
38 ibid., p.136.
39 ibid., p.163.

40 ibid., p.164.

41 ibid., p.117.

42 In its original form the work was a series of newspaper reports, with Kawabata in his own capacity as famous writer and connoisseur of *go* reporting and commenting on a championship match.

43 ibid., pp.117–8.

44 ibid., p.32.

Chapter Six: Time and Anti-time

1 Erich Auerbach, *Mimesis: The Representation of Reality in Western Literature* (Princeton: Princeton University Press, 1968), p. 544.

2 A.A. Mendilow, *Time and the Novel* (New York: Humanities Press, 1965), p. 6.

3 ibid., p.3.

4 Oswald Spengler, *The Decline of the West*, trans. Charles Francis Atkinson (New York: Alfred A. Knopf, 1926-29), II, p.49 n. p.421 n.).

5 Lionel Trilling, *A Gathering of Fugitives* (New York: Harcourt Brace Jovanovich, 1956), p.158.

6 Leon Edel, *The Modern Psychological Novel* (Gloucester, Mass.: Peter Smith, 1972).

7 Marcel Proust, *Remembrance of Things Past*, translated by C.K. Scott Moncrieff and Terence Kilmartin (New York: Random House, 1981), p.3.

8 Yasunari Kawabata, *The Sound of the Mountain*, trans. Edward G. Seidensticker (New York: Alfred A. Knopf, 1970), p. 7.

9 Proust, *Remembrance,* p. 48.

10 ibid.

11 ibid., p.50.

12 ibid.

13 ibid., p.51.

14 ibid., pp.47–8.

15 Kawabata, *Sound of the Mountain,* p. 108.

16 Milton Miller, *Nostalgia, a Psychoanalytical Study of Marcel Proust* (London: Gollancz, 1957).

17 Kawabata, *Sound of the Mountain,* p. 159.

18 ibid., p.160.

19 Proust, *Remembrance of Things Past,* p. 511, Vol. 1.

20 ibid., p.186, Vol.3.

21 André Gide, *Pretexts*, translated by Justin O'Brien (New York: Books for Libraries Press, 1971), p. 205.

22 Quoted in Georges Cattaui, *Marcel Proust* (New York: Funk and Wagnalls, 1967), p. 104.

23 Proust, *Remembrance of Things Past,* Vol. III, p. 1103.

24 ibid., Vol.3, p.1103.

25 ibid., p.1093.

26 ibid., p.1088.

27 ibid., pp.898–9.

28 ibid., p.900.
29 ibid., p.904.
30 ibid.
31 R.C. Zaehner, *Mysticism, Sacred and Profane* (New York: Oxford University Press, 1957), p.60.
32 ibid., p.59.
33 Proust, *Remembrance of Things Past*, Vol. I, p. 35.
34 Masao Miyoshi, *Accomplices of Silence* (Berkeley: University of California Press, 1974), p.119.
35 Kawabata, *Sound of the Mountain*, p. 274.
36 Paul Valéry, *Aesthetics*, translated by Ralph Manheim (New York: Pantheon Books, 1964), p.66.
37 Kenneth Burke, *Counter-Statement* (Los Altos: Hermes Publications, 1953), p.ix.
38 ibid., p.124.
39 Edward Seidensticker, *This Country, Japan* (Tokyo: Kodansha, 1979), p.119.
40 Yamamoto Kenkichi, 'Kaisetsu', in Kawabata Yasunari, *Yama no oto* (Tokyo: Shinchōsha, 1957), p.318.
41 Nakamura Mitsuo, *Kawabata Yasunari* (Tokyo: Chikuma Shobo, 1978), p.189.
42 Earl Miner, *Japanese Linked Poetry* (Princeton University Press, 1979), p.5.
43 Makoto Ueda, *Literary and Art Theories in Japan* (Cleveland: Press of Western Reserve University, 1967), p.37.
44 See ibid., p.52.
45 Konishi Jin'ichi, 'The Art of Renga', *Journal of Japanese Studies*, Autumn, 1975, p.47.
46 Kawabata Yasunari, *Japan the Beautiful and Myself*, translated by Edward Seidensticker (Tokyo: Kodansha, 1969), p.41.
47 Daisetsu Suzuki, *Zen and Japanese Culture* (Princeton University Press, 1959), p.37.
48 Kawabata, *Japan the Beautiful and Myself*, p.42.
49 Kobayashi Hideo, *Sakka no kao* (Tokyo: Shinchōsha, 1961), p.169.
50 *Kawabata Yasunari Zenshū* xxxiii (Tokyo: Shinchōsha, 1980), p.538. Translated by Donald Keene in *Dawn to the West* (New York: Holt, Rinehart and Winston, 1984), p.829.
51 Kawabata Yasunari, 'Of Birds and Beasts', in *The House of the Sleeping Beauties*, translated by Edward Seidensticker (Tokyo: Kodansha, 1980), p.147.
52 *Kawabata Yasunari Zenshū* xii, p.245.
53 ibid., p.247.
54 Burke, p.125.
55 ibid.
56 Marjorie Hope Nicolson, *Mountain Gloom and Mountain Glory* (New York: W.W. Norton, 1963), p.28.
57 Kawabata, *Sound of the Mountain*, p.5.
58 See Burke, p.128.
59 ibid., p.126.

60 Nakamura Mitsuo, *Kobayashi Hideo* (Tokyo: Chikuma Shobo, 1977), p.163.
61 Burke, p.166.
62 ibid., p.125.
63 Katō Shūichi, 'Saraba Kawabata Yasunari', in *Genzai no naka no rekishi* (Tokyo: Shinchōsha, 1976), p.190.
64 Donald Keene, *Anthology of Japanese Literature* (New York: Grove Press, 1965), p.315.
65 Alain Robbe-Grillet, *For a New Novel*, translated by Richard Howard (New York: Grove Press, 1965), p.27.
66 ibid., p.28.
67 ibid., p.29.
68 Miyoshi, *Accomplices of Silence*, p.119.
69 Burke, p.52.
70 See Graham Good, 'Lukacs' *Theory of the Novel*', in *Towards a Poetics of Fiction* (Bloomington: Indiana University Press, 1977), p.130.
71 Eleanor Hutchens, 'An Approach Through Time', in *Towards a Poetics of Fiction*, p.52.

Chapter Seven: Narcissus in Winter

1 The original Japanese, *Nemureru bijo*, can also be translated as 'Sleeping Beauty', an ambiguity which works well for Kawabata's purpose but is unfortunately lost in English.
2 See Chapter Three, p.106
3 Yasunari Kawabata, *House of the Sleeping Beauties and Other Stories*, translated by Edward Seidensticker (Tokyo: Kodansha, 1980), p.17.
4 ibid., p.16.
5 ibid., p.17.
6 ibid., p.79.
7 ibid., p.39.
8 ibid., p.22.
9 ibid., p.35.
10 ibid.
11 ibid., p.16.
12 ibid., p.20.
13 ibid., p.44.
14 ibid., pp.55–6.
15 ibid., p.24.
16 ibid., p.59.
17 ibid., p.59.
18 ibid., p.76.
19 ibid., p.77.
20 ibid., p.70.
21 ibid., pp.72–3.
22 ibid., p.81.
23 ibid., p.82.
24 ibid., p.84.
25 ibid., p.87.

26 ibid., p.90.
27 ibid., p.98. Kawabata Yasunari, *Nemureru bijo* (Tokyo: Shinchōsha, 1967), p.106.
28 ibid., p.14.
29 ibid., p.53.
30 ibid., p.54.
31 ibid., p.66.
32 ibid., p.98.
33 ibid., p.78.
34 ibid., p.79.
35 ibid., p.79.
36 ibid., pp.46–7.
37 ibid., p.35.
38 ibid., p.36.
39 ibid., p.94.
40 ibid., p.95.
41 ibid.
42 ibid., p.96.
43 ibid., p.96.
44 ibid., p.96.
45 *Japanese Nō Dramas*, translated by Royall Tyler (London: Penguin, 1992), p.73.
46 ibid., p.73.
47 Yasunari Kawabata, *Japan the Beautiful and Myself*, translated by Edward Seidensticker (Tokyo: Kodansha, 1968), p.41.
48 ibid., p.56.
49 Kawabata, *House of the Sleeping Beauties*, p.22.
50 ibid., p.68.
51 Tyler, *Japanese Nō Dramas*, p.16.
52 Makoto Ueda, *Matsuo Bashō* (New York: Twayne, 1970), pp.168–9.
53 Yukio Mishima, 'Introduction', in Kawabata, *House of the Sleeping Beauties and Other Stories*, p.7.
54 ibid., p.16.
55 'Introduction' to *House of the Sleeping Beauties and Other Stories*, p.10.
56 'One Arm', in *House of the Sleeping Beauties and Other Stories*, translated by Edward G. Seidensticker (Tokyo: Kodansha, 1969), p.103.
57 ibid., p.104.
58 ibid., pp.104–5.
59 ibid., p.107.
60 ibid., p.108.
61 ibid.
62 ibid., p.113.
63 ibid., p.116.
64 ibid., p.107.
65 ibid.
66 ibid., p.114.
67 ibid., pp.114–5.
68 Yasunari Kawabata, *The Lake*, translated by Reiko Tsukimura (Tokyo: Kodansha, 1974), p.157.

69 ibid., p.158.
70 *House of the Sleeping Beauties*, p.104.
71 ibid.
72 ibid., p.115.
73 ibid., p.105.
74 ibid., p.106.
75 ibid., p.114.
76 ibid., p.120.
77 ibid., p.122.
78 ibid., p.123.
79 ibid., p.124.
80 ibid.
81 ibid.
82 K. Takeda, editor, *Essays on Japanese Literature* (Tokyo: Waseda University Press, 1977), pp.127–28.
83 *House of the Sleeping Beauties*, p.124.
84 ibid., p.104.
85 ibid.
86 ibid., p.108.
87 ibid., p.124.
88 Dostoyevsky, *Crime and Punishment*, p.198.
89 *House of the Sleeping Beauties*, p.115.
90 ibid.
91 Dostoyevsky, *Crime and Punishment*, p.412.
92 *House of the Sleeping Beauties*, p.122.
93 Dostoyevsky, *Crime and Punishment*, p.406.
94 ibid., p.316.
95 ibid., p.315.
96 ibid., p.244.
97 ibid., p.528.
98 ibid., pp.527–8.
99 D.S. Mirsky, *A History of Russian Literature* (New York: Vintage Books, 1958) p.288.
100 'One Arm' was his last work of fiction published in complete form, but after that he began writing a final novel, *Dandelions* (*Tanpopo*), which was left unfinished at his death.

BIBLIOGRAPHY

Akiyama Masayuki. 'Point of View in Kawabata Yasunari and Henry James'. In *Comparative Literature Studies*, Vol.26, No.3. University Park: Pennsylvania State University Press, 1989.

Arima, Tatsuo. *The Failure of Freedom: A Portrait of Modern Japanese Intellectuals*. Cambridge, Mass.: Harvard University Press, 1969.

Auden, W.H. 'Introduction'. In William Shakespeare. *The Sonnets*. New York: New American Library, 1965.

Auerbach, Erich. *Mimesis: The Representation of Reality in Western Literature*. Princeton: Princeton University Press, 1968.

Axthelm, Peter M. *The Modern Confessional Novel*. New Haven: Yale University Press, 1967.

Beckett, Samuel. *Proust*. New York: Grove Press, 1957.

Benson, Jackson, editor, *The Short Stories of Ernest Hemingway: Critical Essays*. Durham: Duke University Press, 1975.

Blyth, R.H. *Zen in English Literature and Oriental Classics*. Tokyo: Hokuseido, 1942.

Booth, Wayne. *The Rhetoric of Fiction*. Chicago University Press, 1966.

Boothby, Richard. *Death and Desire: Psychoanalytic Theory in Lacan's Return to Freud*. New York: Routledge, 1991.

Borges, Jorge Luis. 'Pierre Menard, Author of the *Quixote*'. In *Labyrinths*. New York: New Directions, 1964.

Bradbury, Malcolm. *The Modern British Novel*. London: Penguin Books, 1994.

Bungakkai. Tokyo: August, 1979.

Burke, Kenneth. *Counter-Statement*. Los Altos: Hermes Publications, 1953.

Cattaui, Georges. *Marcel Proust*. New York: Funk and Wagnalls, 1967.

Cowley, Malcolm. *The Flower and the Leaf*. New York: Viking, 1985.

Dante. *The Divine Comedy*. Translated by C.H. Sisson. London: Pan Books, 1980.

Doi Takeo. *The Anatomy of Dependence*. Tokyo: Kodansha, 1973.

Donaldson, Scott. *By Force of Will: the Life and Art of Ernest Hemingway*. New York: Viking Press, 1977.

Dostoyevsky, Fyodor. *Crime and Punishment*. Translated by Sidney Monas. New York: Signet, 1968.

Edel, Leon. *The Modern Psychological Novel*. Gloucester, Mass.: Peter Smith, 1972.

Edel, Leon. *Stuff of Sleep and Dreams: Experiments in Literary Psychology*. New York: Avon Books, 1982.

Elton, William. *A Guide to the New Criticism*. Chicago: Modern Poetry Association, 1948.

Forster, E.M. *Aspects of the Novel*. London: Edward Arnold, 1927.

Fowler, Edward. *Shishōsetsu in Modern Japanese Literature*. Durham, N.C.: Center for International Studies, Duke University, 1986.

Fowler, Edward. *The Rhetoric of Confession: Shishōsetsu in Early Twentieth-Century Japanese Fiction*. Berkeley: University of California Press, 1988.

Frank, Joseph. 'Spatial Form in the Modern Novel'. In John W. Aldridge. *Critiques and Essays on Modern Fiction 1920-51*. New York: Ronald Press, 1952.

Fraser, James. *The Golden Bough*. London: Macmillan, 1957.

Freedman, Ralph. *The Lyrical Novel*. Princeton: Princeton University Press, 1963.

Freud, Sigmund. *Introductory Lectures on Psychoanalysis 1*. London: Penguin, 1991.

Fujii, James A. *Complicit Fictions: The Subject in Modern Japanese Prose Narrative*. Berkeley: University of California Press, 1993.

Gessel, Van C. *The Sting of Life: Four Contemporary Japanese Novelists*. New York: Columbia University Press, 1989.

Gessel, Van C. *Three Modern Novelists: Sōseki, Tanizaki, Kawabata*. Tokyo: Kodansha, 1993.

Gide, André. *Pretexts*. Translated by Justin O'Brien. New York: Books for Libraries Press, 1971.

Good, Graham. 'Lukacs' *Theory of the Novel*'. In *Towards a Poetics of Fiction*. Bloomington: Indiana University Press, 1977.

Hadori Tetsuya. *Sakka Kawabata no kitei*. Tokyo: Kyōiku shuppan sentā, 1979.

Hasegawa Izumi. *Kawabata Yasunari ronkō*. Tokyo: Meiji Shoin, 1969.

Hemingway, Ernest. 'Big Two-Hearted River'. In *In Our Time*. New York: Charles Scribner's Sons, 1925.

Hemingway, Ernest. *In Our Time*. New York: Scribner's, 1925.

Hijiya-Kirschnereit, Irmela. *Rituals of Self-Revelation: Shi-Shōsetsu as Literary Genre and Socio-cultural Phenomenon*. Cambridge: Harvard University Press, 1996.

Hijiya-Kirschnereit, Irmela. *Shishōsetsu – Gattungsgeschichte und Gattungstheorie einer autobiographischen Romanliteratur des modernen Japan*. Bochum: Ruuhr-Universität, 1980.

Hisamatsu Shin'ichi. *Zen and the Fine Arts*. Tokyo: Kodansha, 1971.

Hutchens, Eleanor. 'An Approach Through Time'. In *Towards a Poetics of Fiction*. Bloomington: Indiana University Press, 1977.

Isogai Hideo. *Shōwa shotō no sakka to sakuhin*. Tokyo: Meiji Shoin, 1980.

Isogai Hideo. '*Jū-roku-sai no nikki to sofu*'. In *Shōkon no seishun*, edited by the Kawabata Bungaku Kenkyūkai. Tokyo: Kyōiku Shuppan Sentā. 1976.

Ito, Ken. *Visions of Desire: Tanizaki's Fictional Worlds*. Stanford: Stanford University Press, 1991.

Itō Sei. *Essays on Natsume Sōseki's Works*. Tokyo: Ministry of Education, 1970.

Jackson, Earl. 'Elaboration of the Moment: The Lyric Tradition in Modern Japanese Literature'. In *Literary History, Narrative, and Culture*, edited by Wimal Dissanayake and Steven Bradbury. Honolulu: The College of Languages, Linguistics and Literature University of Hawaii and the East-West Center, 1989.

Joyce, James. *Ulysses*. New York: Random House, 1934.

Karatani Kōjin. *Origins of Modern Japanese Literature*. Translation edited by Brett de Bary. Durham, N.C.: Duke University Press, 1993.

Katō Shūichi. *Genzai no naka no rekishi*. Tokyo: Shinchōsha, 1976.

Katō Shūichi. *A History of Japanese Literature, Volume 3, The Modern Years*. Translated by Don Sanderson. Tokyo: Kodansha International, 1990.

Kawabata Yasunari. *The Lake*. Translated by Reiko Tsukimura. Tokyo: Kodansha, 1974.

Kawabata Yasunari. *Nemureru bijo*. Tokyo: Shinchōsha, 1967.

Kawabata Yasunari. *Japan the Beautiful and Myself*. Translated by Edward Seidensticker. Tokyo: Kodansha, 1969.

Kawabata Yasunari. *The Sound of the Mountain*. Translated by Edward G. Seidensticker. New York: Alfred A. Knopf, 1970.

Kawabata Yasunari. *House of the Sleeping Beauties and Other Stories*. Translated by Edward Seidensticker. Tokyo: Kodansha, 1980.

Kawabata Yasunari. 'Lyric Poem'. Translated by Francis Mathy. In *Monumenta Nipponica*, XXVI, 3-4 (1971).

Kawabata Yasunari. *The Existence and Discovery of Beauty*. Translated by V.H. Viglielmo. Tokyo: Mainichi, 1969.

Kawabata, Yasunari. *Snow Country*. Translated by Edward G. Seidensticker. New York: Berkley, 1960.

Kawabata Yasunari. *Thousand Cranes*. Translated by Edward G. Seidensticker. New York: Berkley, 1958.

Kawabata Yasunari. *The Master of Go*. Translated by Edward G. Seidensticker. New York: Alfred A. Knopf, 1973.

Kawabata Bungaku Kenkyūkai, editors. *Kawabata bungaku e no shikai*. Tokyo: Kyōiku Shuppan Sentā, 1993.

Kawabata Bungaku Kenkyūkai, editors. *Shōkon no seishun*. Tokyo: Kyōiku Shuppan Sentā, 1976.

Kawabata Yasunari zenshū. Tokyo: Shinchōsha, 1980.

Kawashima Itaru. *Kawabata Yasunari no sekai*. Tokyo: Kōdansha, 1969.

Keene, Donald. *Anthology of Japanese Literature*. New York: Grove Press, 1955.

Keene, Donald. *Appreciations of Japanese Culture*. Tokyo: Kodansha, 1971.

Keene, Donald. *Dawn to the West: Japanese Literature in the Modern Era (Fiction)*. New York: Holt, Rinehart and Winston, 1984.

Keene, Donald, editor, *Modern Japanese Literature*. New York: Grove Press, 1956.

Keene, Donald. *Seeds in the Heart: Japanese Literature from Earliest Times to the Late Sixteenth Century*. New York: Henry Holt, 1993.

Keene, Donald. *World Within Walls: Japanese Literature of the Pre-Modern Era, 1600-1867*. New York: Holt, Rinehart, Winston, 1976.

Kenmochi Takehiko et al, editors. *Nihonjin to ma*. Tokyo: Kōdansha, 1981.

Kierkegaard, Søren. *Either/Or*, vol.1. Translated by David F. Swenson and Lillian Marvin Swenson, with revisions by Howard A. Johnson. Princeton: Princeton University Press, 1971.

Kobata Mizue. *Kawabata Yasunari: sakuhinron*. Tokyo: Keisō shobo, 1992.

Kobayashi, Hideo. *Kobayashi Hideo Zenshū*. Tokyo: Shinchōsha, 1955.

Kobayashi Hideo. *Sakka no kao*. Tokyo: Shinchōsha, 1961.

Konishi Jin'ichi. 'The Art of Renga'. In *Journal of Japanese Studies*. Autumn, 1975.

Kōno Toshirō, Miyoshi Yukio, Takemori Tenyū and Hiraoka Toshio, editors. *Taishō no bungaku*. Tokyo: Yūhikaku, 1972.

Kuwabara Takeo. *Japan and Western Civilization: Essays on Comparative Culture*. Edited by Katō Hidetoshi. Translated by Kano Tsutomu and Patricia Murray. Tokyo: University of Tokyo Press, 1983.

Leavis, F.R. *A Selection from Scrutiny*. Cambridge: Cambridge University Press, 1968.

Lodge, David. *After Bakhtin: Essays on Fiction and Criticism*. London: Routledge, 1990.

Lubbock, Percy. *The Craft of Fiction*. London: Jonathan Cape, 1939.

Marcus, Marvin. *Paragons of the Ordinary: The Biographical Literature of Mori Ōgai*. Honolulu: University of Hawaii Press, 1993.

Mascaró, Juan, translator. *The Upanishads*. London: Penguin, 1965.

Mathy, Francis. *Shiga Naoya*. New York: Twayne Publishers, 1974.

Matsuzaka Toshio. Kawabata Yasunari *'Tanagokoro no shōsetsu' kenkyū*. Tokyo: Kyōiku shuppan sentā, 1983.

Mendilow, A.A. *Time and the Novel*. New York: Humanities Press, 1965.

Mie Yasutaka, editor. *Kawabata Yasunari nyūmon*. Yūshindō, 1975.

Miller, Milton. *Nostalgia, a Psychoanalytical Study of Marcel Proust*. London: Gollancz, 1957.

Miner, Earl. *The Japanese Tradition in British and American Literature*. Princeton: Princeton University Press, 1966.

Miner, Earl. *Japanese Linked Poetry*. Princeton University Press, 1979.

Mirsky, D.S. *A History of Russian Literature*. New York: Vintage Books, 1958.

Mishima Yukio and Bownas, Geoffrey. *New Writing in Japan*. Harmondsworth, Middlesex: Penguin Books, 1972.

Mishima Yukio. '*Izu no odoriko* ni tsuite'. In *Izu no odoriko*. Tokyo: Shinchōsha, 1950.

Mishima Yukio. *Mishima Yukio Zenshū*. Tokyo: Shinchōsha, 1973-76.

Miyoshi, Masao. *Accomplices of Silence*. Berkeley: Univ. of Calif. Press, 1974.

Miyoshi, Masao and Harootunian, H.D., editors. *Postmodernism and Japan*. Durham, N.C.: Duke University Press, 1989.

Miyoshi, Masao. *Off Center: Power and Culture Relations between Japan and the United States*. Cambridge: Harvard University Press, 1991.

Morris, Ivan. editor, *Modern Japanese Stories*. Rutland, Vermont: Charles E. Tuttle, 1962.

Mumonkan. Edited by Hirata Takashi. Tokyo: Chikuma Shobō, 1969.

Nakamura Mitsuo. *Kobayashi Hideo.* Tokyo: Chikuma Shobo, 1977.

Nakamura Mitsuo. *Ronkō: Kawabata Yasunari.* Tokyo: Chikuma Shobō, 1978.

Nakamura Hajime. *Ways of Thinking of Eastern Peoples.* Honolulu: East-West Center Press, 1964.

Napier, Susan J. *The Fantastic in Modern Japanese Literature: The Subversion of Modernity.* London and New York: Routledge, 1996.

Nicolson, Marjorie Hope. *Mountain Gloom and Mountain Glory.* New York: W.W. Norton, 1963.

Ooka Shin, Takahashi Hideo and Miyoshi Yukio, editors. *Gunzō Nihon no sakka 13: Kawabata Yasunari.* Tokyo: Shogakkan, 1991.

Petersen, Gwenn Boardman. *The Moon in the Water: Understanding Tanizaki, Kawabata, and Mishima.* Honolulu: The University Press of Hawaii, 1979.

Pollack, David. *Reading against Culture: Ideology and Narrative in the Japanese Novel.* Ithaca: Cornell University Press, 1992.

Proust, Marcel. *Remembrance of Things Past.* Translated by C.K. Scott Moncrieff and Terence Kilmartin. New York: Random House, 1981.

Rico, Gabriele. *Writing the Natural Way.* Los Angeles: J.P. Toucher, 1983.

Rimer, J. Thomas, editor. *Culture and Identity: Japanese Intellectuals During the Interwar Years.* Princeton: Princeton University Press, 1990.

Robbe-Grillet, Alain. *For a New Novel.* Translated by Richard Howard. New York: Grove Press, 1965.

Roden, Donald. *Schooldays in Imperial Japan: A Study in the Culture of a Student Elite.* Berkeley: University of California Press, 1980.

Roggendorf, Joseph. *Studies in Japanese Culture.* Tokyo: Sophia University Press, 1963.

Rosenberger, Nancy R. *Japanese Sense of Self.* Cambridge: Cambridge University Press, 1992.

Rousseau, Jean Jacques. *Emile.* Translated by Barbara Foxley. London: J.M. Dent & Sons, 1911.

Sasabuchi Tomoichi. 'Kawabata bungaku to shūrurearizumu'. In *Kawabata Yasunari,* edited by Nihon Bungaku Kenkyū Shiryō Kankō-kai. Tokyo: Yūseidō, 1973.

Satō, Tadao. *Currents in Japanese Cinema.* Tokyo: Kodansha, 1982.

Seidensticker, Edward. *This Country, Japan.* Tokyo: Kodansha, 1979.

Seidensticker, Edward. *Low City, High City: Tokyo from Edo to the Earthquake.* New York: Alfred A. Knopf, 1983.

Shiga Naoya. *A Dark Night's Passing.* Translated by Edwin McClellan. Tokyo: Kodansha, 1976.

Shiga Naoya. *Shiga Naoya Zenshū.* Tokyo: Iwanami Shoten, 1955-56.

Shirane, Haruo. *The Bridge of Dreams: Poetics in the Tale of Genji.* Stanford: Stanford University Press, 1987.

Shively, Donald. *Tradition and Modernization in Japanese Culture.* Princeton University Press, 1971.

Sibley, William. *The Shiga Hero.* University of Chicago Ph.D. dissertation, 1971.

Silverberg, Miriam. *Changing Song: The Marxist Manifestos of Nakano Shigeharu*. Princeton: Princeton University Press, 1990.

Smith, Julian. 'Hemingway and the Thing Left Out'. In Jackson Benson, editor. *The Short Stories of Ernest Hemingway: Critical Essays*. Durham: Duke University Press, 1975.

Spengler, Oswald. *The Decline of the West*. Translated by Charles Francis Atkinson. New York: Alfred A. Knopf, 1926-29.

Starrs, Roy. *Deadly Dialectics: Sex, Violence and Nihilism in the World of Yukio Mishima*. Honolulu: University of Hawaii Press and Folkestone, England: Japan Library, 1994.

Starrs, Roy. *An Artless Art: The Zen Aesthetic of Shiga Naoya*. Folkestone, England: Japan Library, 1998.

Steiner, George. *Language and Silence*. London: Faber and Faber, 1967.

Steiner, George. *What Is Comparative Literature?* Oxford: Clarendon Press, 1995.

Suzuki Daisetsu. *Zen and Japanese Culture*. Princeton University Press, 1959.

Tajima Yoko. 'A Rereading of *Snow Country* from Komako's Point of View'. Translated by Donna George Storey. In *U.S.-Japan Women's Journal*, No.4, January 1993.

Takeda, K., editor. *Essays on Japanese Literature*. Tokyo: Waseda University Press, 1977.

Tanizaki Jun'ichirō. *Tanizaki Jun'ichirō Zenshū*. Tokyo: Chūō Kōronsha, 1958.

Tanizaki Jun'ichirō. *In Praise of Shadows*. New Haven: Leete's Island Books, 1977.

Trilling, Lionel. *A Gathering of Fugitives*. New York: Harcourt Brace Jovanovich, 1956.

Tsuruta Kinya. *Kawabata Yasunari no geijutsu*. Tokyo: Meiji shoin, 1981.

Tsuruta Kinya. 'Kawabata bungaku ni okeru jiden-teki yōso'. In *Jiden bungaku no sekai*, edited by Saeki Shōichi. Tokyo: Asahi Shuppansha, 1983.

Tsuruta, Kinya and Goossen, Theodore, editors. *Nature and Identity in Canadian and Japanese Literature*. Toronto: University of Toronto-York University Joint Centre for Asia Pacific Studies, 1988.

Tyler, Royall, translator. *Japanese Nō Dramas*. London: Penguin, 1992.

Ueda, Makoto. *Matsuo Bashō*. New York: Twayne, 1970.

Ueda, Makoto. *Literary and Art Theories in Japan*. Cleveland: Western Reserve University, 1967.

Ueda, Makoto. *Modern Japanese Writers and the Nature of Literature*. Stanford: Stanford University Press, 1976.

Valéry, Paul. *Aesthetics*. Translated by Ralph Manheim. New York: Pantheon Books, 1964.

Waley, Arthur. *The Nō Plays of Japan*. London: George Allen and Unwin, 1921.

Washburn, Dennis C. *The Dilemma of the Modern in Japanese Fiction*. New Haven: Yale University Press, 1995.

Weeks, Robert. *Hemingway: a Collection of Critical Essays*. Englewood Cliffs, N.J.: Prentice-Hall, 1962.

Wilson, Edmund. *Eight Essays*. New York: Doubleday, 1954.

Yamamoto Kenkichi. 'Kaisetsu'. In Kawabata Yasunari, *Yama no oto*. Tokyo: Shinchōsha, 1957.

Yanagida Izumi, Katsumoto Seiichirō and Ino Kenji, editors. *Zadankai: Taishō bungaku shi*. Tokyo: Iwanami shoten, 1965.

Yoshida Sei-ichi. *Bunshō to buntai*. Tokyo: Meiji Shoin, 1963.

Wilson, Colin. *The Outsider*. Boston: Houghton Mifflin, 1956.

Zaehner, R.C. *Mysticism, Sacred and Profane*. New York: Oxford University Press, 1957.

Zweig, Paul. *The Heresy of Self-Love*. Princeton: Princeton University Press, 1980.

INDEX